AFRICAN WOMEN

BOOKS BY MARK MATHABANE

Kaffir Boy
Kaffir Boy in America
African Women

WITH GAIL MATHABANE

Love in Black and White

AFRICAN WOMEN

Three Generations

MARK MATHABANE

HarperCollins*Publishers*

HarperCollins books may be purchased for educational, business, or sales promotional use. For information please write: Special Markets Department, HarperCollins Publishers, Inc., 10 East 53rd Street, New York, NY 10022.

FIRST EDITION

Designed by Jessica Shatan

Library of Congress Cataloging-in-Publication Data

Mathabane, Mark.
    African women : three generations / Mark Mathabane. — 1st ed.
       p.   cm.
    Includes index.
    ISBN 0-06-016496-4
    1. Women, Black—South Africa—Social conditions. 2. Family—
South Africa. 3. Apartheid—South Africa. 4. South Africa—
Social conditions. I. Title.
HQ1800.5.M38   1994
305.4'096—dc20   93-43514

94 95 96 97 98 ❖/RRD 10 9 8 7 6 5 4 3 2 1

TO AFRICAN WOMEN WHO,

WITH INDOMITABLE COURAGE

AND UNDYING FAITH,

DAILY FOUGHT TO SUSTAIN HOPE

IN THE DEPTHS OF DESPAIR AND BONDAGE.

Black woman,
        You are a vital part of this country called South Africa,
        This is your land!
                Land of your birth,
                Land of your children's children.
        This is your land!
            Claim it!
—BETTIE J. DURRAH, *What Color Is Economic Justice?*

Men, their rights and nothing more;
Women, their rights and nothing less
    —SUSAN B. ANTHONY

The masters of women wanted more than simple obedience, and they turned the whole force of education to effect their purpose. All women are brought up from the very earliest years in the belief that their ideal of character is the very opposite to that of men; not self-will, and government by self-control, but submission, and yielding to the control of others. All moralities tell them that it is their duty as women, and all current sentimentalities that it is their nature, to live for others, to make complete abnegation of themselves.
    —JOHN STUART MILL, *The Subjection of Women*

Women are more than 50 percent of the world population, they perform two-thirds of the world's work, receive one-tenth of the world's income, and own one-hundredth of the world's property.
    —UNITED NATIONS STATISTICS

CONTENTS

PREFACE

The earliest idea for this book occurred to me following publication of my first book, *Kaffir Boy*, in 1986, which is about my coming of age in apartheid South Africa. *Kaffir Boy* elicited from its readers around the world hundreds of letters condemning the apartheid system for its inhuman treatment of blacks and supporting the black majority's struggle for liberation and justice.

This epic struggle, fought since the arrival of the first white settlers in 1652, has culminated in negotiations for a nonracial, nonsexist, and democratic South Africa. It is my fervent hope that such a country, the fondest dream of millions, thousands of whom sacrificed their lives for it, is gloriously realized.

Most of the letters I received also expressed admiration for my family, particularly my mother. Readers were keenly interested in the story of her life, as she had played a pivotal role in preventing me from self-destructing amid the raging hell of ghetto life. She raised seven children and put up with physical abuse at the hands of my father, all while groaning under the yoke of triple oppression: she was black in a white-dominated and racist society, a woman in a patriarchal culture, and illiterate in a world where those who could read and write had control over her life and the lives of others like her.

The stories of my mother's struggles and experiences—and those of African women like her who battle for survival every day—have waited too long to be told. Women, after all, are the unsung heroines of many a liberation struggle that rid Africa of the galling yoke of colonialism and white oppression. Unfortunately, many of their exploits, accomplishments, and sacrifices have gone unrecognized.

Yet without such women, victory would have been impossible.

In South Africa, women fought alongside men in the battlefield, as part of *Umkonto We Sizwe* ("Spear of the Nation"), the military wing of the African National Congress (ANC). They marched, protested, and died in the streets. They slaved for a pittance as maids for white people. In their own homes they strove valiantly to keep families together and to sustain hope in the young, who are the future and salvation of the new South Africa.

My mother endured insults, humiliation, and beatings to see me educated. She encouraged me to shun gangs, to read books, and to pursue my dream of using tennis as a stepping stone to freedom. She even helped me make the hard decision to accept a tennis scholarship to America at age eighteen, when my parents and six siblings relied heavily on me as the primary breadwinner and my departure was certain to plunge them back into grinding poverty and hopelessness.

Though I already knew a great deal about my mother's life, especially that portion of it which is intertwined with my own, I knew there was much more about her past, her struggles, her growing up without a father, her marriage at seventeen to a man almost twice her age who abused her, her bout with insanity, and her staunch faith in God.

In 1992 my sister Florah came to America. During her visit my wife, Gail, and I had long conversations with her about her life, particularly her relationship with men and her struggles as a woman in a male-dominated society and culture. She was then attempting to extricate herself from an abusive relationship with a former gangster. She had become involved with him during a period of great pain and turmoil in her life, when the young man she thought would love her forever, the father of her only daughter, began cheating on her.

As Florah recounted her story, patterns began emerging about her life that paralleled my mother's. Though belonging to different generations, both had been purchased by men following the *lobola* custom, after which the men changed and the relationships turned oppressive and abusive. With no knowledge of Western feminism or law, my mother and sister instinctively refused to accept their inferior status and degradation as women, and they fought doggedly for their rights as they then understood them to be.

Intrigued, I probed deeper and discovered much about their lives that had remained hidden and buried or had failed to register with me when I was growing up, absorbed as I was in my own struggles for freedom and rendered blind to sexism by seeing it accepted and condoned in the world around me.

Knowing that my maternal grandmother, Ellen, another victim of *lobola* and a survivor of male abuse, was still alive, I decided to investigate her story, too, from her childhood in the tribal homelands to her life as a single mother in a strange city, raising three children on her own after her husband had abandoned her for another woman.

What emerged when I followed the three stories was a harrowing, poignant, heroic, and inspiring saga of three women who, in their individual ways, refused to buckle under tradition, custom, and oppression. They fought against daunting odds to preserve their individuality and independence, their dignity and pride, their hearts and souls. They worked and raised children in a culture and society where black women had hardly any rights, were daily discriminated against by apartheid, and were regarded as the property of their husbands or fathers by custom. Any attempt to liberate themselves—as the lives of Granny, my mother, and my sister revealed—was condemned and harshly dealt with.

The stories of these three women are told in their own words. They are distinct yet interwoven memoirs of abuse, oppression, and witchcraft, of being cheated out of inheritances, of being sold at a young age to older men, of mysterious deaths and insanity, of rape, silent pain, endurance, of survival, triumph, faith, and, above all, undying love.

In telling these stories in the first person, through the eyes of each of the three characters, I have sought to avoid intruding on the ways my grandmother, mother, and sister saw, felt, thought, and acted. I was surprised by how differently we often saw the same thing and reacted to the same experience. For instance, my father, with his strange moods and domineering and stubborn pride, was far more of a tyrant and abuser than I had let myself remember.

This book does not claim to be a representative study of all South African women, let alone of all African women. Nor are the men described in it supposed to represent all African men. Yet the oppression of women is widespread in South Africa, largely because as apartheid over the years has emasculated and degraded black men, and stripped them of their manhood by depriving them of the means to provide for their families and loved ones, many of these men find convenient targets for their rage, frustrations, and bitterness in those under their immediate and absolute control: women.

As in the case of my father, this abuse of women is made easy because apartheid, for its own devious ends, has encouraged and rewarded tribalism among blacks. Thus my father continued to cling to customs and traditions that had long outlived their usefulness, mainly out of a sense of desperation. Under tribalism men have power, authority, and respect, while in the modern world ruled by the white man they are powerless, get no respect, are called "boys," and treated as less than dirt.

Yet many African men and women have heroically retained their dignity and sense of self amid the horrors of apartheid. Their lives in many ways have been the opposite of the lives depicted in this book.

It is a fact that some African women like the custom of *lobola*, despite its abuses, and take pride in going for the highest price. They have their own reasons, just as my mother, Granny, and sister had their own for their love-hate relationship with the custom. For some African women, seeing a man pay money for them is the only moment in their lives when they feel valued.

The issue of witchcraft is particularly sensitive and complex. There are many who dismiss it as primitive superstition. To people brought up under the influence of Western culture and Christianity, whose lives are steeped in modern technology and science, belief in witches and voodoo may sound fantastic, straight out of the Middle Ages. But readers of this book must bear in mind that there are various ways to perceive and interpret the same reality.

In South Africa, given the horrendous state of health care among blacks, endemic illiteracy, and the sway of tribal beliefs, it is easy for people whose mental and physical well-being has been devastated by apartheid to believe in supernatural causes. Yet there is something about the nature of witchcraft that defies Western scientific explanations and cannot be easily dismissed as mumbo-jumbo, just as there is a lot about Christianity and other major religions and faiths that cannot be explained using logic and reason. Such beliefs exercise a profound influence on people as they search for answers to the conundrums of life, to the eternal questions of who and why we are. The challenge is not for one culture to pass judgment on another—no one possesses absolute knowledge about the nature of things—but for us to seek to understand, learn from each other, and respect the complex differences among the various belief systems in this world.

Through these simple stories of the lives of my grandmother, mother, and sister, I hope to pay tribute to the millions of grandmothers, mothers, and sisters worldwide who continue to do so much to preserve hope and peace in our troubled world, despite suffering long and often in silence at the hands of outmoded customs and traditions that serve only to stifle their growth, strangle their dreams, and prevent them from becoming what they have the God-given potential to become: full human beings and equal partners of men.

Kernersville, North Carolina
1994

ACKNOWLEDGMENTS

This book is the result of the generous contributions of many wonderful people. First on the list are my grandmother, mother, and sister Florah, who courageously opened up their souls to tell their individual stories of pain, struggle, love, and triumph.

Second, a multitude of thanks to my wife, Gail, who journeyed to South Africa in April 1993—a tumultuous month during which Chris Ḥani, head of the South African Communist Party and a popular black leader, was assassinated—to conduct the interviews that form the basis of this book. As a woman, she was able to unlock many of the doors that would have been inaccessible to me when talking to my mother, grandmother, and sister about intimate details concerning their lives. As my best and severest critic, she constantly challenged me to make the stories come alive. And as a superb photographer, she captured imperishable images for the insert.

Third, I would like to thank Terry Karten, my new editor at HarperCollins, who brought sensitivity, constructive criticism, and enthusiasm to the manuscript of *African Women*. I would also like to thank my former editor at HarperCollins, Craig Nelson, who eagerly embraced the idea of a book on three generations of African women, when we originally had an agreement for a different book. I wish him well at his new home, Hyperion.

Fourth, I wish to thank my agents, Fifi Oscard and Kevin McShane, for proving such steadfast friends and supporters over the years.

And last but far from least, I wish to thank my children, Nathan and Bianca, for patiently putting up with me during those many months of intense, solitary labor, when I constantly took time away from reading, playing, and walking with them in the woods to "work on the computer." I wrote this book, my darlings, to always remind you that along with Mommy, there are other special women Daddy has been blessed to know.

PART 1

1

FLORAH

LOBOLA
COMPLICATES LOVE

One day in the summer of 1980, three of my boyfriend's relatives—
his stepmother and two uncles—came to my father's shack on 13th
Avenue to pay *lobola* for me. They brought no cattle as the bride
price, as had been the custom back in the days of my grandmother.
They came to pay cash.

For days my family had eagerly anticipated their coming. Elaborate
preparations had been made to welcome them and to dignify our
poverty. The small dirt courtyard in front of the two-room shack had
been swept clean. The cement kitchen floor had been scrubbed and
polished to a shining red. The two cracked windows with faded cur-
tains had been washed till they shined like mirrors.

The furniture had been polished and dusted over and over again,
to hide the fact that it was old and cheap. The single bed in one corner of the kitchen, on which my brother slept at night, had its sagging mattress replaced with a thick piece of sponge and decorated

with throw pillows to resemble a sofa. The large, secondhand coal stove, which was propped up on three sides with bricks because its legs were missing, had been cleaned, and its yellow enamel plates sparkled. A linen tablecloth, embroidered by my mother with patterns of colorful flowers, had been washed, ironed, and spread conspicuously across the table.

Everything in the shack was spic-and-span. And I, the bride-to-be, assisted by my two sisters, Mirriam and Maria, had done all the work. I wanted to impress my prospective in-laws and show them that I was worth every penny they had come to pay as *lobola*.

The table was decked out with a sumptuous meal. It was easily our best meal for the year. It consisted of a chicken my father had bought and slaughtered, rice, pumpkins, green vegetables, beetroot, custard and jelly, cake, soda drinks, and beer. Everything was served on the special dining ware that had taken me months to purchase on layaway and was used only for special occasions such as Christmas celebrations.

The smiles and nods of satisfaction on the faces of Collin's stepmother and uncles told me that they were indeed impressed. After they had feasted, the *lobola* proceedings began. My father, dressed in a well-worn black suit, white shirt, and gaudy tie, was accompanied by a male neighbor, similarly spiffed up, who acted as witness. The two sat solemnly at one end of the table, and Collin's relatives sat at the other.

I quietly removed myself to the bedroom of the shack, where I remained cloistered with the rest of the womenfolk in the house. The bride-to-be was forbidden to be present during *lobola* discussions. But I could overhear everything, as I listened intently through the thin walls.

"We've come to make a down payment of R100 [about $35] on your daughter Florah," Collin's uncle said. "Our son Collin has known her for nearly two years now. He's been so happy with her that he wants her for a wife."

"I trust you've already been informed that I want R1,000 for my daughter," my father said.

"Yes, we've been informed," said Collin's stepmother.

"She's worth more, you know," my father said. "You're getting her at a bargain price. She's the oldest and prettiest of my daughters. And she's been to school and is a hard worker."

"Yes, we know her virtues," said Collin's uncle. "They're well displayed in the beautiful appearance of the house, and in the fine meal we've just enjoyed. We appreciate your generosity in asking only R1,000 for such a splendid daughter. We're certain she's worth more."

"I guarantee you that," my father said. "She's been well raised and will be a boon to any man."

"We're confident our son will be most happy with her," Collin's uncle said. "As for the rest of the *lobola*, it will be paid to you in several installments. That is our solemn pledge."

Thus the bargain was struck, making me, at eighteen years old, Collin's betrothed. Once he had paid the balance of R900, I would be completely his, a permanent part of his household, his property.

At first I didn't mind that Collin had paid *lobola* for me. In fact I was relieved. Our love was real and only *lobola* remained to legitimize it in the eyes of society and of our parents. Now that he had paid part of it meant I could start living with him and his family without shame or violating any taboos. Most important, the move would place me beyond the reach of my father's tyranny.

I so much wanted to be away from my father. I was fed up with his domineering over everything and everyone in the shack. And females were his special target. Whenever we bought things without consulting him, talked back to him each time he lectured us about our duties, or fought for our rights, he always became irate and would remind us he was the ruler of his own home.

"As long as you live under my roof," he would bellow, "you'll do as I say."

Being a *makoti*, a bride, also filled me with a sense of pride. For some time several of our neighbors had openly gossiped that my headstrong attitude would scare men away and leave me a childless spinster.

"Your daughter, Musadi (woman)," one neighbor had told my

mother, "is good only for *vat en set* [shacking up]. She's too loose with her tongue. And men don't like that in a woman."

My mother partly believed this. She feared that her enemies had somehow bewitched me into acting contrary to my matrimonial interests, in which case I was unlikely to find a husband willing to pay *lobola* for me.

My mother often shared her fears with me.

"Florah, my dear," she said one day, "stop talking back to men the way you do."

"But I have my own mind, Mama," I replied.

"Of course you do, child," my mother said. "But men don't like women with an attitude."

"But, Mama," I said, "I have to speak out to let people know how I feel. After all, I'm not a rock or a doll."

"You don't know men, my child," my mother said. "You're still young and inexperienced. I do. The one thing they hate the most is a woman who can't bridle her tongue."

"But you talk back to Papa," I said.

"Yes, and you know the consequences," my mother said. "He beats me up and chases me out of the house. I just don't want the same to happen to you, child. I don't want you to suffer the way I have."

"Well," I said, "maybe it's best not to get married."

"Don't talk like that, child," my mother said in an alarmed voice. "It's bad luck."

"What's wrong with not being married?"

"What sort of a woman will you be without a husband?"

"A free woman," I said.

"Now don't be foolish, child," my mother said. "What will you do for children?"

"I don't have to marry to have children, do I?" I said.

"Oh, Lord," my mother cried. "What's gotten into you child? You're indeed bewitched. Do you know what it's like to raise children without a husband? Ask your grandmother. She'll tell you. And do you want to be called a *skeberesh* [whore]?"

"Times have changed, Mama," I said. "I know many unmarried

women with children who are doing just fine. They feel no shame."

"But in our family it is shameful," my mother declared.

So when Collin finally agreed to pay *lobola* it came as a great relief to my mother, and to me. Yet I hated the feeling that I had been bought, that I was my husband's possession, that he now had control over my destiny.

In many ways I considered myself a modern woman, and the thought of losing my independence as part of the bargain over *lobola* scared me. But what could I do? Good men were hard to find. And I was living in black South Africa, where tradition ran deep, and *lobola* was still a revered institution, despite its abuse and the bondage and untold pain it has brought many a woman, as I vividly saw in the lives of my mother and grandmother.

I could only hope that the Collin I knew before *lobola*—respectful of me and my opinions, and supportive of my ambitions—would not be transformed into a sexist tyrant by the knowledge that I now belonged exclusively to him. I could only pray that he would not abuse the tremendous power *lobola* gave him over me, as my father did his power over my mother.

My mother had been bought cheap. Her *lobola* amounted to no more than R50. Maybe that partly explains why my father, in a long, abusive marriage which has lasted over twenty-five years and produced seven children, constantly demanded her total submission and obedience. Whenever she rebelled, which she had the habit of doing even when she was counseling me to submit to men, he would beat her and chase her out of the shack, calling her all sorts of degrading names and threatening to return her to her mother and demand his *lobola* back.

I was determined to let no man treat me the same way. I went about choosing my life mate very carefully. Women friends called me "picky" and warned me that my "attitude" was a guarantee that no man would want to marry me.

"The man I marry," I said to my friend Hlekani (laughter), "has to take me as I am."

"You don't know our men, Florah," Hlekani said. She was six years older and had been in several relationships, none of which ended up in marriage. Yet in all of them Hlekani had been the perfectly submissive and obedient girlfriend. "They don't like a woman who's too cheeky. They want a woman they can control."

"Do you think wanting to be treated right is being cheeky?" I said.

"No. But there's a way for a woman to get what she wants from a man without being too aggressive about it," Hlekani said.

"Why should we always be changing ourselves to suit men's tastes?" I said. "Why don't they change themselves to suit our tastes for once? Why should we always pretend we're nothing when we know our worth? I hate playing these games."

"They're not games, Florah," Hlekani said. "This is the way things are. That's how we've been raised. That's what men expect and want."

I believed I had found Mr. Right in Collin. I met him when I was seventeen and he two years older. I was returning home from work one day at the piano store in the white suburbs, where I helped polish and refurbish old pianos. My best friend, Joyce ("Tears") and I worked there together. Tall, light skinned, and street smart, Joyce was my age and we were inseparable. Each time I found a job, I made sure Joyce got one too at the same place—and she did the same for me.

Joyce and I had shared many secrets and experiences growing up in the same yard on 13th Avenue. We had even wanted to attend the same school, but because Joyce was a Mosotho and I was Venda the authorities required that we go to separate tribal schools.

Every day when Joyce and I walked home from work we would pass a group of about a dozen boys hanging out on the street corner. Always we stopped and chatted with them. Joyce teased me for being shy and fearful of boys. She taught me to flirt. Collin vied with the other boys to gain my attention. He was tall, slender, and a snappy dresser, preferring a popular fashion called "hippies" or "American style." He wore small caps, colorful, baggy shirts, and three-quarter-length jeans. He was laid back and fond of making jokes.

One day when Joyce and I paused to talk to Collin's group, he took me aside and whispered in my ear, "You're the loveliest girl I've ever seen. I especially like your smile and your big eyes."

"Thanks," I said softly, embarrassingly averting my eyes from his steady gaze. I thought myself ugly because I was skinny, even after I quit school and started working and dressing up in the latest fashions.

"Did anyone ever tell you you look like Mirriam Makeba?"

"Do I?" I said with a smile, feeling flattered.

Mirriam Makeba was not only my favorite singer, she was also the most beautiful woman I had ever seen. She had the looks of an African queen, the voice of a nightingale, and her haunting songs came from and touched the soul.

"Yes you do."

"You're just flattering me."

"No, I'm not."

"As a matter of fact, several people have told me the same thing," I said, "and I think they lie. No one is as beautiful as Mirriam Makeba, I mean naturally beautiful."

"Well, you come close," Collin said. "Can you sing?"

"Like a frog," I said. "That's why they kicked me off my mother's church choir."

We both laughed.

Again he whispered into my ear, "I dig you, Florah."

In South Africa when a boy says that to you, it usually means, "Let's go to bed."

"NO!" I said. "I don't *do* that."

My reaction seemed to please him and he became determined to win me. Collin's parents were divorced and he traveled back and forth between his mother's place in Vereeniging, where he attended school, and the home of his father, stepmother, and stepsiblings in Alexandra. His father, a musician who used to perform in a band, had many children by different wives, but Collin was his favorite son.

Collin came to Alexandra often during school holidays to visit his father, and that's when we got to see each other. When he matriculated he moved to Alexandra to look for work and to be near me.

Our relationship became serious. In my family, as in many others where tribal tradition still held sway, it was taboo for mothers to talk to their daughters about sex, yet I knew more or less what it was all about, mainly from talking to friends and cousins. When I brought up the issue of birth control, at first Collin laughed and didn't want to talk about it.

"You don't expect me to wear a rubber, do you?" he said.

"That would be the easiest form of birth control," I said. "But if you don't want to, I can go to family planning."

He said nothing, which meant I could go. Many black women often asked their husbands or boyfriends for permission to use birth control. Many men were not satisfied simply with controlling women's lives, they also wanted to control their bodies. If a man wanted a baby, you had the baby. If you refused, that was often the end of the relationship or marriage.

There were four family planning centers in Alexandra. I went to the nearest one, located in a huge women's hostel. The center was a tiny, spare, unpretentious room staffed entirely by overworked black nurses who often took out their frustrations by being rude to the steady stream of young girls and illiterate women who came for services.

When I arrived there I found a long line already formed outside the facility. I was not surprised to see only women. For a variety of reasons, many black men, especially the uneducated, opposed any form of birth control. Some saw it as part of a devilish plot by the government to keep the black population down. Others regarded having lots of children, particularly girls, as wealth in the form of lobola. Still others believed that a woman who was perpetually pregnant was easy to control and to keep honest. And then there were the men who expressed their virility by the number of children they could father, usually by different women.

While I stood in line I started talking to a young woman named Precious, about twenty-one, who had already had four children, in rat-tat-tat fashion, one after the other.

"I envy you for not having any children and working," Precious said. She was accompanied by all of her children—three girls and a boy, the oldest almost seven and the youngest still nursing. They wore rags and had no shoes. But despite their poverty the children looked beautiful.

"But your babies are gorgeous," I said.

"People tell me so," Precious said with a heavy sigh. "But if I had to do it all over again, I would want only one. They're such hard work. They make me feel so old and helpless. They often get sick and they like playing in the streets, which are so dangerous nowadays. My husband and I are very poor. He never went to school and makes only R14 a week. That's hardly enough for food and rent. No one helps me take care of the children. I want to have a future. I want to work. I want us to have a better life. I want to be able to send my children to school and buy them nice things. That's why I'm here. I want to stop working at having babies. I want real work. But if my husband finds out I've been here, he'll kill me."

"Kill you?"

"Yes. He's warned me against using birth control," Precious said. "He doesn't believe in it. He wants more children. And he has this strange idea that birth control will affect his virility. Will it?"

"I don't know that much about birth control," I said. "But I don't think so."

"Don't you think four children are enough?" Precious asked plaintively.

"They're more than enough," I said. I wanted only two.

"So I'm right in coming here?" she asked dubiously. "A few of my women friends have told me I shouldn't come here. They say that birth control will make me sterile or make me have deformed babies."

"You're doing the right thing," I said reassuringly.

Yet the fears Precious had were not totally unfounded. At one time, black women were being secretly sterilized at government-run family planning centers. And recently, in one factory in Natal, black female employees had to submit to monthly injections of Depo-Provera—a crude form of birth control with dangerous side effects—every three months or lose their jobs.

"Thank you for your support," Precious said.

"You're welcome," I said.

I don't know if her husband ever found out she had been to family planning. I prayed he wouldn't.

My turn came. A short, fat black nurse with a brusque manner asked me my age and what form of birth control I wanted.

I told her I was eighteen, and since I hardly knew a thing about the various birth control devices, I simply said I wanted a device that worked and was safe.

"No form of birth control is 100 percent safe, girl," she said.

Without giving me a choice or explaining any bad side effects, the nurse told me that an IUD was the proper birth control device for me. She ordered me to pull up my dress, remove my underwear, and lie on a bunk. She proceeded to insert the IUD inside me. She did it hastily, and I felt stabs of pain which made me wince. But I didn't say anything, as there were many other young women there, most of them schoolgirls, eager for some form of birth control, presumably because their boyfriends were pressuring them into having sex and their mothers, like mine, hadn't told them a thing about it. Most of the girls were not yet eighteen.

Several days after the IUD was inserted, I started having cramps and bleeding. I went back to the clinic and was told my symptoms were normal. All women feel discomfort from an IUD, the nurses said, especially after each monthly checkup. Every month I complained of the pain and bleeding, but no one listened or seemed to care.

At last I had the damn thing removed. Collin wanted a baby. I was madly in love with him and wanted to prove my fertility so that he'd marry me before a magistrate. Without a marriage license, *lobola* or no *lobola*, I had no rights whatsoever should Collin leave me for another woman, as often happened in *lobola* marriages in which the woman bore no children.

Children are so precious to African men that sterility is frequently grounds for divorce. A married woman without a child is living on borrowed time. At any moment she might be returned by the husband to her parents, in disgrace and shame. The husband considers himself wronged, deceived, as if the woman and her parents should have known beforehand that she couldn't bear any children, which is absurd.

To appease a childless husband, and desperate to save their daughter's marriage, the parents of the infertile woman sometimes purchase him a second wife. If they can't afford to do so, they offer a younger sister or niece as a second wife. Some of my relatives have done that. But I shuddered at the thought of sharing a husband with any of my younger sisters.

When a year and a half passed and I didn't get pregnant, I became extremely worried. To go that long without a child after *lobola* was paid was considered strange. Collin and his family began wondering too.

"Where are the grandchildren, Florah?" Collin's stepmother said. "Remember, you're never quite a wife without children."

"They'll come," I said.

There had been tension between Collin's stepmother and me ever since I moved in with his family. She was a shrewd and domineering woman, accustomed to getting her way and running things. She resented my headstrong attitude, and thought that I was trying to remove Collin from under her control. Before I arrived on the scene, she was used to running Collin's life.

She demanded that he give her his wages, she set his priorities, and she monitored his comings and goings. When I tried to change all that she considered me as meddling in the affairs of "her house," and treated me almost like a stranger, an interloper, especially since I was from the Shangaan and Venda tribes, tribes many Xhosas looked down upon.

I tried making Collin aware of the problems and strains his step-mother's behavior was causing in our relationship.

"I'm tired of having to seek your stepmother's approval before doing anything in this house," I said.

"It's her house, Florah."

"Granted it's her house," I said. "But we are grownups, man and wife, and have the right to make up our minds about things. For instance, why do you always give her your wages? I'm tired of having to beg her for money whenever I need to buy something." I even had to get her approval to buy a dress and a pair of shoes with my husband's money.

"My stepmother knows how to handle money," Collin said.

"I do too," I said, "and I'm your wife. Don't you trust me?"

"I trust you," Collin said, "but my stepmother will get mad if I stopped giving her money. Until I'm done paying lobola for you and we have a place of our own, it's best that I do things her way."

"But I'm your wife, for God's sake," I cried. "Your stepmother has no business telling you what you can and cannot do. You're not a child."

"She's not telling me what to do, Florah," Collin said. "I just don't want any trouble. So why don't we leave things as they are until we have a place of our own?"

We left things as they were. While Collin's stepmother treated me with coldness, suspicion, and disdain, his father, on the other hand, was a darling. He was easygoing, full of laughter, and treated me with the kindness and respect I deserved as his son's wife. But his wife clearly had the power in the house, and he often had to defer to her judgment, albeit reluctantly.

When Collin's stepmother realized that I was determined to wrest Collin from under her control, she started watching me like a hawk. It wasn't a hard thing to do in the tiny two-room house. She scrutinized my cooking, washing, and cleaning and was on the lookout for excuses to use things against me. I gave her none. She then latched on to the issue of children. She started telling me that Collin was complaining to her because I was unable to conceive, and that under no circumstances would he make further lobola payments without a baby. This of course was a veiled threat that either I conceive or the marriage would soon be over.

When I confronted Collin about his stepmother's threats, he was evasive.

"You know children are important, Florah," he said.

"Yes, I know," I said. "And we've been trying, haven't we?"

"Yes, but—"

"But what?"

"You haven't had any."

"So I have to go?"

"I didn't say that."

I wanted him to repudiate his stepmother's threats but he didn't. Instead he became somewhat distant and impatient with me. He started hanging out in *shebeens* (speakeasies) with his friends and would come back home drunk. Sometimes he didn't come home at all.

The pressure to conceive came not only from Collin and his family, but also from my family.

"Any child on the way?" my mother asked me one day.

"I don't think so," I said.

"Is there anything wrong?"

"No, I don't think so," I said in a doubtful voice. "We've been trying but have had no luck."

"Well," my mother said. "You shouldn't worry too much. They'll come."

"But Collin and his parents are concerned."

"Your father is concerned too," my mother said. "He thinks the reason Collin is behind in his *lobola* payments may be because of your inability to conceive. But I told your father not to worry and the babies will come."

"I love Collin, Mama," I said. "I badly want to give him a child. I don't want to lose him to another woman."

"You won't," my mother said. "Trust me you won't. The God of Israel will see to it that you and Collin have a tribe of children."

My mother was such a fervent Christian that she thought nothing beyond the power of her God. But I wasn't leaving my matrimonial fate only to the God of Israel. I consulted a *nganga,* a traditional healer, who prescribed some herbs and roots that were supposed to increase fertility. I even went to a Zionist prophet, who recommended ablutions and laxatives, and still nothing happened. And although my IUD had been removed, the cramps and bleeding continued.

I was now frantic. I began wondering if I was unable to conceive because I had used an IUD. I asked questions but no one provided me with satisfactory answers. On the contrary, I discovered evidence that there was something terribly wrong with the IUDs they were putting in us. I saw children born with IUDs embedded in the flesh behind their ears and in their cheeks. I heard other women talk about cramps and bleeding. I couldn't see a gynecologist because they were white and expensive. I could only pray and keep trying to conceive.

At last, I conceived. For several months I did not realize I was pregnant because I continued to bleed. I thought I was still menstruating. The IUD had messed up my uterus so badly that I had pain, cramps, and bleeding all through my pregnancy. I was working at a fiberglass factory on the outskirts of Alexandra at the time. The work was hard, the fiberglass material was itchy, maybe even toxic, and I was always sick. Because my precarious health made it impossible for me to work long on the assembly line, I was often sent to buy lunch food for fellow workers. Frequently I ended up at the clinic and people would tell me I had passed out while waiting in line at the store. The clinic told me I had low blood pressure and needed to stop working.

But I was reluctant to quit my job. I needed the money to support myself so I would not have to rely on Collin's stepmother, and to help my parents and siblings because my father was unemployed and my mother was sick. I continued working until the eighth month, when cramps, bleeding, fatigue, and fainting spells often made it impossible for me to leave the house.

On the 13th of August 1982, four months before my twenty-first birthday, I gave birth to a baby girl and named her Angeline Nonqeba. *Nonqeba* in Xhosa means a sensitive, kindhearted person who is always eager to help others. I continued to experience pain and cramps and bleeding, but now I knew that whatever the IUD had done to my womb, even if I never conceived again, at least I had had one child.

Without any income or job, I had to constantly beg Collin's step-mother for money for food, diapers, trips to the clinic, and baby clothes. This sort of humiliation was intolerable. Shortly after Ange-line was born I began combing the want ads for jobs. Luckily I was hired as an assistant at a store in the city, and my mother and sisters took care of Angeline when I was away at work.

Collin was very happy when I had the baby. He doted on her. Collin's parents too were happy, even though I had given birth to a girl—a boy is often preferred as the firstborn because he ensures that the family name and line will be perpetuated. I was now finally one of the family.

With Angeline's arrival, Collin's stepmother's attitude toward me changed from one of coldness, resentment, and suspicion to one of tolerable warmth. One thing, however, didn't change. I was still the family drudge. Despite nursing an infant and working, I was still expected to clean the whole house alone, do laundry, and cook for everybody. When I complained to Collin he told me that his parents had a right to expect the woman he had paid *lobola* for to do all the work around the house, because that was her duty. Most African women are such slaves, and they mourn in silence.

2

GELI

SOLD TO A MAN
I DIDN'T LOVE

Despite the hard work my daughter Florah was expected to do as a *makoti*, which was normal in *lobola* marriages, I regarded her as lucky to have married the man she loved. I wasn't so fortunate. The day Jackson paid *lobola* for me, making me his wife, was the most miserable day of my life. I wasn't in love with him. My heart belonged to someone else. But I was young, seventeen years old, and my mother and Aunt Matinana conspired to determine my fate. I pleaded with them in vain to let me marry my distant cousin David, with whom I had grown up. He had already paid R9 (about $3), a respectable sum, especially in the 1950s, as down payment for *lobola*.

David was my age, had a good job as a laborer, and possessed a gentle heart. His deeds told me he would keep his promises, despite the fact that men often made many promises to women they wanted to marry, only to end up hurting and abusing them, just as my grandmother and mother were deceived and abandoned by their husbands.

When David proposed through his mother and sister, as was the custom, I was living with my mother and three siblings in a one-room shack in Alexandra. My mother was having difficulties caring for us since my father, John Mabaso, deserted her several years earlier for another woman.

One evening my mother and I were sitting on the floor around the brazier knitting mats out of corn sheaves. The family had just finished a skimpy dinner of *pap* (cornmeal porridge) and *murogo* (greens), and my siblings were out playing. My mother slowly raised her eyes from her work and said, "David's mother and sister were here this morning."

"I saw them," I replied. My heart pounded with excitement, as I thought they had come to make another *lobola* payment.

"I gave them back their *lobola*," she said without emotion.

I was stunned. For several minutes I could not speak. Finally I said, in a voice choked with emotion, "Why, Mama?"

"I don't want you to marry David."

"Why?" I asked again. There was deep pain in my heart.

"He's too young. I don't want you to end up like me. I married your father when he was too young. He grew tired of me and left me for another woman. And look what a miserable life I've led ever since."

"What makes you think the same will happen to me if David marries me?"

"All young men are the same."

My mother went on to say that she preferred I marry an older man who had already sown his wild oats and was therefore more likely to be faithful.

"It's better to be an old man's darling than a young man's fool," she said.

I couldn't argue with my mother. She always had the final word. She was a strict woman, very short-tempered, and ever since my father left her she had been drinking heavily. She would often beat me and my siblings with a switch if we disobeyed her. But I was disappointed, troubled, and hurt by her attempts to kill my dream of marrying the man I truly loved.

David was also living in Alexandra. When he heard from his mother and sister that his suit had been rejected, he sent word asking to see me. I dressed in my best *mucheka*, tribal dress, and went, taking elaborate precautions that my mother wouldn't find out. It was taboo for a young woman to visit a man without her parents' permission or an escort. But I had grown up in the city, and didn't subscribe to all the customs.

I found David alone in his neat, tiny shack. It had a small bunk bed, milk crates for nightstands, a small three-legged wooden table with pieces of newspaper for a tablecloth, and the walls were plastered with newspapers serving as insulation and wallpaper. A half-spent candle flickered on the table.

David didn't believe in wasting money. With his wages of R3 a week, he could have afforded a nicer place, fancier clothes, and a more lavish life-style, like many of his friends from the homelands. But he was frugal. He wore overalls, didn't drink, and, ever since he started working, had been saving most of his earnings for *lobola*, as many men did who had no sisters on whose *lobola* they could count to get themselves wives. David had sisters, yet he preferred working and saving for his *lobola*. He said earning his own *lobola* gave him a sense of pride and independence, and prevented complications should the marriage of the sister who was the source of the *lobola* not work out. David was also a Christian, and the church discouraged the practice of *lobola* and only reluctantly sanctioned it in cases where the man earned the money rather than sold his sister to obtain it.

"Why doesn't your mother want us to marry?" David asked. "Is it because I'm a relative?"

"No. I don't think so."

"What's the reason, then?"

David was sitting on a tin chair, and I sat on the floor. My head was slightly bowed to the side and my eyes looked shyly down. We were at a respectful distance from each other.

At first I didn't want to tell the truth. I didn't want to speak ill of my mother. But I loved David, and I could feel the disappointment and pain in his heart. So I said, "My mother doesn't want me to marry someone young."

David bristled. "But I'm a grown man now. I've been to mountain school. I work. I can afford the *lobola*."

"I know," I said.

"And I love you."

"I know that too."

"And I will make every effort to make you happy."

I didn't say anything. But the tears flooding my eyes spoke for my heart.

David went on. "Why does your mother think that an older man will make you happy?"

"I don't know. But she feels that a young man in a few years is more likely to leave me for a younger woman. Just like my grandfather left my grandmother, and my father left my mother. Both married young men."

"But I won't do that," David said passionately. "I love you and will be faithful to you, as a husband should."

"My mother doesn't believe that."

"Don't you believe it?"

"I'm still young. I don't know what to believe. My mother has the bitter experience."

"Don't you love me?"

"I do. But you know I can't go against my mother's wishes."

"Does she have any specific old man in mind for you?"

"I don't know."

"Doesn't your mother know that older men often have other wives? Sometimes many of them?"

"She does."

"Won't you mind sharing a man with other women?"

"I will never be a second, third, fourth, or fifth wife to any man," I said vehemently. "I'd rather die."

David came over to where I was sitting, squatted, and gently held my hand. He ran his eyes admiringly over my *mucheka*, which he had told me many times was the prettiest he had ever seen and became me well. For a while neither of us spoke. Finally he proposed that we elope.

"We can live in another township," he said eagerly, "far away from here where we won't be found."

I was mortified.

"I love you, David," I said. "But I can't run away and leave my mother and siblings alone and suffering. She depends on me, especially now that my big sister Mphephu is married and lives far away. It would wound her deeply. And what if I ran away with you and you proved untrue to your promises, as so many men do?"

"I swear I would never be unfaithful to you," David said.

"But what if I do something to anger you and you start to beat me, where would I go? I couldn't return to my mother."

"I'll never lay a hand on you."

But when I persisted with my arguments, David finally understood the obligation I felt to my mother and siblings, even if it meant foregoing a chance at my own happiness. We said farewell to each other, and held out hope that my mother would change her mind and let us marry, because our hearts belonged together.

At first Jackson's courtship was indirect. He was a regular drinker at a *shebeen* in an adjacent yard, operated by a woman named Mrs. Makhemisi. Whenever I hung laundry to dry on the line, swept the courtyard, or made the brazier, I would peep over the fence and often see him sitting among a cluster of men, drinking beer and talking boisterously.

He was a man of about forty, a trifle short, dark skinned, with a face hardened by years of manual labor and drinking. He spoke Venda, a language we Shangaans scorned. He struck me as conceited, and acted as if he could get whatever he wanted, including me. He first approached Mrs. Makhemisi, who was my mother's friend, and asked questions about me.

"Who is that girl?" Jackson asked.

Mrs. Makhemisi told him my name—Magdaline Mudjadji Geli Mabaso—and added that I was fresh from the homelands and had just graduated from ritual school. Ritual school, *tikhomba*, was a sort of rites of passage during which girls in their puberty were transformed into marriageable, sexually active women.

"I want her," Jackson said. "She'll make me the perfect wife. She's a hard worker. I always see her working when I come over to your place. And she's pretty too."

"But she's too young."

"So much the better."

"She won't like you," Mrs. Makhemisi said. "I know her. She's too cheeky. She'll say you're too old."

"I said I want her, and I'll *have* her, or my name isn't Jackson Mathabane."

"Why do you want such a child?" asked Mrs. Makhemisi. "There are many other women your age, Jackson. I can set you up with any one of them. And they'll be all too glad to have you for a husband. You have a job."

"I don't like city women," Jackson said. "They're too independent. I want her. She seems well raised. Didn't you say she used to live with her older sister in the homelands?"

"Yes. She just got back."

"And you say she's been to ritual school?"

"Yes."

"Then she's the wife for me."

Makhemisi then set to work, especially after Jackson had promised to bring her more of his drinking buddies. Competition for customers among *shebeens* was fierce, and Jackson was staying in a men's compound and had many friends.

One afternoon as I was building a cooking fire outside, Mrs. Makhemisi came to the fence and called me over. I went. She said she wanted to introduce me to someone who liked me very much.

"Who?" I asked.

She pointed at Jackson, who was sitting in his usual place. He grinned as he saw me staring at him.

"Him," I said scornfully. "He's old enough to be my grandfather."

"He'll take good care of you," said Mrs. Makhemisi. "He's got a good job."

"I'm not interested."

"He makes $1.50 a week."

"I wouldn't be interested even if he made a hundred times that."

Mrs. Makhemisi then went to work on my mother. She knew that if she could get her to approve of Jackson, then I would be his. She described Jackson's virtues to my mother: he was older, was not a *tsotsi* (gangster), had a steady job and earned $1.50 a week—not too many men earned that much—and had promised that once we were married, he would not take me far away from my mother. Mrs. Makhemisi knew that my mother was eager to have me settle near her once I was married.

At this time my mother was again having financial problems and we were forced to leave our shack. We moved back with Aunt Matinana, my mother's stepsister. Though Aunt Matinana and her siblings had inherited all of my late grandfather's wealth and knew we were destitute, they had never offered to help us. Several of the siblings even disavowed any kinship with us. And Aunt Matinana condescended to assist us on condition we were willing to work for her. She offered us a tiny room in her big house. A month later she began charging us rent, even after promising us rent-free lodgings.

At Aunt Matinana's I became a slave. I cleaned the house, washed the laundry, and cooked, even though she had several young daughters. They were sent to school while I worked. Granny helped Aunt Matinana with beer selling. When Jackson found out we had moved, he tracked us down and persisted in his courtship. He was in luck. He found a powerful ally in Aunt Matinana.

"Why won't you marry Jackson?" Aunt Matinana asked me one day.

"He's too old, Auntie. He's more than twice my age."

"What's the matter with that?" she retorted. "Old men make better husbands. Besides, he has a job and can help you and your mother."

"I don't love him, Auntie."

"What's love got to do with it?" Aunt Matinana snapped. "Now stop being foolish, girl, and next time Jackson calls treat him nice."

Jackson had become one of Aunt Matinana's favorite customers but I refused to treat him nice. I was often rude to him and gave him stale beer in the hope that he would stop coming. Sometimes, when he made me particularly angry with his advances, I even spit in it. When Aunt Matinana found out she beat me while my mother looked on, afraid to intervene lest we find ourselves homeless.

One late afternoon Jackson stopped by and found me alone in the house, getting ready to cook dinner. There was a pot of hot water on the stove and I was busy preparing meat. He asked where everyone was.

"They're out," I said brusquely.

"That's a pretty *mucheka* you're wearing," he said.

I made no response.

"Once you become my wife," he said, "you'll lose all that stubbornness."

"I'll never be your wife, you old geezer."

"We'll see about that. You'll not only be my wife but you'll bear me lots of children."

"Never."

His conceit and arrogance infuriated me. When he touched me I lost my head. I grabbed the pot of hot water and drenched him with it. Luckily for him, the water was not yet boiling, but it was hot enough to make him scream. Soaking wet from head to foot, astonished, and doing his best to contain his anger, Jackson got up and stormed out, mumbling curses and threats under his breath.

When Aunt Matinana and my mother returned and heard the news from neighbors, Aunt Matinana soundly thrashed me with a piece of wood. She threatened to call the police and have me arrested for what I had done to Jackson.

The water incident sealed my fate. The following day Aunt Mati-nana informed Jackson that he should bring his *lobola* down payment immediately and it would be accepted. From then on David was to be only a memory of what could have been, and Jackson the night-mare that haunted me for the rest of my life.

3

GRANNY

ABANDONED FOR
ANOTHER WOMAN

I thought Jackson, being an older man and not a relative, would make a good husband for my daughter Geli. I married a young man and a relative, and have regretted it the rest of my life. I didn't even know I was getting married until my parents called me into the hut one afternoon, in the Shangaan homeland of Gazankulu ("Big Home"), and said, "John Mabaso, the son of your Uncle Mzamani, is to be your husband. He's going to marry you."

I had to say then and there whether I liked him or not. I said, "Yes, I will marry John Mabaso." Had I said no, my decision would have been overridden because my feelings as a woman didn't matter.

John and I had never courted. Our parents had arranged everything. Custom said they knew best about such matters, and possessed the experience and judgment to choose the right partners for us. I was told that if young girls were left to choose their own husbands, they would be blinded by love into forgetting their duty. Love, I was told, was unimportant in a marriage. Women were foolish to want such a frivolous thing as love, especially when there were more important things to desire in a marriage: being the first wife, marrying rich, and having many children. Those women who wanted love were told it would grow with familiarity.

As John was a first cousin, my maternal grandmother's brother's son, the rite of *dlaya shilongo* (killing the blood relation) had to be performed. Among our tribe the marriage of the *bashaka* (close relatives) was taboo unless this rite was performed, so John's parents brought the ox with which to "open the hut" and to announce their son's intention to marry me. A few days later both our relatives assembled and the rite was performed.

John and I sat on a ceremonial mat on the cow-dung floor inside my parents' hut. The ox was slaughtered and an offering made to my ancestors to witness that any shame that arose from being blood relations was being killed in the daylight, as there was nothing to hide, and that they should bless us with children. If the rite wasn't performed, I would have been cursed to remain childless.

Getting married to John made me the proudest woman in the village. I was twenty-one, which was considered very old. My mother and relatives had worried that I would never get married. Most women became brides at fifteen and sixteen, and some while as young as twelve. As soon as girls started menstruating and graduated from ritual school, they got married.

In fact, groups of men often waited outside ritual schools, to have their pick as soon the *tikhomba*, the newly initiated, made their grand appearance after a three-month seclusion, wearing veils and decked out in spectacular outfits showcasing them as prospective brides. It was like a cattle market. But girls liked it and found the attention flattering, especially because most of the men dazzled them with trinkets such as bracelets, beads, mirrors, and *doeks* (head scarves) they had bought in the city where they worked.

But I wasn't so easily snared. I wanted to postpone marriage as long as I could. I was in love with myself. I had the habit of strolling down the village road dancing and singing, like a carefree spirit. I wanted men to see that I was now a woman but admire me only from a distance. I didn't yet want to be owned by any man. From watching my mother I knew that the best years enjoyed by a woman were when she was young and unmarried, able to do whatever she pleased, unburdened by the unending responsibilities of obeying her husband's will and looking after his house and children.

In my youth, suitors preferred girls who were proven hard workers. Another important requirement for marriage was that no one in the girl's family be implicated in witchcraft. The ideal of beauty was tallness, strong limbs, and large breasts, which were considered proof that the girl would have no trouble suckling strong children. A father could demand more *lobola* simply on the basis of the size of his daughter's breasts.

To parade their beauty, girls wore nothing above the waist, except tons of gorgeous colorful beads they made themselves. They went about with naked breasts, bras were unknown, there was no shame, and virgins could be distinguished by their erect breasts, compared to the drooping ones of married women, who had suckled many children.

Women stopped going around half-naked when the missionaries came and called the practice "heathen" and inspired by the devil. They spoke to our chief, who reluctantly put an end to it. We started wearing dresses. I was among those who first wore dresses in our village, because my father was a lay preacher in the Swiss mission church. I looked pretty in dresses, even though I preferred the tribal outfits, as they felt more natural and were more lovely because we made and embroidered them ourselves. As a compromise between tribal and modern dress, I took to wearing my *mucheka* with a bushy skirt called *tinguvu* under it, a T-shirt, usually white, along with an intricately folded *doek*, which resembled a turban, on my head. But I never gave up the colorful bracelets which covered my legs, from the ankles to the knees, and arms, from the wrists to the elbows.

Most women made these bracelets themselves, from metal wires, and never took them off, whether bathing, sleeping, or making love.

They always jangled when we moved, which gave our dances a special rhythm.

Across my stomach I had a lovely tattoo, a tribal beauty mark. My mother made it by cutting tiny notches in my stomach with a razor blade when I was about ten. I remember it hurt, there was no anesthesia, but I was proud because when I went to the river to bathe with other girls, I was no longer the butt of jokes for not having *tinhlanga*. We also chewed tobacco, and girls who didn't were considered strange.

My wedding day was a memorable affair. I was decked out in resplendent tribal regalia, from head to foot, and there was great feasting on homemade beer and cooked and roasted meat from a freshly slaughtered cow. We sang and danced under the open, starry sky, out in the courtyard. I most enjoyed the dancing. Before I was married my mother often took me on trips to dance contests in other villages, where I won numerous prizes.

John and I weren't together long after our wedding before he returned to work in Johannesburg, where he earned $2 a month, standard wage for a black man in the 1930s and 1940s.

"I will send for you as soon as I've found a place for us," he said.

"I will wait faithfully, my husband," I said.

For the next six years John and I saw each other twice or thrice a year, when his white employers allowed him leave from work. Our children—two girls, Mphephu and Magdaline, and a son, Reuben—were conceived during these brief visits.

I vividly remember when Mphephu, my first child, was born. Midwives, *tinsungakati*, from the village were summoned to the hut where I was in labor. My mother, young girls in the family, and men were forbidden inside the hut because their presence would harm the child.

I screamed and sweated profusely as I clung to the big wooden mortar I had been given by the midwives to lean on. The earthen floor of the hut was covered with special straw mats to help ease some of my discomfort. But pain was regarded as part of childbearing. A woman was supposed to have the strength to bear it. One reason the mother and sisters of the woman in labor were not allowed to be present during delivery was that they might be ashamed of her screams.

As it was my first child, I didn't quite know what to do or how to cope with the pain. I was afraid. The midwives reassured me, told me to grit my teeth and rely on my strength. They held my knees as I fought through each contraction, and occasionally gently rubbed my stomach to make me comfortable. From time to time they gave me sips of warm water to drink.

When only one child, a baby girl, finally appeared, after several hours of labor, I was relieved. Had I given birth to twins, it would have been a bad omen, and one of them would have had to be killed. Then the villagers would have buried the dead twin in the wet soil of the river bank. If the tiny corpse were buried in dry soil, the gods would be angry and withhold rain, causing drought and famine.

The afterbirth, *yindlu ya nwana* ("the house of the child"), was attended to with great care and buried in a place where hyenas and other wild animals couldn't unearth it, which was taboo.

Three months after Mphephu was born, I presented her to the new moon. I took her outside the hut, in private, on a beautiful cloudless evening, when the moon was full and the sky glittered with stars. I tossed her up into the air and said, "There is your moon, my dear child." I did this so her ears would be opened and she wouldn't be stupid. And now that I had "given her the moon," I could start singing her lullabies.

Each time before I sang her a lullaby, I would cook some corn, invite several of my relatives' small children, and give them the corn so they could throw grains at the baby while I sang. This always delighted Mphephu and she would giggle and wave her tiny limbs.

I took Mphephu with me everywhere, bound securely to my back with the goatskin she had received at her coming-out celebration, performed shortly after her birth when her umbilical cord had dried and fallen off. We went to the river together to fetch water, to the fields to sow and reap, and to the forest to gather firewood. She would go to sleep on my back. Whenever she was hungry I would simply swing her round in the goatskin sling and let her suckle, wherever we happened to be. When she got a little older, I dug a shallow hole in the ground and put her in it from time to time to help her learn to sit. Sometimes I would put her under the tree to sleep on a blanket. Whenever she cried, I would strap her to my back again, and rock from side to side, singing a lullaby. Invariably, she grew quiet.

It was taboo for any mother to conceive a second child until the first was weaned, around two and a half or three years old. I was told that the first child would die if I became pregnant, since it was impossible for a single womb to feed two children simultaneously.

I knew of a woman in my village whose child died mysteriously after she had violated the taboo, and she was blamed for killing the baby. In reality the elders of the village had poisoned the baby, but the woman believed she had killed her baby by allowing her husband to have intercourse with her before her child was weaned. She felt terribly guilty. She tried explaining that she hadn't meant to violate the taboo, but that her husband had forced her to have sex.

No one believed her. People constantly pointed accusing fingers at her and said, "You are the one who should have said no to your husband when he wanted to sleep with you." But it was hard for us women to say no to our husbands, because they had paid *lobola* for us and we had to obey them unconditionally.

Fortunately John Mabaso's visits were few and far between, and my children were always weaned before we had the opportunity to sleep together again. In fact, the youngest of the three, Geli, began talking while still breast-feeding. She would go to the river with other children to play and return at intervals to be breast-fed. She stopped when her playmates began singing ditties making fun of her.

The long separations from my husband, and our infrequent sex, made it easy, I believe, for another woman to replace me. I had heard that city women had no misgivings about sleeping with men before infants were weaned, or when they were menstruating, or right after they had had an abortion. To them, rituals and taboos and tradition meant little. They didn't even care whether a husband paid *lobola* or not. In fact they often preferred he didn't, so they could leave whenever they pleased.

When John stopped writing and sending me money I suspected another woman but had no proof. The impassioned letters I sent him, which a relative in the village who knew how to read and write wrote for me, reminded him of his promise to send for me. I begged him to send me money for food and to please visit every once in a while as the children and I missed him terribly.

"If you have taken a second wife, my dear husband," I wrote, "don't let that be an obstacle to your coming back. I don't mind a second wife. Most men have them. I understand your feeling lonely sometimes in that big city. But please come back, because I am your first wife and we have children together."

My letters were returned undelivered. John had apparently left his old address and moved to an unknown one. This was after our third child was born.

I started crying every night, fearing the worst, feeling alone and abandoned, just like my mother had been by my father, who went to Johannesburg and never came back, taking another woman there for a wife. I thought how cruel was the system that forced men to journey alone to the city to work, and forbade their wives and children from being with them.

My mother, who had never been quite the same since my father left her—she was constantly depressed, absentminded, and seemed sapped of the will to live—feared that I had been cursed with her fate. She was at a loss what to tell me to do, except to wait, and pray for John to come back, just as she had done.

Dissatisfied with this advice, I consulted various relatives. They too told me to be patient, that John would come back, that he hadn't forgotten me. Some relatives tried comforting me with dismal stories with happy endings, of men who went to the cities leaving their families in the homelands, and were not heard from for years, only to turn up again one day having amassed a fortune, and reunite with their families, and everyone lived happily ever after.

Months went by and John never wrote or came back.

Burdened with three children, and without any money to feed and clothe them, I began relying heavily on my relatives.

My only sibling, my brother, Johannes Shibalu, had died a few years earlier after he mysteriously fell ill during a trip to Giyane to fetch my *lobola* so as to get himself a wife. He had just come from Alexandra, where he and my father owned property.

At first, relatives were willing to help. Then I started hearing whispered criticisms that I and my children were a burden, that we were creating an imbalance in the village, and that I should go to Johannesburg and seek my husband, even though I would be breaking the law that prohibited wives and children from being in the city without permits.

One day, I said to my mother that I had decided to go to Johannesburg and search for my husband.

"Maybe that's the best thing to do, child," my mother said.

"But I don't have a place to stay in the city," I said.

"Go to your father's," my mother said.

"Will he help me," I asked, "with that Elizabeth telling him what to do?"

Elizabeth was my father's second wife. He had married her after leaving the village. Elizabeth was a shrewd and ambitious woman, known for her strong will, fierce temper, and ruthlessness. She couldn't brook the thought of being a junior wife to my mother and forbade my father from ever visiting my mother.

Elizabeth and my father were married before the magistrate and had several children, among them two daughters named Matinana and Elsie. She knew that according to tradition my mother, as the first wife, had precedence over her, thus she prevented any contact between my mother and father, in the hope that she and her children would be his sole heirs. She was so ruthless that even my father, a strong-willed man, had been cowed by her threats to kill him and my mother if she ever found them together.

"Certainly he will help you, child," my mother said, "despite that witch Elizabeth. Your father is your father, regardless of how Elizabeth may feel. He won't turn you away. You're his own flesh and blood."

I hoped my mother was right, that my father, despite Elizabeth's hatred of my mother, would allow me to stay at his house while I searched for my husband and sought a reconciliation. So in 1944 I packed my three children and our meager belongings and headed for Johannesburg.

4

FLORAH

INFIDELITY

Granny's husband left her for another woman. I left Collin and started living with my boyfriend, Walter, because of other women. When my father found out, he was livid.

"Is it true you've left your husband?" he demanded, a snarl on his face. I had just come home to fetch some of my belongings and found him alone in the kitchen, seated by the table repairing the sole of one of his worn-out shoes.

"Yes."

"Why did you leave?"

"Collin has been cheating on me."

"Cheating on you?" my father said skeptically. "Collin wouldn't do such a thing. I hear you're the one who's been cheating on him. Where have you been living these past few weeks?"

"I've been staying with Walter."

"Who's Walter?"

"My boyfriend," I said reluctantly.

"You see," my father said accusingly. "What sort of married woman are you to be running around with boyfriends? Are you a *skeberesh?*"

"No."

"Then why aren't you with your husband?"

"I told you," I said, my anger rising. "He's been sleeping with other women behind my back. I've put up with it for years, now I've had enough."

"I don't believe you," he said. "You're making up these accusations as an excuse to be with this Walter. You should go back to your husband. Remember, he paid *lobola* for you."

"I'm not going back to him."

"Then get out of my house!" he shouted. "Get out this minute."

"I need my things," I said.

"What things? Get out!" he started menacingly toward me. I ran outside and stood several feet away from the door. We engaged in a shouting match. He called me all sorts of insulting names and I returned the favor. Angeline, three years old, had run out after me and stood next to me, tugging at the hem of my dress, saying, "Mama, let's go. Let's go. I don't like Grandpa."

I felt embarrassed, humiliated, and angry at my father. My mother, who might have diffused the situation as she had done many times before, was away testifying (sharing Christ with non-Christians) with a group of women from her church. Two of my younger sisters, Mirriam and Maria, had been next door and the commotion brought them home. But they simply stood by helpless, afraid to intervene lest my father attack them too, as he often did.

I left with my daughter for Walter's place as soon as clusters of nosy neighbors began peering through windows and congregating about doors to witness the spectacle of my father and me vilifying each other. Our yard on 16th Avenue, about the size of an average white suburban home, contained nearly a hundred people, most of them with an insatiable appetite for gossip and scandal.

The spectacle of my father abusing members of his family was highly entertaining to many of our neighbors. It made them feel superior to us, despite their abject poverty and misery.

Ever since my family moved into the yard, after our old shack on 13th Avenue collapsed one afternoon—fortunately no one was home at the time—many of our neighbors had taken a perverse delight in our troubles. Some were jealous of us because my brother, Johannes—who took on the name Mark in 1976 in an effort to hide his identity from the police—was studying in America. Others disliked us for striving to lift ourselves from poverty by working, sending children to school, and buying nice things for the shack, such as kitchen cabinets, a secondhand mattress, and cheap linoleum to cover the bare floors.

Even when my father added a lean-to as a kitchen to the tiny two-room shack, by slapping together some zincs, cardboards, and cement blocks, a few neighbors with tinier shacks were heard murmuring, "The Mathabanes are moving up in the world now. Soon they'll start looking down on us."

For some strange reason my father didn't want any money—including my own—spent on home or personal improvement. Materials for the lean-to were mainly scraps he had picked up in junkyards and abandoned buildings. One time, while I was still living at home, he threatened to burn a pair of new cheap dresses I had purchased after I got a new job at a flower shop.

"Aren't your old dresses good enough?" he asked.

"They're worn out, Dad," I replied.

"I wear worn-out things and nobody laughs at me."

"But Dad, I work among white people all day," I said. "I have to look presentable."

"We can't eat dresses, you know," he said.

"But Dad, every week I buy groceries for this house," I said. "And I do need these dresses. Besides, it's my own money."

"It may be your money," he retorted sharply, "but this is my house. And I lay down the rules."

He would have been most happy had I given him the money to spend on himself. He was constantly demanding a share of everybody's hard-earned wages: my mother's, Maria's, mine. When we refused to give him any, he threatened to toss us out of the house.

Money was also the main reason he opposed my leaving Collin. He had already spent the *lobola* Collin had paid thus far, mostly on liquor for himself and his unemployed buddies, with whom he sat in the sun all day, drinking and talking about the latest violence and killings or the latest cases of witchcraft.

He therefore feared that if I left Collin permanently he would be unable to refund his *lobola,* and stood to lose the unpaid balance. Collin still owed my father nearly R850, having made only one payment since the down payment of R100. My father also worried that my leaving my marriage might set a bad precedent for my four as yet unmarried sisters. What if they, too, after *lobola* had been paid for them, were to get it into their heads to leave their husbands? My father would be a poor man indeed.

He regarded my four sisters and me mainly as a form of wealth and often boasted to his drinking buddies, "I am a rich man, now. I have five daughters."

One time one of his drinking buddies asked him, "Are all your daughters working?"

"No," my father said. "But they'll soon be married. And that's better than working. A working woman is nothing but trouble. She thinks that because she now earns a few pennies she can start wearing the pants around the house."

"You're quite right, Jackson," the man said. "I know such women. I'm married to one. And since I was laid off and she's working, she's taken to giving orders around the house. I keep thrashing her but she's too stubborn. But as for your daughters, don't count your chickens before they're hatched, it's bad luck."

My mother constantly warned my father against making these boasts to strangers.

"Do you want your daughters to be bewitched into not getting married?" she asked him one time.

"No one can bewitch them," my father said confidently. "The Mathabanes are well protected." By this he meant that he had taken care to obtain powerful *muti* to protect his investment.

For the first two years of our marriage, despite my being a slave to

Collin's family, and despite minor problems having mostly to do with newly married couples adjusting to each other, Collin and I had been relatively happy. He was faithful and we were very much in love. We worked near each other and we often walked home together. He would buy groceries for my family when my parents had no money, and was highly respected by my mother, who never believed a bad word said against him.

But our marriage began floundering when Collin started sleeping around with other women. His philandering began around the time I was having trouble conceiving and he began drinking and visiting *shebeens* packed with single women. I confronted him when friends told me they had seen him staggering out of *shebeens* with his arms embracing various women.

At first Collin categorically denied that he had ever been unfaithful. Then he began reminding me that I had no right to ask him such questions, that I was forgetting my role as an obedient and dutiful wife by impugning his integrity. His parents took his side and told him that he should have married a good Xhosa girl, rather than a stranger, a cheeky and infertile one at that, from another tribe.

Anxious to save my marriage, I forgave Collin and kept my mouth shut. Then Angeline was born and our marriage improved somewhat. He became a caring father and husband. For a while he even stopped seeing other women. But try as I did to pretend nothing was wrong in our relationship, his infidelity had wounded me to the core. I now distrusted him. I felt betrayed, for I had truly believed he'd be unlike other men, especially after I had given him a daughter, a child he and his parents so desperately wanted and without whom I was considered incomplete as a woman, and felt that way myself.

I left Collin reluctantly, as a last resort. I wanted desperately for our marriage to last. I dreamed of our working hard together and leaving the ghetto for one of those lovely houses they were constructing in the decent part of Alexandra—Phase 1, Phase 2, or East Bank—which had electricity, indoor toilets, extra rooms, and a yard for children to play in and friends to gather for weekend *braaivleis*, cookouts.

I wanted us to make both our families proud. Both of us had grown up the hard way, and were making something of ourselves through sheer hard work. But my dreams of matrimonial bliss evaporated when Collin's infidelity became a regular habit. They were replaced by pain, anger, a sense of betrayal, self-doubt, and self-blame. What did I do wrong? We seemed so happy and everyone thought us the perfect couple. Didn't I satisfy him enough? Was I sexually inadequate? Was there some woman out there who wanted Collin so badly she was using voodoo to take him away from me?

Soon I could no longer deal with the enormous pain of constantly forgiving Collin and taking him back.

My hurt and anger turned to rage when I found out that Collin had even tried to seduce my own cousin, Florence, who used to visit me and often gave me advice and support whenever I had problems with Collin or his parents.

Florence was two years older than I, a single woman and a mother of two. She used to live with her husband in a section of Soweto, but they fought constantly because he wanted a third child and she didn't—not for a while anyway. She wanted a career, and operated an unlicensed beauty salon, which provided her with an independent income. She specialized in straightening women's hair according to the latest American style. Her husband opposed her having an independent income, and must have thought that if Florence were perpetually pregnant she would have no time to work.

When Florence continued resisting having a third child, he started having affairs with other women. When she found out, she kicked him out, confident she could take care of herself and her children without a man. I admired Florence's courage and strength.

One day, when Angeline was a few weeks old, Florence came to visit me. She wanted to go to the store to buy me some food and Collin offered to accompany her. Florence later told me that on the way Collin said to her, "You know, Florence, I find you ravishing."

"What?!" Florence cried, horror-struck.

"I want to go out with you," Collin said. "I dig you."

"Please stop making such jokes," Florence said, trying her best to control her anger. "Not only are you married, but you're married to my cousin and my close friend! How dare you even say that!"

"Florah and I aren't really married," Collin said. "I haven't even finished paying *lobola* for her."

"But she has your child."

"We'll make sure she doesn't find out."

"You don't know me well, Collin," Florence said. "I can never do that to any woman, let alone my own cousin. And you know what, I've lost all respect for you."

"Take it easy, Florence," Collin said. "I was only joking."

"Please stop making such tasteless jokes," she said.

When Florence told me this I was furious with Collin, but he made light of the matter when I confronted him, repeating that he had only been joking.

The second time, he took Florence to the *shebeen*, thinking he could get her drunk and take advantage of her. After a couple of drinks he made a pass at her.

"Go to hell," Florence said to him. "You must be some low, creeping, double-crossing vermin to act like this when you're married to such a good woman as my cousin."

"But Florah won't know," he said.

"Yes, she may not," Florence said. "But I *will*."

Florence had thought the first attempted seduction an innocent mistake, but realizing Collin was dead serious about having an affair with her, she came straight home and told me to pack my bags and leave the bastard.

"If he has no shame trying to seduce me, your own cousin," Florence said, "I can just imagine how many other girls he must be sleeping with."

"But I can't leave, Florence," I said, sobbing. "I have a tiny baby. It needs a father. And I have no money. And I'm physically exhausted from the difficult pregnancy."

"But you can't allow him to go on hurting you like this," Florence said. "Go back home and tell your parents what he's doing. Surely, they'll understand."

"No, they won't," I said. "Not my father. He'll tell me it's my fault."

"Go back only for a few weeks then," Florence said. "Just long enough to show the bastard that if he doesn't stop his philandering, you'll leave him for good."

I listened to Florence and packed my bags and left. When I got home I didn't tell my mother what had happened—I doubted she would have believed me, so fond was she of Collin. Instead I said that I was only visiting for a couple of weeks. When Collin found out I had left he came and pleaded for forgiveness, blaming his behavior on drunkenness, and promised to stop hurting me. He sounded so sincere in his repentance I forgave him and went back.

I also forgave Collin when I found out that he had been sleeping around with women I had considered friends. It was the 1980s, a dangerous and violent time in Alexandra township. Women were losing their husbands, brothers, and boyfriends to police bullets, to insanity, and, as blacks killed each other for complex political reasons, to revenge and simple jealousy. People were sometimes killed for having a job by those who didn't. Some were killed for their shacks or because they owned used cars. Some of my girlfriends used the shortage of men as an excuse to start sleeping with Collin.

One day I confronted one of these snakelike friends, who had an extraordinarily big butt, which she stuck out even farther in her tight-fitting pants to show off whenever she went past a group of men, and they whistled.

"What are you doing sleeping with my husband?" I said angrily.

"My dear, don't be greedy," she said calmly. "We have to share our men now. There just aren't enough to go around."

"You can share other women's men, bitch," I said. "But keep your filthy paws off my husband."

"If I want him, I can have him," she retorted. "Any time. And there's nothing you can do about it."

She was right, there was nothing I could do about it. In the ghetto, women outnumbered men. At times it seemed like there were ten women to one man. How could a man not be tempted to sleep around when the numbers were so skewed and women were taught to feel incomplete without a man, and poverty and lack of education made many of them economically and emotionally dependent?

When Collin's infidelity didn't stop, I knew I had to act decisively. I had to let go of him, the pain had become unbearable. I knew I needed to live apart from him, to heal, to reassess things, to see if I could have my own life and be independent of him. I told myself I was through with him unless he completely changed his behavior.

But Collin refused to accept my leaving him. He threatened to take Angeline away from me if I did. Like a lot of men, he believed he had a right to sleep around while it was my duty to stay at home, cook, clean, take care of his children, remain faithful, and never complain.

He never thought of the pain his womanizing caused me. He never considered the dangers of AIDS and other sexually transmitted diseases. Like a lot of men, he thought himself immune to such diseases, even though daily there were stories of children born with syphilis, herpes, and gonorrhea. And AIDS, little known to most blacks at the time, had started its silent and deadly rampage in the ghettos, and in a few years was to reach epidemic proportions.

Though I considered Collin and I married, we hadn't done so before a magistrate, so I had no legal rights to sue for divorce, alimony, or custody, and under the *lobola* custom children belonged to the husband. I feared losing my little daughter.

Even with that possibility I again packed my bags and returned to my parents' home a second time. Mindful of my mother's fondness for Collin, and my father's eagerness for *lobola*, I was again evasive about the reason I had come back home. I told my mother that Collin and I weren't getting along too well and I needed time away from him to sort things out.

Collin again came and begged for forgiveness and for me to come back home.

"No way am I coming back," I said to him. "I'm through with you.

I gave you plenty of chances to clean up your life but you've refused."

"You know that if you don't come back I can no longer support you," he said.

"Is that a threat?"

"It's up to you."

"Don't worry about me," I said. "I can take care of myself."

"What about Angeline?"

"Do you mean you'll stop supporting her because I've left you?"

"As I've said, it's up to you," Collin said. "If you come back that won't be necessary because we'll all be together. But if you don't I want my daughter back."

"I'm not giving her to you."

"We'll see about that."

With that threat, Collin left. The support stopped. I trudged all over the suburbs looking for work. Luckily I found employment at a flower shop, and was able to earn enough to take care of myself and my daughter, who was almost three. Shortly after I began working at the flower shop I started seeing Walter. This was nearly six months after Collin and I separated.

Walter was short and muscular, owned a jalopy and operated a taxi for his brother. He had a thirteen-year-old son who attended boarding school. At age thirty-six he was thirteen years older than me. Before I met him, he had a reputation as a *tsotsi*, a gangster, but he never talked about his past. I thought him a good catch, especially for a vulnerable young woman living in a violent ghetto. He was tough, sober, street smart, and had his own place, in a yard belonging to his family that had a famous disco and *shebeen*.

At first, spending nights with Walter was merely a way for me to get back at Collin for hurting me. I wanted to make him jealous. I wanted to show him that he wasn't the only man in the world, that, *lobola* or no *lobola*, I could be with another man who respected me and treated me better. Yet in the back of my mind I kept hoping that Collin would change his behavior and we would reconcile. But with time I fell in love with Walter, and he with me, or so I thought.

As custom still said I belonged to Collin, and would continue to do so until he was refunded his *lobola*, I hoped that Walter would agree to pay back the money. But I soon had second thoughts about whether or not he should. I wondered if his paying *lobola* for me would change him in the same way it had Collin.

5

GELI

A CHILD IS BORN

While my daughter's marital problems troubled me deeply, I knew only too well how difficult life could be for a new wife, a *makoti*. One moment you are single and free; the next, a household drudge heaped with responsibilities and having to cope with the vagaries of men.

I was sold to Jackson in the winter of 1958. There was no wedding celebration and no exchange of rings. I was in no mood to celebrate. I simply moved into his tiny basement room on 14th Avenue. It had no furniture, except for a rusty single bed with a hard mattress and without a headboard, a small unpainted table and cupboard, two unpainted chairs, and some milk crates used for storage. The cold room had no windows and was heated with a brazier, which was also used for cooking.

For two months after I moved in I refused to let him touch me. I spent most of the time alone, as if in mourning. He tried acting affectionately, buying me things, improving the appearance of the room, and giving me money; but I was indifferent to everything. We hardly talked. I grew depressed whenever I thought of David and imagined how happy we could have been together.

"You're mine now," Jackson said one day. "And nothing you do can change that. So you might as well forget about David."

"I may be yours," I said, "but you'll never have my heart."

"We'll see about that."

He went to my mother and Aunt Matinana and complained about my "stubbornness." Afraid that he might demand his *lobola* back, part of which had already been spent, they summoned me home and Aunt Matinana gave me severe lectures on my duties as a wife, which boiled down to pleasing Jackson, obeying his every command, and conceiving as soon as possible.

Then Aunt Matinana said, "Ellen, talk to your foolish child. I don't want the family to be disgraced by her headstrong behavior." She went out of the room, leaving my mother and me alone.

My mother sidled over to where I sat on the mat, and held my hand, gently stroking it.

"My child, I feel the unhappiness in your heart," she began. "It gives me sleepless nights and makes me wonder if I did the right thing in letting Jackson marry you. But I did it to help the family and to secure your future. Some good has come out of it."

"How can you say that, Mama, when I'm so unhappy?" I said.

"Well, you may not know this," my mother said, "but the money Jackson paid in *lobola* has been put to good use. I no longer have to depend on your Aunt Matinana. I have it saved. I draw from it bit by bit to pay rent, buy food, and most important, to pay for your brother's schooling."

My heart was glad to hear that. Having been prevented from attending school because I was a girl, even though I begged to be allowed to go, I had developed a passion to see my brother Reuben educated.

While my grandfather was alive and we were living with him, I had eagerly looked forward to Reuben returning home from school and sharing with me his lessons for the day. He would laugh at my clumsy attempts to copy what was in his books. But he was a patient teacher and helped me learn to count and recite the ABCs. If there was anything redeeming in my having been sold to a man I loathed, it was the knowledge that the *lobola* was helping my mother and siblings survive, and my brother learn.

I went back to Jackson and continued doing the duties expected of me: cooking for him, washing his clothes, which always had a bad smell, darning his socks and sewing his few shirts, and taking care of his house. I did not yet consider it my home. I did these things less reluctantly than before, and without complaining, and Jackson took my changed attitude to mean that I had come around to loving him. If only he had known the true state of my heart, he would have understood that *lobola* can buy a woman, but it cannot purchase her affections. Those have to be given willingly. They have to be deserved. They have to be reciprocated.

For four months I refused to sleep with him. I slept alone on the floor, and whenever he tried joining me I always rebuffed him. One ruse I was fond of using was that I was having *tinweti*, "the months," knowing it was taboo for a man to sleep with a woman when she was menstruating. At other times I pretended to be sick. In short, I did everything to avoid conceiving by him.

One night I had a dream in which my maternal grandmother came and talked to me about Jackson.

"Why are you married to this horrible man?" she asked.

"I didn't want to marry him, Grandma," I replied. "They forced me to."

"Tell your mother, my poor dear little daughter, that what she did was wrong. The ancestors are angry."

The next day, early in the morning, I went and told my mother about the dream. At first she reacted defensively, angrily, and accused me of having fabricated the dream. Then she calmed down, and lamented that there was nothing she could do to undo the deed, as Jackson's *lobola* had already been spent.

"My child," she said, "despite having put Jackson's *lobola* to good use, had we not moved in with your Aunt Matinana, I doubt now if I would have let you marry him. She made me do it, even though I'm partly to blame for going along. I was desperate, child. Your Aunt Matinana was hounding me for rent money. And had she kicked us out, where would we have gone?"

"We could have found work, Mama," I said.

"Where, my child?" my mother said.

"There are lots of jobs at the Indian place," I said.

"Huh. Don't you recall the many times I've trudged from one Indian place to another and been told there was no work? Even robust men can't find work. And those with jobs are being laid off. They say it's the same situation all over the country."

"But there are always jobs for maids in the suburbs," I said.

"Yes, child," my mother said, "but not for people without permits."

I fell silent. I had forgotten about apartheid and its demands that black people have permits to work in white areas. Survival was such a daily preoccupation, and there were so many laws governing black people that one seldom thought of them until one ran afoul of them.

"That's why I'm thinking of using the little money that's left from your *lobola* to start brewing and selling beer. But I can't do that here. Your Aunt Matinana won't let me because she sells beer herself. So we'll have to move soon. I'm waiting for an affordable shack to become available somewhere."

This was the first time I had heard of my mother's intention to move. I became anxious. "Don't move too far, Mama," I said. "I want you near so I can have a place to run to when trouble starts with Jackson, as I know it will."

"I won't go too far, my child. You and your siblings are all I have left in the world."

She then invited me to join her in offering a propitiatory sacrifice of snuff to my angry ancestors for causing them pain through my marriage to Jackson. We embraced, solaced each other with words of hope, and I left.

When I didn't conceive immediately after my marriage to Jackson, people began to wonder. Aunt Matinana confronted me and inquired if I had been "naughty" before I got married. She wanted to know if I had slept with any man, who might now be tying up my womb, thereby preventing conception.

I replied no. Had I had any sexual relations before marriage I would have had to confess all my lovers in front of my husband so that my womb would be untied.

"Then where are the children?" Aunt Matinana demanded.

"I don't like this man," I said.

"You better bear him children," Aunt Matinana said. "You're now stuck with him. Don't disgrace the family. And remember the *lobola* he paid for you is gone. And you know who spent it. Your mother."

A month after the talk with Aunt Matinana I became pregnant. As soon as Jackson found out, he was elated. He became more understanding, no longer shouted at me, and allowed me to buy whatever my appetite craved. He even made a deposit at the clinic so that nurses would come and attend to me at childbirth.

The pregnancy went tolerably well until about a week before I was due, when I had a visit from a strange old woman. She was short, with greying hair, wrinkled skin, and ferretlike eyes. Her name was Mrs. Malotsi and Jackson told me she was his distant relation.

"I would have married her daughter if I had gone back to the homeland for a wife," Jackson said.

How I wished he had.

Jackson seemed to know the old woman well, and the two spent evenings reminiscing about old times. There was hardly any room for her in the shack, so Jackson partitioned it into two with a piece of burlap stretched across the room.

I thought Mrs. Malotsi kind to have come at such an opportune time and offer to act as a midwife. She cooked for me, cleaned the house, and washed laundry. My own mother, who normally would have served as midwife and done all this, was away in Soweto visiting various *ngangas*, seeking treatment for a nagging foot injury.

Mrs. Malotsi went out of her way to coax me into eating meals she had prepared, and kept asking me if I needed anything. I didn't suspect her of anything evil until I began having contractions. It was on a Tuesday. The pain was most excruciating. Mrs. Malotsi reassured me that the pain was normal, and that all would be well. I had heard of pain during childbirth, so I didn't make much of it.

Wednesday came and still the baby wasn't any nearer to being born, yet the unbearable contractions persisted. I was now completely bedridden and growing weak from the ordeal. Jackson became concerned.

"Don't worry," Mrs. Malotsi told Jackson. "Go to work tomorrow and when you get back, the baby will be here. I'll take good care of Geli."

Jackson returned from work and still there was no baby. Thursday came and still no baby. Yet the strange, wrenching pain continued. I thought I was going to die. I was sweating profusely. I spoke in labored speech. I told Jackson that I suspected something was terribly wrong and asked him to call the clinic people. The clinic was about a mile away and Jackson had to walk there.

On the way to the clinic, Jackson decided to stop at 4th Avenue and consult with his brother, Silas, who owned and operated a tailor shop. He found Silas with his wife, Aunt Sarah, who happened to be visiting from the homelands.

As soon as Aunt Sarah heard that Mrs. Malotsi was acting as my midwife, she was indignant and alarmed.

"How in the world did you let that witch into your house?" she berated Jackson. "Don't you know that she's never forgiven you for not marrying her daughter?"

"But I thought that was in the past," Jackson said sheepishly. "Ever since she came she's been very helpful."

"Of course, you fool," Aunt Sarah said. "She had to give the appearance of being helpful in order to work her evil."

"What should I do?" Jackson said, bewildered.

"What should you do?" Aunt Sarah retorted. "Get that witch out of the house at once or your wife and child will die."

Jackson didn't even bother proceeding to the clinic. He promptly returned home, accompanied by Aunt Sarah, and the two told Mrs. Malotsi to pack and leave. Mrs. Malotsi left without a word, but as she was packing I noticed that her face had a smirk of malevolent satisfaction.

Aunt Sarah immediately took over as midwife. The first thing she did was to throw out all the food Mrs. Malotsi had prepared. She ordered Jackson to go buy fresh groceries. She then gave me a sponge bath and made me something to eat.

I slept a little better that evening, but I still had those wrenching contractions. Jackson was so beside himself with worry that the next day he reluctantly went to work. He came back around noon.

"I couldn't work," he said. "I told my boss that I just had to go home as my wife was very sick."

"You didn't have to," Aunt Sarah said. "Geli is feeling a bit better now."

"Well, I simply couldn't concentrate on anything," Jackson said.

I was deeply moved by the gesture. It meant that he had lost half a day's pay out of concern for me, and might even have been fired for making such a request if he had had a common employer. I became even more determined to have the baby. Jackson then left to consult a *nganga* in an effort to get to the bottom of the matter. He returned with a stocky, jet-black man with deep-set eyes and dressed in animal skins. The *nganga* was renowned among the Vendas of Alexandra, yet his price was reasonable. He asked me detailed questions about Mrs. Malotsi's behavior since she came, then consulted his divinatory bones.

A while later he delivered the terrible news: Malotsi was indeed a witch. She had come with plans to kill me and the baby because of the grudge she still bore Jackson for not marrying her daughter. She had worked her voodoo by putting *muti* in the food she had been giving me.

The *nganga* gave me the antidote, and then performed a purification ceremony, but couldn't guarantee if I or the baby would make it.

"It's now in the hands of the gods," he said.

That evening Jackson sent word to my mother in Soweto that I was seriously ill and she needed to come despite her foot injury. Saturday morning my mother hobbled into the shack. She broke down in tears when she saw my haggard look and the pain I was in. She thanked Aunt Sarah for her timely intervention and then took charge of things, constantly reassuring me that all would be well. I was very pleased to see her. Every half hour she prayed to our ancestors for assistance and made offerings. I continued taking the *muti* the *nganga* had prescribed and gradually felt better.

During the night the contractions again began in earnest. Jackson went to the clinic and summoned the nurses, and at around seven o'clock Saturday morning, after five days of excruciating pain, I gave birth to an eight-pound, nine-ounce baby boy. I named him Johannes, in remembrance of my dead uncle Shibalu, my mother's only sibling. Aunt Sarah had the honor of giving the baby the tribal name Thanyani, which means "Be Wise."

"The name has a message for you and the child," Aunt Sarah said to me. "It admonishes you to wise up, to stop being gullible and naive, and too trusting of strangers. For the child it advises him to remember when he's grown and working that wisdom lies in taking care of those who with difficulty brought him into the world."

Scarcely were my mother, Aunt Sarah, or myself aware that this little manchild who almost didn't make it into this life, with whom I almost died at childbirth, would one day go to America, and as Mark write books about black life under apartheid.

After Johannes was born, my mood changed. I now had something to live for. I was proud to be a mother and doted on my baby, often dressing him in girl's clothing, as his features so much resembled a girl's. He cried a lot though, and was short tempered and didn't like being breast-fed.

Jackson, too, was overjoyed at the birth of our son. He now had an heir, and he openly expressed a desire that my future children be all girls, who would bring him lots of *lobola*. He showered the baby with presents and I never lacked for diapers, baby clothes, and rattles. He even bought my mother and Aunt Matinana gifts. He became very supportive of me, attentive to my every need, and even loving, in his own way.

Every Friday he brought me his entire wage, and asked me if there was anything I or the baby needed. My resentment of him gradually softened, and I hoped that our newfound understanding would last, and maybe ripen into something akin to love.

Jackson had an uncle called William in Hammerskraal, outside of Pretoria, the capital of South Africa. He took me there on a visit one weekend. He only stayed a day, as he had to get back to work, but he told me that I could remain as long as I wanted to regain my strength and get to know some of his relatives.

We began visiting Hammerskraal regularly. Uncle William worked for the railway and owned a large farm, on which he planted mealies, fruit trees, and various vegetables. The crops provided his growing family and other occupants of the farm with much needed sustenance and income. His wife treated me well, as soon as she found out that I was a hard worker. There were several other families living on the farm, mainly William's relatives, and I always accompanied everybody to the fields, cooked, washed laundry, and helped with whatever work needed to be done.

During one prolonged visit there, a year and half after Johannes was born, he suddenly became sick. He kept vomiting every morsel of food given him, including my milk. He was lethargic, cried all the time, and slept fitfully. Jackson hadn't visited in nearly a month, nor did he send any money for food or diapers with his uncle, who visited Alexandra every two weeks. The only word from Jackson had been that he had no money.

Now my child was stricken. The nearest clinic was several hours away. No one owned a car, and the bus came around only once a week. Fortunately Johannes fell ill on Friday, and the next bus was due to come Monday. Uncle William's wife used her expertise in raising children to help stabilize Johannes by forcing him to take some *muti*, which temporarily stopped the vomiting. But Johannes still wouldn't eat, and remained very sick.

"Here's some money," Uncle William's wife said Sunday evening, handing me 20 cents. "It's enough to buy you a one-way ticket back to Alexandra. Pack your things tonight and tomorrow go find out what's wrong with your husband. Find out why he hasn't sent you any money or responded to your letters."

I packed my few belongings and strapped my child on my back with his goatskin blanket. He was so lethargic he slept the entire journey of several hours to Alexandra.

A shock awaited me at home. Jackson no longer lived at 14th Avenue. The landlord had repossessed the room. A neighbor told me that Jackson was now living with Silas, his brother, on 4th Avenue. Tired and hungry, I trudged there on foot, and found Silas at work mending pants in a room cluttered with jackets, pants, and overcoats needing fixing. He told me that Jackson was at work.

"Why is he living with you?" I asked.

"He was evicted about a month ago for not paying rent," Silas said.

"That's strange," I said. "That's exactly when he stopped sending me money. Has he told you anything?"

"He's told me many things," Silas said. "But it's better he told them to you himself. He's got a lot of explaining to do."

"And Johannes is very sick," I said.

"I can see that. Clearly Jackson has been irresponsible."

Silas gave me some money and I went to the local grocery store and bought a loaf of brown bread, came back, and made some tea. I tried giving Johannes some of the food but he turned his head away, fussed, and went back to sleep. Feeling exhausted, I slept too, and awoke when Jackson returned from work around 5 P.M. He was startled to see me but tried not to show it.

I told him about the child's illness and asked him why he had stopped sending me money.

"I don't have any," he said, a touch of shame in his voice.

"What have you been doing with your wages?"

"I don't have to answer that," he said defensively.

"And what happened to our home?" I asked.

"I moved out."

"Why?"

"The rent was too high," he said.

"Tell her the truth, Jackson," Silas said. "Lies won't be of any help."

Jackson hesitated a few minutes, then launched into a convoluted and unconvincing explanation of how he came to be evicted. He said that three weeks ago, just at the time he stopped sending me money, he and three friends at work had begun a payback scheme called *muholisani*, through which they sought to augment their meager wage of R3.25 a week. The scheme worked this way: Each Friday, payday, three buddies contributed R2.00 each and gave the sum to the fourth, thus increasing his take-home pay by R6.00 to R9.25. The four partners took turns and Jackson was last in line, which meant that next Friday, the fourth payday, it would be his turn to take home R9.25.

At this Silas let out a suppressed laugh and said, "Next Friday will soon be here. We'll see if you'll be that rich."

Jackson then attended to the child. He went to consult the same Venda *nganga* he had consulted when I had trouble giving birth because of Mrs. Malotsi's witchcraft. At the appearance of any illness, Jackson's first instinct was not to go to the Alexandra Health Clinic but to head straight for the *nganga*. He openly said he had little faith in white medicine. "Where were white people with their pills and injections when our ancestors cured strange diseases and performed miracles?" he would often say.

The *nganga* told Jackson I should bring the child the next morning, and reassured him all would be well.

The following day I went to see the *nganga*. One of his several attendants ushered me into his consulting room, where I sat on the floor cradling my baby. When the *nganga* entered, with an air of self-importance and a serious look on his face, he took Johannes in his hands, turned him this way and that, then ordered me to strip him naked while he prepared him a bath in a tub filled with warm water mixed with *muti*. He carefully bathed him. He then shaved his head with a razor blade and smeared more *muti* on top of it. Finally, he mixed some *muti* with soft porridge and ordered me to feed him the traditional way, with my fingers and not a spoon.

At first Johannes turned his head away from the porridge, but the *nganga* started humming a soothing song while waving his *choya* (animal hair tied to a stick in the shape of a feather duster) in front of him, as pungent incense from a clay calabash filled the room. Gradually Johannes began to eat. He ate the whole bowl. I stood by expecting all of it to come back up. It didn't. The *nganga* told me to dress him, which I did, and he led him outside to the backyard, the fence of which was festooned with animal skins hung up to dry. There, for the first time in nearly a month, my child played. He was so content and reassured, and his broad, sunlit face displayed the smiles and innocence I was accustomed to seeing and rejoicing over. The *nganga* gave me more *muti* with instructions to add a little to his meals and bath. I went home, where Johannes continued playing and was soon back to his healthy self.

6

GRANNY

JOHN AND I
ARE NOT EUROPEANS

Geli relied on me for support whenever she had marital problems, but I didn't have my mother nearby when I arrived in the city and John rejected me, so I turned to my father for assistance.

My father, Lazarus Khosa, was unlike most men I knew. Though born and raised in the Shangaan homeland toward the end of the nineteenth century, he had early embraced the white man's way of life and religion, even while remaining faithful to the traditions and worship of his ancestors. He was an educated man and became a lay preacher with the Swiss mission church, in which his father had been a full-fledged minister.

He left the homeland to seek work in the city shortly after my brother, Shibalu, was born. He finally made his way to Johannesburg, where he settled in Alexandra and worked at various jobs. He was soon joined by my brother, and together they earned enough money to start buying several *stands*—small plots of land.

Back then blacks were allowed to own land in Alexandra because no whites were interested in the flat, arid dust bowl twelve miles north of the City of Gold, as Johannesburg was then called. In 1912 Alexandra was officially declared a "non-European township," and land was sold at giveaway prices to blacks and other "non-Europeans," mainly Coloreds (people of mixed race), who provided the city and nearby suburbs with a ready source for cheap labor.

After he left the homelands for the city, my father, despite still being married to my mother, met and married Elizabeth.

I remember the pain my mother felt when she learned that my father had taken a second wife without consulting or informing her, as was the custom. Everyone said that such a union was unhealthy, and predicted it would end in disaster.

"Why did he do that?" people asked. "There are plenty enough women in our village who would have made fine second wives."

"When our men go to the white man's city they take on strange customs and lose their attachment to the village and the tribe."

"They say that this Elizabeth has bewitched him. That's why he's never been back here since he married her."

When my brother, Shibalu, after coming of age, first went to the city and lived with my father, Elizabeth resented his presence.

"I don't want to have anything to do with the children of your first wife," she said. "Besides, she isn't your *real* wife. I'm the one with the ring."

"In the eyes of God and of our tribe we are married," Lazarus said. "And Shibalu is my firstborn. My own flesh and blood."

"You're married to *me*," Elizabeth retorted. "I gave you children too. And I am not the sort to share you with any woman."

"But you're only my second wife," Lazarus said.

"Second what?" Elizabeth exploded. "You might as well get that idea out of your head. I won't play second fiddle to any woman. I won't stand idly by and see my children disinherited. I am your one and only wife and you better get that straight. If I ever catch you with that woman I'm going to pour hot water over both of you. I'll kill you."

My father still loved my mother and us children, but after his marriage to Elizabeth he stopped coming to visit us. He showed his love by his willingness to help me and my brother, despite Elizabeth's threats. Sadly, he died without ever seeing my mother again. Even in death, when custom demanded they be buried side by side, my mother and father were forcibly separated by Elizabeth's machinations.

The Alexandra that met my eye when my three children and I arrived in 1944 was a vibrant township. It was not yet a slum and there weren't as many shacks as there are today. Most of the houses were large and made of brick. They had yards with gardens where people planted crops and kept chickens, goats, and cows. Much of Alexandra was owned by black landlords, who rented their property mostly to Shangaans and Vendas. Shangaans and Vendas flocked to Alexandra after the First World War to work in the gold mines of Johannesburg, because back then the Zulus and Xhosas considered mine work degrading, and preferred working on the railroad.

My father took us all in, despite Elizabeth's objections. He owned a big house, with several rooms, including a dining room My three children and I had two rooms, and he supported us while I sought a reconciliation with my husband. Elizabeth showed her aversion to our presence in many ways. She frequently accused me of having left my husband, and not the other way round.

"He couldn't have left just like that," she said. "You must have done something wrong."

"I did nothing wrong."

"I know you devious women," she said. "Your husband leaves for the city and you start having *shigangus* [lovers]."

"Don't say such a thing," I said angrily. "I can never do that to my husband. He's the one who left *me*."

I wondered if Elizabeth saw the irony of her baseless charges. She was, after all, the one who ought to know what it meant to steal another wife's husband.

My father finally located my husband. John's second wife, a Mosotho woman, had already left him, taking the furniture and everything in the house. He had tried going after her. When he arrived at her homeland her relatives beat him up and told him to leave her alone. John was shocked to discover that the woman he had called his wife for nearly two years already had a husband and children back home when they were married. In fact, he knew the husband. He had visited John and his wife from time to time, and the deceitful wife would say to John, "This is my brother. He's brought me news from home. He would like to stay with us a few days, do you mind dear?"

"I don't mind, my sweet love," John would say. "Your brother is always welcome here."

So when John was away at work, his wife and her "brother" had a wonderful time. The Mosotho woman had also deliberately avoided having any children with John so that he would have no claim on her.

In my days this was a common practice. Married women would come to Johannesburg to work, and, earning little, feeling lonely, and unable to be with their families because of Influx Control laws, they would get another husband, called the "city husband," through whom they supported their true husband and children back home. When they grew tired of the city and had amassed a small fortune, they emptied the house and returned to the homeland. The "city husband" would come back from work only to find wife and everything gone. She would even take his clothes, to give to her true husband in the homelands. It served John right to be so bamboozled. Still, I pitied him.

After being deceived by the Mosotho woman, John had taken a third wife, Melinda, and moved to Diepkloof, a section of Soweto. Melinda bore him four children. My father was an influential man and managed to get John served with a subpoena to appear in the Bantu (black) court. Our case came before a white judge.

"My husband has left me," I said to the judge. "Together we have three children. I have no job. I want him back, and if he refuses I want him to support me and the children."

The judge replied that he had no legal basis on which to compel John to return to me or to pay alimony as we were not married under civil law and, most important, John now had a wife under civil law.

"But I'm his first wife," I argued. "He paid *lobola* for me. Melinda is only his third wife. I mean second wife, now that the Mosotho woman has left him. I don't mind John having many wives, as long as he fulfills his obligations to me, the first wife."

The judge hemmed. "It doesn't quite work that way among us Europeans," he said.

"But John and I are not Europeans."

"I mean," said the judge, "the white man's law says a man can only have one wife at a time. And under that law Melinda is John's lawful wife."

"But John didn't pay *lobola* for her," I said. "How can she be his lawful wife?"

"She's his lawful wife," the judge said, "because of this piece of paper called a marriage certificate." He held up the marriage license for me to see.

I was incredulous. I said, "Is that piece of paper worth more than the cattle John paid for me?"

"It's not worth more," the judge said. "It simply means more."

"I don't understand." I shook my head and took a little snuff.

John made a suggestion in the hope of resolving the matter. "Your Honor," he said, "I'm willing to take the children and so free my former wife to remarry."

Women with children had a hard time getting remarried because many men balked at the thought of having to support offspring not their own.

"If you don't want the wife," said the judge, "you can't have the children."

"How dare you even suggest that?" I said to John. "I won't be separated from my children. If you want them, you have to take me too."

John said no.

I returned to my father's house husbandless. Elizabeth's resentment of me increased, especially when she saw that I continued to be my father's favorite, despite her attempts to drive us apart. My father continued to support my children and me generously. He paid for the schooling of my son Reuben, and often spoke of giving me some land he owned in Donaldton, near Pretoria, where my children and I could live without too much hardship.

One day he told Elizabeth, "I want to take my grandson Reuben with me to Donaldton and show him the land I bought so that when I die, my daughter Ellen and her children can go live there."

"No," Elizabeth said. "I won't permit that. That property belongs to *my* children."

"Don't worry," my father said, "your children will be well taken care of. But Ellen and her children must have their share too."

My father was being generous to Elizabeth. Under tribal custom the children of the first wife usually inherited everything.

My father defied Elizabeth and went to Donaldton anyway. Before he left he promised that when he returned he was going to make a new will, dividing his wealth equally between my son Reuben and Elizabeth's son, Manuel. He never came back alive.

Soon after my father arrived in Donaldton, he suddenly became ill, complaining of a pain in his side. He became bedridden, and was unable to return to Alexandra. The pain grew worse and he died. Neither Elizabeth nor any of her children informed me that my father was dead or when or where he was to be buried.

I only heard of his death when my son Reuben came to me crying.

"What's wrong?" I said.

"Don't you know grandfather is dead?" he replied.

"What?"

"Yes, he's dead," Reuben said, overcome with tears. He had heard the news from one of my half-sibling's children. "Now I'll have no money to go to school."

I was never invited to attend my father's funeral. I tried to go without an invitation but one of my stepsisters prevented me. My brother Shibalu's death had left me as the only surviving child of his first wife, and according to tradition I had a right to a portion of his wealth, and deserved it more because I was destitute. But I got nothing.

To add insult to injury, Elizabeth drove me and my children out of the two rooms my father had provided for us, into a tiny room just large enough for a small bed. My three children had to sleep cramped together on the floor. This in my father's house.

And I later learned that I had been mentioned in my father's will, that he provided well for me and my children, partly, I believe, to atone for his having hurt my mother deeply by leaving her, and partly because he loved me and I was the only surviving child from his first marriage. I was told that he had left me property with houses on it, a farm, and a store. I never got a penny. All this wealth, with prudent management, could have set me and my children up for life. I would never have had to worry about sending them to school, providing them with a home, buying them food and clothes. I would have never had to beg and borrow and scrounge for the rest of my life.

PART II

7

FLORAH

THE RAID

One night in March of 1985 as I slept beside Walter in the darkness, I awoke with a start at hearing noises outside the shack. At first the sounds were barely audible. Low hurried whispers. The soft shuffle of feet. The scraping of something metallic against the thin walls of the small bedroom where Walter and I were sleeping. Angeline was asleep on a pallet on the kitchen floor.

I wondered who could be outside. Was it the police? Thieves? Inkatha *impis* after ANC supporters? Most people in Alexandra, including Walter and myself, supported the ANC. And just recently, in another part of the ghetto, ANC supporters had been massacred in their sleep. The victims included children. They had been stabbed and mutilated to death by *pangas* (long, homemade knives) and spears, favored weapons of the Zulu followers of Inkatha.

The metallic scraping grew louder, as did the voices, but still I couldn't make them out. Could it be those mysterious hooded gun-men who lately had been terrorizing township residents, swooping down suddenly and disappearing without a trace, leaving behind only bullet-riddled corpses? Rumors were rampant about these gunmen. They were believed to be Afrikaner neo-Nazis disguised as blacks, and it was thought that their goal was to foment black-on-black violence.

Perhaps it was Walter's enemies come for their revenge. Former *tsotsis* like Walter often had many enemies: mainly people they had robbed, stabbed, or double-crossed.

Perhaps it was my estranged husband, Collin, who, having finally tracked me down, was about to wrench Angeline from me, as he had lately threatened to do.

"Walter, Walter," I whispered anxiously, gently shaking him. "Wake up, wake up!"

"Huh?" He stirred sleepily.

More low whispers and scraping outside, this time very close to the window.

"Walter, wake up," I said. "Did you hear that?"

His eyes flew open. He said "Yes" as he propped himself up on one elbow, leaning over me protectively. He craned his neck toward the window, listening intently. He squeezed my arm.

"Get up. Go get Angeline. And don't make any noise."

"Who's out there?" I asked.

"Don't ask questions, just get up."

I tossed aside the blanket draped across my shoulders, leapt out of bed and groped for my clothes. Angeline was now awake and crying softly. I dressed hurriedly and fumbled for her in the semidarkness. I dared not light a candle.

Walter turned to his side of the bed and felt for something under it. He sighed with relief when he found whatever he was groping for. A noise made him turn sharply.

"What is it?" I asked.

He made no reply. His silence was worse than anything he could have said. I saw his face, alert and tense, in the pale moonlight seeping in through the room's tiny window. For a minute or two the noises outside seemed to die down. It was merely the calm before the storm. Suddenly there erupted from the darkness on all sides of the shack a cacophony of sounds. Barking dogs, screams, shattering glass and wood, blaring sirens, and commands shouted in Afrikaans.

"Oh, shit," Walter said. "It's a raid."

"Oh, my God, not again."

It was the second surprise predawn raid in a month. After the first raid it had been rumored that police had targeted our section of the ghetto because it was thick with guns and was a hotbed for Comrades, young militants who pledged allegiance to the ANC.

Ever since the forced resignations of members of the white-appointed city council, who were vilified by many in the community as Uncle Toms and sellouts for working in structures created by the white minority regime, the Comrades ruled the ghetto with an iron hand. They were the law. During funerals for those slain by the soldiers and the police, and during boycotts and marches, they rounded up the masses and enforced obedience and discipline. Those who ignored the decrees of the Comrades ran the risk of being necklaced (necklacing involved hanging a gasoline-soaked tire around the neck of the victim and setting it on fire) or beaten up. One woman who violated a shopping boycott was lucky to escape with the lenient punishment of having her groceries scattered in the middle of the street and forced to drink the bleach she had bought to clean her clothes.

"Quickly," Walter whispered. "Take Angeline and get the hell out of here."

Walter crouched by the door, the whites of his eyes gleaming in the translucent darkness. A piercing crash froze me where I stood. The kitchen window had been shattered. Walter grabbed me and hustled me over to the back door as I clutched Angeline close to my breast. He made sure that his body was between me and any bullets that might come whizzing in through the broken window.

"Out the back door, fast, and keep your head down," he said.

He then pressed something cold, hard, and metallic into my trembling hands.

"Hide this," he whispered.

I looked at what I held in the pale darkness. It was a gun. Instinctively I tried to hand it back to him. I had not seen the gun since the day I spotted it while packing clothes into the drawers and realized that a rumor I had heard about Walter was true: he had once been jailed for armed robbery.

"So you *are* a jailbird," I had said.

"That was my *old* life," Walter had replied defensively.

"If it was your old life why do you still carry a gun?"

"For self-defense. Every man in Alex carries a gun. If you don't you're a fool. This is a war zone, Florah, a jungle. It's kill or be killed."

And now he was telling me to hide the deadly weapon for him. I wanted to have nothing to do with guns or killing. The sight of guns made me sick. They infested Alexandra like a plague. Everyone now seemed to own a gun. It was said that in South Africa's ghettos there were four guns for every person. And people used them, indiscriminately, at the slightest provocation. Where in the past fists and knives would have been used, bullets now blazed. It was like the Wild West. Guns were the cause of the almost weekly mass funerals I attended. A day never went by without someone being shot. I had lost many friends and neighbors to guns. There were so many guns that black children now scorned cartoons on television and had voracious appetites for violent movies with bloody shootouts.

As I prepared to slip out the back door I heard a loud banging on front door.

"THIS IS THE POLICE," a voice with a thick Afrikaner accent shouted. "OPEN UP!"

"Please, Walter, don't make me take this," I said, paralyzed with fear. "What if I'm caught?"

"Don't get caught."

"But what if?"

"They don't frisk women, now go. Or do you want me back in jail? Do you want me killed? Do you know what they'll do to me if they find that gun on me?"

"But what should I do with it?"

"Hide it! Anything! Go!"

"OPEN UP I SAY!" The pounding grew louder.

Walter held Angeline while I slid the gun under my skirt. I took Angeline back. The barrel was pressed tight against my abdomen by the skirt's narrow waistband. What if the gun was loaded and went off accidentally, killing me and my child? I shuddered at the thought. Angeline and I vanished into the opaque darkness and chaos just as the door of Walter's shack burst open.

I ran quickly, my bare feet pounding the dusty alleyways between yards filled with *mkhukhus,* ramshackle shacks made of corrugated tin, handmade bricks, newspapers, cardboard, plastics, and sticks. This had been my world for over two decades. I knew its every nook and cranny. I had to in order to survive. The poverty, the police, the squalor, the desperation, the violence, the death, and the madness were all a part of daily life, of being quarantined in a ghetto, of the nightmare of being black in apartheid South Africa.

Angeline and I crawled under a barbed-wire fence, and as we were about to emerge into a dark alleyway, I heard the rumbling sound of *hippos* and *caspers*—huge yellow armored trucks that blacks ironically nicknamed "Mello Yello." Instantly I crawled into a nearby *donga* (ditch), still clutching Angeline.

Two *hippos* thundered past, a few yards away, and I could see, in the pale moonlight, automatic rifles protruding from their turrets, ready to fire.

I had only one goal: to get to my parents' home on 16th Avenue, a few blocks away. Once I thought the danger past, I took double-ups and shortcuts, as I raced toward my parents' shack.

The first streaks of dawn were faint in the east. A naked child of about three stood terrified in the middle of the road, crying shrilly for its mother as black men and women sprinted this way and that, fleeing in terror from the police. Some woman scooped up the child and dumped her in a yard across the street.

When I reached my parents' shack I was exhausted. I knocked on the door and slumped against the corrugated tin wall, gasping to catch my breath. I saw my ten-year-old sister, Diana, peep timidly out the grimy window.

"It's me—Florah!" I whispered. "Let me in."

Diana unbolted the door and I entered the darkened two-room shack. My mother was asleep on the single bed in the back room. My father had left for the Venda homeland a few days ago, to attend the funeral of one of his relatives. My sisters Maria, Mirriam, Linah, and Diana and my nephew Given were randomly scattered about the kitchen floor, some curled up under the table and others stretched out by the coal stove. The single bed with the sagging mattress, on which my brother George, twenty-two, slept, was empty.

My mother awoke and entered the kitchen in her tattered nightgown.

"Where have you been?" she demanded.

"There's a police raid down on 14th Avenue," I said. "I was lucky to escape."

"I thought Collin lived on 9th Avenue," my mother said.

"I wasn't with Collin."

My mother didn't ask who I was with—she knew. Like my father, she disliked Walter and refused to accept my relationship with him.

"Look at the trouble you're bringing upon yourself because of that *tsotsi*," my mother said. "Look at my poor grandchild, she's scared to death. Come to Grandma, dear Angie." She took Angeline from me and gently wiped the tears from her small ebony cheeks while rocking her.

"The raid wasn't exactly Walter's idea, Mama," I said.

"But what were you doing at his place? Don't you already have a husband? And a child by him?"

"I've decided to leave Collin for good."

"Leave him for good?" she exclaimed, shocked. "He paid *lobola* for you, didn't he?"

"He may have paid *lobola*," I said, "but that doesn't make me his property for life."

"Did Walter pay a cent for you? Or are you simply his mistress? I see, your father is right in calling you a whore. Is that what you are?"

"No," I said.

"Then what are you, a married woman with a child, doing with a man who's not your husband? Walter didn't pay *lobola* for you."

"He'll pay it someday," I said.

My mother stared skeptically at me and said, "We'll see. You'll regret having left Collin."

I made no reply. I was tired of being held up to my mother's high moral standards, which had made her stay with my father despite his abuse and infidelity. Our lives were different. Times had changed. The pain Collin's unfaithfulness caused me was real and deep. I could no longer ignore or sublimate it. I couldn't see myself sacrificing my own chance at happiness to fulfill obligations under a tradition that was grossly unfair to women.

My mother went on talking as she prepared some space on the crowded floor for Angeline to sleep. She recited a familiar litany of Collin's virtues, as she saw them: "Collin is a good responsible young man. He's educated. He's never given you a black eye or tried to strangle you" (my father had done this a lot to my mother). "He doesn't gamble or drink too much" (my father did). "He supports you and the child. How many men do that today!"

"Not many," I said.

"Then what are you doing running around with this Walter?" she asked. "What future does he have? And he's an ex-con too. Maybe that's why the police are after him."

"But Collin has been cheating on me, Mama," I said.

"I don't condone his cheating," my mother said. "But men have their weaknesses. You should forgive him."

"But I've forgiven him many times. I can no longer deal with the pain."

"So you go take off with another man? Will that cure the pain?"

"I don't know. What I do know is that I'm through with Collin."

"To tell you the truth, I don't believe the things you're saying about Collin," my mother said. "He doesn't strike me as the kind to fool around."

"I knew you'd say that," I shot back angrily. "You seem to have such faith in men, despite being married to a good-for-nothing husband who abuses you."

"Don't say that about your father. You'd be in trouble if he were here."

"But it's true. And what I'm saying about Collin is true also."

"That's just a phase men go through."

"Just a phase? Is Dad's abuse just a phase? How long will this so-called phase last? How much pain do I have to endure? How many more times do you want me to cry all night waiting for Collin to come home, imagining him in bed with another woman? I don't have your kind of strength to endure pain, Mama. I'm not a martyr."

"I don't believe he meant to hurt you."

"Don't give me that rubbish, Mama," I said. "He knows exactly what he's doing."

"Watch your tongue, child," my mother said. "You should have had more patience with him. Men often hurt women. Look at what your father did to me. But I had patience with him, for the sake of you children. You too must save your marriage for the sake of Angeline. That's most important. You know how hard it is to raise a child alone, and to remarry when you already have a child by another man. What if you get pregnant by that *tsotsi*? Your life would be ruined."

I made no answer. I was sick of such pious lectures. It was clear that my mother and I inhabited vastly different worlds with diametrically opposed realities. Her world was one of fidelity at any cost, of standing by your man despite his trampling upon you. I couldn't tell her that though *lobola* had been paid for me, I wasn't prepared to stay in an abusive marriage, that I now loved Walter so much I desperately wanted to have his baby, *lobola* or not.

Walter sometimes said, "I wish you could get pregnant, then I could marry you."

I knew I had to prove my fertility to him. Walter had told me that he wanted to make sure I could bear him children before he would marry me. That wasn't an unusual request. Many men made it. Yet I just couldn't get pregnant, despite the fact that I wasn't using any birth control. I felt so low. I wanted to get pregnant badly. I wanted to keep Walter.

"Mama," I said with finality. "I mean it when I say I am through with Collin. I no longer love him."

"Florah, *love* is a word thrown around by foolish girls. You're a grown woman now. You have a child and duties as a wife and mother. I didn't love your father. In fact I hated him. I was forced into marrying him. But once that marriage took place and you children came along I stayed in it for your sake."

"But you didn't have to."

"If I hadn't, what would have become of you children, growing up without a father?"

"But he's never been a real father to us," I said. "He's a bully. He beats you. He takes my hard-earned wages and yours and buys liquor. We'd be a hell of a lot better without him."

"Don't say such things about your father, child," my mother said. "He has his faults, I admit. But he's helped me raise you up. You listen to him instead of me. And it was his strict rules that prevented you from going astray like other kids raised without fathers."

"Mama," I said, "you can deal with a loveless marriage. I can't."

"I see that you've become too much of a city girl. You no longer think like a true African woman. What did they teach you at ritual school?"

I didn't respond. My mother's arguments wearied me. I let my mind wander. I thought of the gun in my waistband and wondered what to do about it.

"Mama, I'm very tired," I said, as I prepared to lie down next to Angeline. "Please, let me and my child get some sleep."

"Okay, child," she said. "I hope you come to your senses and go back to Collin."

She took a roll of toilet paper from the cupboard, went back to the bedroom and got a shawl, draped it around her bony shoulders, and left the house for the communal toilets. People brought their own toilet paper when using the communal toilets; those who couldn't afford any simply used pieces of newspaper.

As soon as my mother was gone, I quickly got up and headed for the bedroom, where I frantically searched for a place to hide Walter's gun. I hid it behind the old wardrobe, where people seldom searched or cleaned. I went back to the kitchen and tried in vain to go to sleep. Though I had pretended not to listen, my mother's words had sunk in. For the first time in months, I thought fondly of Collin and felt that, just maybe, a reconciliation might still be possible.

Though I no longer lived with Collin, whenever he heard that I was back at my parents' home, he would come by to see Angeline and attempt a reconciliation. Depending on my mood, I would either raise his hopes or dash them. Whenever I dashed them he would issue veiled threats about taking Angeline away from me. He still worked near me and would sometimes walk me to work.

One day, as he was walking me to work, Collin said, "Florah, I've changed. I no longer fool around. Why don't you come back home? Then we can go to the magistrate and get married officially. That way we can qualify for a permit to buy one of those nice houses in East Bank you're always talking about. Angeline needs a real home and we belong together."

His offer was tempting, for a number of reasons. Once we were married before the magistrate and I had that license and ring, I would have rights under civil law that women were denied under traditional law. For instance, I could divorce him, sue for custody, force him to pay child support and alimony, be his legal survivor in case he died, and so on. Under *lobola* the woman had no such rights. The husband kept the house, the children, the furniture, the savings, and anything he had bought his wife, including her dresses, if he chose. He was under no obligation whatsoever to give her anything. If the husband died, his parents and relatives had a right to claim all his property, including his wife.

Granny and my mother found out the hard way about the unfairness, the cruelty, of *lobola*. I didn't want the same to happen to me. Collin knew too that if we married before a magistrate, he had obligations toward me and Angeline that could be legally enforced, rather than left to his whim.

And once we had that marriage license, we could qualify to buy one of the new low-income homes that were being constructed on a filled-in garbage dump on the east bank of the dried-up river across from the sea of shacks that made up the rest of Alexandra. Collin had a steady job at a computer company and was making a decent salary, and I worked full-time at a flower shop. Our combined incomes would probably be enough to secure us a loan.

Most of the new houses being built and trumpeted as the "New Alexandra" were begging for tenants because few blacks could afford them. The typical cost of one such house was R60,000, unemployment in the ghetto was 50 percent and rising, and most of those who were lucky to have a job earned barely enough to survive on, let alone afford a down payment for a new house.

As I lay awake and the morning grew lighter outside the shack, I pondered about what to do. Go back to my husband or stay with Walter? If I went back to Collin, would I find him truly changed, and would Walter let me go without a fight? If I stayed with Walter, as my heart told me to, would he follow through and marry me, or would he want me simply as his girlfriend?

8

GELI

WITCH DOCTOR'S
SPELL

One reason I liked Collin as a son-in-law, especially in the early stages of his marriage to my daughter, is that he was everything my own husband was not when we were first married. As far as I knew, Collin respected and trusted Florah. My husband Jackson had been the very opposite.

The Friday after I returned from Hammerskraal, Jackson brought home his pay. It was only R3.25, instead of the R9.25 he had told me he would bring. He was furious, saying that his *muholisani* buddies had double-crossed him.

"How did they do it, Jackson?" his brother, Silas, asked, in a voice suggesting that he thought his explanation a cock-and-bull story.

"They all have emergencies back in the homelands," Jackson said. "They promised that next week I will get the money."

"And what if they have more emergencies next week?" pursued Silas. "Will it be the next, and the next, and the next?"

"They will give me the money," Jackson vowed, "otherwise they'll find out what it feels like to double-cross a Mathabane."

"May heaven protect them," Silas said facetiously. "I forgot you're the most dangerous man in Alexandra."

I took Jackson at his word, despite my suspicions his explanations didn't ring true. Something was wrong.

The next morning I went to see the landlord on 14th Avenue about getting our basement room back. The landlord accepted the rent owed him but said that he had already rented the room to someone else. He offered us a shack, smaller, with one tiny window, a rotting door, a leaky roof, and a cracked floor through which vermin crawled. It was close to the communal toilets, which stunk and were constantly surrounded by puddles of urine, created by the nightly stream of drunkards from the yard's several *shebeens*. And the shit buckets regularly overflowed with feces or were overturned, producing such a stench that it was impossible to cook or sleep at night.

Without a permit to look for better housing in government-owned yards, we had no choice but to take the shack. I went back to 4th Avenue and packed our meager belongings, carrying most of the heavy boxes balanced on my head. I was my own moving van. Jackson hired two teenage boys and paid them pennies to help transport the bed, carpentry tools, table, and chairs. Jackson was a good carpenter, and after Johannes was born he had made a pair of handsome chairs and a table, from material he had stolen from his job. Thieving from the job was common among blacks, for we were paid so little. We saw it not as theft, but as part of our just wages.

When I went back to 4th Avenue to pick up the last belongings, Silas took me aside and said, "The true reason Jackson hasn't been sending you money is that he's been naughty."

I asked him to elaborate.

"Wait until next Friday and you'll find out."

Friday came. Jackson returned from work and gave me R2—about a dollar—with orders to go buy all the groceries we would need all of next week.

"Is this all the money you've earned?"

"I'm keeping the rest."

"All of it?"

"Yes, how much do you think I make a week?" he retorted.

"Isn't it your turn for *muholisani*, which means you should have R9.25 altogether?"

He laughed, but, quickly composing his face into a serious look, said, "I forgot to tell you. My *muholisani* buddies all quit their jobs this week."

My suspicions that he'd been lying about this *muholisani* business were confirmed, but I couldn't bring myself to tell him so. I wanted to avoid a scene and a possible beating.

"Did you say I should buy groceries with this money, including meat?" I asked.

"Yes."

"Where will we store the meat? We don't own a fridge."

"Then buy *murogo* and *sonjas* [prickly worms resembling leeches]," he said. "They don't have to be refrigerated."

"Why are we suddenly buying all the food at once?" I asked. "Won't it be better to buy things as we need them, like we used to? That way they won't spoil and the rats won't eat them."

"Do as I tell you, woman," Jackson snapped.

He then took off his overalls, donned his faded pants and shirt, and went out, stopping by the door to tell me that he was going to see a witch doctor about something that had been bothering him of late. He added that I shouldn't wait for him, but should leave his dinner covered on the table and the door unlocked.

His visits to the witch doctor began occurring every Friday. Whenever he returned, he had no money, his temper was savage, and for fear of being beaten I said nothing and asked no questions.

One Friday evening Jackson gave me money and I bought mealie meal, sugar, bread, tea, and some canned goods. As a result I had only 5 cents left. But I figured that since I spent most of the day at my mother's, and we needed nothing special, and Jackson never asked me for any money during the week since we hardly had any, the 5 cents would do, in case of emergencies, till next payday.

Monday evening came. I discovered that I had run out of salt, so I bought some with the last 5 cents. Jackson returned from work in a bad mood. He demanded that I give him bus fare.

"I don't have any money," I said.

"What? What did you do with the R2 I gave you?"

"I bought groceries, as you told me to."

"With all of it?"

"Yes."

"Dammit," he said. "Don't lie to me. How could you have spent all that money on food? Are you feeding elephants? I hardly eat anything, so the groceries you buy ought to last us more than one week."

"But we have a child," I said, "and I'm nursing."

"Even with nursing you can't devour R2 worth of food each week. Where's my money?"

"I don't have any."

"Where is it?" he fumed. "You gave it to your relatives, isn't that so? They're getting rich from my sweat."

"I did no such thing."

"Then where's the money? I want it here," he slammed an open fist on the table. It shook. As we were talking, Jackson had slowly been moving toward the door. He now bolted it and came toward me. Johannes had been sleeping, but the raised voices woke him up and he began crying. I quickly went over and picked him up, clutched him closer to my breast as a shield, thinking that Jackson would not strike me while I was holding the child.

"Put that child down," he demanded. "I'm going to teach you a lesson."

"But he's crying."

"Put him down!"

I didn't.

He wrenched the child from my breast and flung him on the bed. He then grabbed me by the throat and shoved me up against the wall with a thud. I struggled, Johannes bawled. Jackson's back was turned away from him. I had a flash of insight.

"Watch out, Jackson," I managed to scream despite his choke-hold. "Johannes is about to fall off the bed."

He let go of my throat and swung round to catch the baby. That was all the time I needed to lunge for the door, unbolt it, and dash outside.

"You lying bitch," Jackson cursed as he realized I had tricked him.

I stood outside the shack, gathering my breath, a safe distance away from the door. Jackson stood by the threshold, fuming. Johannes wailed inside.

"Come and get the child," he demanded.

"You must think me a fool," I said. "So you can throttle me again?"

A crowd of neighbors began to assemble, attracted by the noise of the scuffle. The landlord came and Jackson's demeanor promptly changed. The demonic fury in his face was replaced by a fake placid-ity.

"At it again, I see," the landlord said to Jackson. He was familiar with our almost weekly fights.

"It's nothing, Murena [Mr. landlord]," Jackson said meekly. "My wife and I just had a slight misunderstanding."

"A slight misunderstanding, you say," the landlord said. "Look how that 'slight misunderstanding,' as you call it, has disturbed the peace of the yard." The landlord pointed at the crowd with his fat arm.

"I'm sorry, Murena," Jackson said.

"Let this be the last time," the landlord said, wagging a thick fore-finger at Jackson. "Another disturbance like this and you're out. No more reprieves, you understand? There are dozens of people eager to rent that shack."

"I understand, Murena."

I took advantage of the landlord's presence to dart into the shack and grab my child. Jackson could do nothing, with all those wit-nesses watching him. He just stood there gaping at me while I hur-riedly packed a bag and then went out the door.

"Where are you going?" he asked.

"Away from this hell," I said.

When I arrived at my mother's I found her seated by the stove with Aunt Matinana, chatting about something. My unexpected appearance surprised them.

"What's wrong?" Aunt Matinana asked.

I explained.

"Why is this Mbvesha doing this?" she said angrily. Mbvesha is a disparaging description of a Venda by a Shangaan.

"I don't know," I said. "You and my mother should know. After all, he's your husband, not mine. I didn't want to marry him and you forced me to."

Aunt Matinana threw a glance at my mother, who sat silently, her head bowed. My mother was clearly in anguish over my bad marriage. She had grown markedly thin since I started complaining of Jackson's abuse. Her cheeks were hollow and her long limbs had the emaciated look of someone whose heart was being gnawed by guilt. Aunt Matinana vowed to confront Jackson and get him to change his ways.

Speaking of the devil, at that very moment, an angry Jackson burst in through the front door.

"Where's my wife and child?" he demanded. "I've come to take them home."

"Your wife isn't here," Aunt Matinana said coolly.

"What do you mean?" Jackson bellowed. "There she is over there!" He pointed at me. I was sitting on the floor next to my mother.

"You must be blind, Mbvesha," Aunt Matinana said, "that's not your wife."

"That is my wife," Jackson retorted. "I paid lobola for her."

"Never mind lobola," Aunt Matinana said. "If this woman were truly your wife, you would treat her with more respect, rather than abusing her."

I was surprised by Aunt Matinana taking my side and defending me. She rarely did that.

"She's stubborn," Jackson said. "She deserves a thrashing now and then. Give her back to me or give me my child and my lobola right this minute."

"You are getting nothing," Aunt Matinana said. "Either you start treating your wife better or you'll lose her, the child, and the lobola."

"Who are you to tell me what I can and cannot do with my wife?" Jackson fumed. "I didn't steal her from you. I bought her. I own her."

"I'm your match, Jackson," Aunt Matinana said, straightening her tall wiry frame and squaring her shoulders. "I'm no ordinary woman. I am no pushover."

"Give me back my wife and child or give me my money," Jackson insisted.

"I said you'll get nothing. Now, get out of this house. You disgust me."

"I won't. You make me."

"Okay, you asked for it." The temperamental Aunt Matinana instantly seized a fire poker hanging from the side of the stove and charged Jackson like a mad bull. Jackson was bewildered, unconvinced that a woman would dare assault a man. Aunt Matinana raised the fire poker and brought it crashing down, smack on Jackson's head. "Here, you *Mbvesha*, this ought to teach you a lesson!" she yelled as she struck again and again, driving Jackson toward the door with each blow.

Realizing that Aunt Matinana wasn't going to stop, a confounded and grimacing Jackson turned and fled. Neighbors appeared, drawn by the noise and shouts, and asked what was happening.

"Nothing," Aunt Matinana said. "Just a *tsotsi* who got what he deserved."

The following day Aunt Matinana told me to pack my belongings. She took me and Johannes to Donaldton to stay with her mother, Elizabeth, until the feud with Jackson was settled, one way or another. I spent several weeks in Donaldton, working hard for Elizabeth: cleaning, making fire, hauling wood, and cooking. I was also able to see my grandfather's grave for the first time, the one my mother had yet to see. I was deeply moved and offered prayers to his departed spirit, and beseeched him and my ancestors to intervene to end the miseries in my life.

Elizabeth, as soon as she saw I was a hard worker, started encouraging various men to come courting, saying I needed a new husband to replace Jackson. I was cool to their proposals. I distrusted Elizabeth's motives, and worried about how my son would be treated if I remarried. Many men mistreat sons if they are not of their blood; the son inherits nothing, and he in turn is unlikely to obey his stepfather and is ever ready with the disrespectful retort, "You can't tell me what to do. You aren't my real father."

A month went by. I longed to return to Alexandra, to be among familiar sights and trusted faces.

One day word arrived that Aunt Matinana had resolved the matter with Jackson and wanted me to come back. A contrite Jackson came to Aunt Matinana's place full of apologies and promised to be a good husband. He even brought gifts to appease my mother and Aunt Matinana. Aunt Matinana warned him to keep his word or next time I would leave him for good.

"And you're already such an old man," Aunt Matinana added scornfully, "that I doubt any other woman would want you. You should consider yourself extremely lucky to have married my niece."

Once we were back home, Jackson told me that he had decided we should move to another shack at the other side of the ghetto. I interpreted the move to be an attempt by him to take me farther away from my mother and Aunt Matinana so they wouldn't interfere should he resume his abuse.

9

GRANNY

WITCHCRAFT KILLS

MY ONLY BROTHER

Jackson was able to get away with abusing my daughter because there was no man to defend her. My father was dead, and so was my brother. Both, I believe to this day, were victims of witchcraft. Though I was raised in a Christian home, my father having been a lay preacher in the Swiss mission church, I never ceased believing in witchcraft. Neither did my entire family nor most people in the village.

While we attended church every Sunday, we never thought belief in our ancestors and witchcraft incompatible with Christianity. Witchcraft was real to us. Its powers were part of the mysterious forces of nature, which only the initiated understood and could exploit, either for good or evil. Even the Bible we found to be full of stories about witchcraft; the devil was the instigator of most it, and God through his grace and mercy gave his prophets and disciples the power to combat evil for the benefit of humankind. We regarded the *nganga* as one such disciple of God.

A *nganga* performs good witchcraft, which is sanctioned by the chiefs, our rulers, and brings us rain, heals the sick, protects the village and the warriors in battle, strengthens the bonds of family and of community by fostering the common good, and smells out wizards and sorcerers, the practitioners of bad witchcraft.

Sorcerers and wizards are those evil-minded, antisocial individuals who, either from greed, jealousy, or mere perversity, become enemies of the tribe by creating discord, stealing, blackmailing, and killing.

My mother was once bewitched by a woman who wanted her husband. She became sick. She consulted a *nganga*, who told her, "Someone has put something in your drink and tried to poison you." The *nganga* then gave my mother *muti* to drink. The *muti* made her vomit everything, including the poison, and she became well again.

I was thrilled when my firstborn, Mphephu, was chosen by the ancestors to become a *nganga*. This is how it happened. She got sick and no cure could be found for her strange illness. She vomited blood and had fainting spells. Her sickness was on and off. Finally a *nganga* was consulted, and after reading his divinatory bones, he told us that Mphephu could only be cured by becoming a *nganga* herself.

She underwent the initiation, first becoming an apprentice to an experienced *nganga*, with whom she lived for several months. She would rise early in the morning, around 3 A.M. or 4 A.M. to cook and clean the *kaya*, home. She wore no shoes, even during bitterly cold winter days. The *nganga* taught her the art of divination, and how to find in the forest various medicinal herbs and roots, how to mix them into potent *muti*, how to diagnose diseases of the mind and of the body, and how to administer the doses of *muti* to effect a cure. She also learned everything about witchcraft: how to identify witches and sorcerers and how to stop their mischief.

At the end of her apprenticeship, the length of which had been determined by our ancestral spirits, Mphephu was completely cured of her strange sickness of vomiting blood and fainting. She was now qualified to set up her own practice. She became a popular *nganga*. Her *muti* was so powerful that people from cities as far as hundreds of miles away flocked to the village to consult her on various cases of sickness and witchcraft. She also dispensed love charms and good luck charms, and performed religious and purification ceremonies.

It's been so many years since then—times have changed and much has happened in my life and in South Africa to alter the traditions and customs of my ancestors, but I still firmly believe in witchcraft. I still believe that most of the misfortunes that have befallen me and my children are in a great measure due to the evil practiced on us by witches and sorcerers.

From as far back as I can remember, witchcraft has always hovered over the household of my family like a dark storm cloud ready to burst. It is intimately connected to those events in my past which are full of mystery and pain and grief, events which have shaken my soul to the core and made me wonder if the gods of my ancestors and the God of the Christians have forgotten me, have shut the gates of mercy and pity on me and those from my womb whom I love the most.

After all the heartaches and sorrows I have had in my life, I sometimes feel like Job, and am tempted to curse the Christian God and the gods of my ancestors. Sometimes I feel there is no God, gods, or justice in this world. If there is a God, if there are gods, why did my father and only brother die from witchcraft? If there is justice, why do evil doers go unpunished, why are they allowed to prosper from the misery and pain they have inflicted upon others?

It is from the deaths of my father and brother that I trace the beginnings of my misfortunes in life. Their deaths broke my mother's heart, and when she died in 1954, I was left all alone in a world where the hearts of many men and women, including those of my own relatives, are so hard, so greedy, so selfish, so full of hate and evil.

My mother, Tsatsawana, was a beautiful, proud woman, sweet natured and soft-spoken. She could easily have been a daughter of chiefs. She was one of six children and had married my father the traditional way when she was seventeen. She bore me in the northern Transvaal town of Louis Trichardt, in 1912 or thereabout, the year when great swarms of locusts came and ate all the mealies in the fields. Those of my age are uncertain about dates, but we remember experiences of long ago as vividly as if they had just happened, because memory is our only link with the past and with reality.

My family moved to Giyane when I was about seven, after the Boers (Afrikaners) came and drove us off our land, insisting they needed more space for their farms. We didn't understand why they needed all that land when they were so few, but they had guns and they kept few of their promises. And the law—the white man's law—always took their side.

From my mother I learned a great deal of woman's work: I learned to grind mealies with mortar and pestle, to carry water in a jug on my head from the river, to fetch wood from the forest, carrying bundles of it on my head, to cook, and to polish the floor of the huts with cow dung mixed with clay and smeared by hand. From watching her I also learned the role a woman was supposed to assume in village life.

But the lesson she taught with the most strictness was respect for my elders, an important element of tribal life. One time I heard two women gossiping about my mother and I ran home and told her.

"Mama," I said, "those people were saying bad things about you."

"Eavesdropping on the conversations of your elders is wrong, my child," she scolded me. "Don't do it again."

"But they were saying bad things about you, Mama," I said.

"That may be true," my mother said, "but that still does not excuse your eavesdropping."

My only brother, Shibalu, was much older than I, so we seldom played together. And as a boy he was taught different lessons about his role in the family and in the village. He was being groomed to take charge, to be head of the household. When he was little he tended goats and cattle, and as a young boy he was sent off to mountain school, where he was circumcised and initiated into the secret rites of passage into manhood, which made him hard, stern, aloof, and dictatorial, especially with women, as a way of showing them that he was now a grown man and they were his inferiors.

But still he regarded me, his only sibling, with tender affection, especially in private when other eyes were not there to censor him for showing his true feelings and being human.

I was filled with sadness the day he left the village for Johannesburg to seek work. For a while, Shibalu lived in Alexandra with my father and his second wife, Elizabeth, but she didn't like him at all, because he was my father's heir. Shibalu sensed this, so he moved into his own house. Yet he and my father continued to work together and to purchase property all over Alexandra. Soon it was time for Shibalu to get himself a wife.

Normally a man goes back to his village in search of a wife. Shibalu informed our father of his intention to do so. Elizabeth knew that if Shibalu were to come back to Alexandra with a wife and start a family, as the firstborn son of the elder wife, he would inherit my father's wealth.

She approached my father and told him that there was no need for Shibalu to travel all the way to Giyane for a wife. She said she knew of a pretty young girl who would be a perfect match for my brother. She introduced them. Shibalu must have liked the girl, for he wrote to my mother and informed her he would be coming home to fetch my *lobola* to purchase himself a wife.

"My son," my mother wrote back, "you're a man now, and have the right to make your own decisions. And it's your prerogative to claim your sister's *lobola* so as to get yourself a wife. But I beg you, on my knees, in the name of God and of our ancestors, don't get a city wife. Obey the custom of our ancestors and come back home to look for a wife among your own people. I stand ready, as is my duty, to help you in the search. There are many young maidens who would make you splendid wives and give you many children. So please come back."

Shibalu shared the letter with my father, and he said, "Your mother is right, my son, tradition has to be obeyed. You must go back to the village in search of a wife. Your mother and relatives will help you pick out the best wife among our people."

Shibalu listened to our father, and journeyed to Giyane, but it was his fate never to return to Alexandra alive. The day Shibalu died was the darkest of my life. How he died remains a mystery, but I know deep in my heart that witchcraft was the cause and that I'm forever linked to his death.

Shortly after his arrival in Giyane, Shibalu became very ill. He had a fever, his eyes grew glazed, his body was wracked with pain, and, most frightening, when he urinated, blood came out.

A *nganga* was summoned. He consulted his divinatory bones, performed various rites, and then started explaining what was wrong with my brother.

"He's hovering at death's door," the *nganga* said ominously. "There's little I can do to save him. The *muti* that bewitched him has already done its wicked deed. But I will try my best."

"What's the matter with him?" my mother said in tears. "What have they done to my poor son?"

"A woman did this to him," the *nganga* said.

"Which woman?" my mother asked. Her voice was choked with grief.

"The woman that he knows."

Those of us standing at Shibalu's bedside were puzzled. What did the *nganga* mean? Did he mean that one of us had bewitched my brother? Women looked at each other with searching, suspicious eyes.

The *nganga* must have read our thoughts, for he said, "No, the woman who did this to him is not in this hut. She is far away."

"Where far away?" asked my mother.

"She's where he came from."

Shibalu had just come from Alexandra. Who could this strange woman be? Elizabeth?

"And this woman was to have been his betrothed," the *nganga* said.

There were gasps of horror all around the hut. My mother emitted a shrill cry, and burst into tears.

"He slept with her," the *nganga* said. "That's how he was bewitched. I can't tell any more."

Oh, my poor dear brother, my heart sighed with anguish. There was no doubt in my mind as to the identity of the woman Shibalu had slept with. It was the woman Elizabeth had planned for him to marry. I wondered if this strange woman had recently had an abortion; the *muti* used to kill the fetus was said to be powerful enough to kill a grown man. Or perhaps she was menstruating; intercourse with such an unclean woman was supposed to make a man sick. Or did the strange woman have a deadly disease contracted from sleeping around with many men?

The *nganga's* stentorian voice roused me from my meditation over possible motives.

"The only consolation I can offer you," he said, addressing my mother, "if it is any consolation, is that if Shibalu dies, so will the person who killed him."

The *nganga* then performed the closing rites. All the time, my brother lay there, almost in a deep sleep, though from time to time his body writhed in pain. He never spoke a word or regained consciousness. The following morning I was aroused from a fitful sleep by the uncontrollable wailing of my mother and the women of the village, and I knew that my only brother had died during the night.

For years I mourned Shibalu's death. I somehow felt implicated in his death, guilty, for had I not married, there wouldn't have been any *lobola,* and possibly he wouldn't have yielded to the temptation to get married, which proved fatal in his case. And did my own marriage fail because everything associated with my *lobola* become contaminated with the evil of my brother's death?

My mother, too, mourned the loss of her only son. She had lost a husband to a strange woman, and now her son was dead because of another strange woman. She became even closer to me, her only surviving child.

It came as little comfort when we later learned the fate of the woman supposed to have killed Shibalu through voodoo. She went on to marry a policeman who one day found her in the arms of another man. In a fit of rage he bludgeoned her to death with an axe.

Grief from losing her dear ones continued to gnaw at my mother's heart. Her soul grew weary of this life and finally, in 1954, departed for the peaceful realm of my ancestors. She had requested to be buried next to my father in Donaldton, who had died three years earlier. It was her sacred privilege as the first wife, but Elizabeth forbade it, as she wanted the grave for herself. So instead my mother was buried in our ancestral ground on land owned by one of my uncles.

Though my mother was denied her last wish, I know that her soul, uncorrupted by any evil, always caring and loving and hopeful, has found a fitting resting place amid the forests, the singing birds, the purling streams, the majestic mountains, the verdant valleys, and the sweet smiling day and soft moonlight of the open African skies. Wherever she is I know she watches over me and mine.

10

FLORAH

COLLIN IS
SHOT

Granny's enormous suffering had left her with the sort of wisdom and experience that would have immensely benefited me had we been in the habit of talking to each other about what life had been for her as a woman. But she largely kept her experiences bottled up, either because the pain of remembering was too intense, or because custom frowned upon such self-analysis. As a result I was left to my own resources, and to whatever advice I could get from friends and distant relatives.

For several weeks I wavered between returning to my husband, Collin, whom my parents refused to believe was having affairs, and staying with Walter, for whom my love was growing each day, maybe because he was the only man who hadn't yet mistreated and deceived me.

Walter was aware of the pressures on me, from my parents and from my own conscience, to reconcile with Collin.

One day he said, "Honey, we should give Collin back his *lobola*."

"Do you mean it?" I said, surprised. "Have you saved that much?"

"Not yet. But soon. I want to marry you. I love you."

This pleased me greatly, but at the same time I rather enjoyed being pursued by two men who competed for me. It occurred to me that I could use this to my advantage. It could help me extract important concessions that would protect me in a marriage to either of them. For instance, I could demand a civil marriage, a no-girl-friends-or-else-I-leave clause, an I-must-have-my-own-career clause, and an I-don't-want-to-be-the-slave-of-your-whole-family clause.

No doubt these demands were ambitious. But since I had leverage I figured I might as well use it to get the best deal I could out of a situation in which the odds were stacked against me as a woman. This was not just time for love, I thought, it was also time for sober calculation that would protect my own interests should the marriage not work out. If it meant being calculating about issues of the heart, so be it.

One Saturday morning in June of 1985 I was awakened by a rapping on the kitchen door and soft weeping. I left Walter in bed and went and opened the door. I was startled to find Collin's sister Tembi trembling outside, tears streaming down her face. She was tall and of a slight build, like her brother, and her thin shoulders shuddered from sobbing. Tembi was the only member of Collin's family to whom I was close. She often took my side during fights with her brother or stepmother.

"What's wrong, Tembi?" I asked.

She attempted to speak but she choked on the words.

I gently took her hand, embraced her, and ushered her inside the kitchen.

"What's wrong, Tembi?" I repeated.

"Collin's been shot and Calvin is dead," she said between breathless sobs. Calvin was my sister Maria's boyfriend and Collin's bosom friend.

"What?!" I said, stupefied with shock.

Several minutes passed before I could utter another word.

"It's so terrible, *Skwiza* [sister-in-law]," Tembi sobbed.

"Did you say 'shot'? 'dead'?" I stammered. "When did it happen? Who did it?"

"I don't know, *Skwiza*," Tembi sobbed. "They took Collin to hospital. A bullet entered through the neck and shattered his spine. They say it's touch and go."

"Oh, my God!" I cried. "When did this happen? Who did it? Was it the police?"

"We don't know," Tembi said. "Maybe it was the police, maybe a hired assassin, maybe *tsotsis*, nobody knows, *Skwiza*. Only Collin might know. That's why I'm here. Will you come with me to the hospital?"

"Of course," I said. "Let me get dressed."

"But I don't know if my brother will still be alive when we get there, *Skwiza*."

I could not believe my ears. My mind swam in a fog of confusion. Everything seemed such a nightmare.

"Please wait here," I said to Tembi, motioning her to a nearby chair. I hastened back to the bedroom where I hurriedly dressed.

"Who's that? Where are you going?" Walter asked sleepily.

"It's Tembi, Collin's sister," I said. "Collin's been shot. He's been taken to hospital. I have to go see him."

Walter made no reply. I returned to the kitchen and went over to where my daughter was sleeping.

"Angeline, get up, get up, we have to go see Daddy."

"Mommy," she murmured, "but I want to sleep."

"Daddy's sick. Very, very sick. Now come on, darling. You can sleep in the car."

I quickly dressed her in a warm outfit and fur-lined boots Collin had bought her. It was the beginning of winter.

It was over an hour's drive from Alexandra to Baragwanath Hospital. The Alexandra clinic was overcrowded, understaffed, and at the time lacked equipment to handle all the serious emergency cases that were routine in the ghetto—gunshot, stabbing, and spear wounds, and the serious burns of those lucky victims of necklacing who survived being torched with gasoline-soaked tires hung around their necks. These cases were often transferred either to General Hospital or Baragwanath Hospital in Johannesburg, or to Tembisa Hospital.

Many patients died en route. Edenvale Hospital was much closer, about fifteen minutes or so away, and had more sophisticated emergency equipment, but it was for whites only.

Tembi, Angeline, and I boarded an overcrowded Volkswagen minibus called a *kombi* (a type of taxi service). Because Putco buses were routinely attacked, robbed, and set ablaze, they had stopped coming into the ghetto. Now a brisk *kombi* service flourished and I usually rode one to work each day.

But you had to know which *kombis* were safe. Lately they were being used as weapons in a deadly turf war raging between rival companies with opposite political allegiances. If you got into the wrong *kombi*—say, one operated by an Inkatha member or sympathizer— you might be attacked by the Comrades. *Kombis* belonging to ANC members or sympathizers were similarly attacked by Inkatha members or white vigilantes.

We boarded the politically correct *kombi*. Angeline sat on my lap, Tembi next to me, and a couple of other passengers sat on top of each other. In this way nearly twenty people were jammed and crammed into a minibus designed to carry half that number legally. The passengers in the back handed their fare from one seat to the next until the money reached the driver.

As some passengers swapped stories in various tribal languages and others sat stoically, Tembi told me what had happened yesterday on 16th Avenue.

"Collin and Calvin were plotting to take the kids away from you and Maria," Tembi said.

Collin and Calvin were not only best friends, they lived on the same street, and had children by two sisters—myself and my younger sister Maria. Both Maria and I were tired of their philandering and drunkenness and had left them, taking our children with us. Maria still had a black eye and bruised ribs from the last time Calvin battered her, after accusing her of sleeping with other men.

"Calvin and Collin went to your parent's place yesterday and demanded their Given and Angeline," Tembi continued. Given, Maria's son, was born the same year as Angeline, when Maria was only fifteen. "Collin was angry that Angeline wasn't there." Though for all practical purposes I had moved in with Walter, I still came home occasionally, and Angeline spent most of the time at my parents' home. But this time I had taken her with me to Walter's.

"Angeline is *my* child," I said. "He can marry one of his mistresses and have kids with her, but Angeline is mine."

"You talk as if you think he'll live, *Skwiza*," Tembi said.

I fell silent. The possibility that Collin might be dead for all we knew had still not sunk in. I stared out the window at the passing scenery of affluent white suburbs to divert my mind from painful thoughts, but I couldn't stop thinking about Collin. I reflected on the most recent argument he and I had had over custody of Angeline.

"You seem to forget that I'm her father," Collin had said. "And I paid *lobola* for you."

"You may have paid *lobola*," I said, "but you don't own me or my daughter. Why don't you go make a baby with one of your many girlfriends? Do whatever you want. But leave me and my child alone."

"You're not taking good care of her, Florah. You dump her on your mother all the time."

"I have to work, Collin. I have to make a living. You aren't supporting us anymore. Besides, my mother doesn't mind looking after her own grandchildren."

"But your mother is overwhelmed. Today I went by your parents' place. Angeline was sitting alone, withdrawn and sulking. You should have seen her. Her hair was dirty and she smelled. Her dress was unwashed. How do you expect your mother to look after her own children and yours and Maria's as well? What are you trying to do? Make your mother go mad again?" (My mother had had a bout with insanity in 1981, which lasted almost two years.)

"Of course not. But what do you expect me to do? Quit my job? I have to help support my parents as well as feed and clothe my child."

"I'm sick of your excuses. You're not taking good care of my daughter and I want her back!"

"Look who's talking. You *never* helped me take care of the baby while we were still living together. I nursed her, diapered her, fed her, and did everything for her, all by myself. Even your stepmother and sister never lifted a finger to help me. Instead your stepmother demanded that I also clean the house, wash laundry, and cook for everybody."

"You never complained until you took off with that jailbird Walter."

"I didn't dare complain because I was in your stepmother's house. And she wields such influence over you. You wouldn't have believed me and would have taken her side, making her hate me even more. Remember that one time I objected when she demanded that your little brother sleep with us in our tiny room? With you, me, Angeline, and our belongings there was simply no space. Also, how could we make love with him there? And do you remember what you said? Nothing!"

"What did you expect me to say?" Collin retorted. "Where should my little brother sleep? In a junkyard?"

"No. But we needed some privacy. He could have slept in the kitchen. Or with your parents."

"There's no room in the kitchen, as you know. Anyway, my parents said he should sleep with us. And it's their house."

"You see what I mean? You forget that I'm married to you and not to your parents."

"I hate arguing, Florah," he said. "Either you come back home or just give me Angeline and my *lobola* back and you can do whatever you want with your life."

With that he abruptly turned and left me standing in the middle of the dusty street, almost in tears. I muttered swear words under my breath, in Zulu and Shangaan. I seethed with rage as I walked the rest of the way to work. I knew he could carry out his threat, because he was a man. Under African culture, a woman's children belong to his husband's family.

But was Collin still alive? The sun had risen quite high in the sky by the time we reached the hospital. Already the corridors bustled with nurses and teemed with black patients waiting their turn for treatment.

Tembi and I led Angeline by the hand to the main nursing station.
"May I help you?" a nurse asked.

"I'm looking for my husband, Collin," I said.

The nurse ran a finger down a list of names. "Sorry, there's no one here by that name."

"But he *must* be here, nurse," I said. "He was shot yesterday afternoon and brought here."

"Dozens of people were shot yesterday afternoon and brought here," the nurse said nonchalantly.

"But we have to see him right away, please nurse," I said. "He was badly wounded and may not have long to live."

Unable to help us further, the nurse directed us to another section of the hospital. We wound our way up the stairs. Angeline tagged along at my heels, whining.

"Mommy, where are we going? Where's Daddy? I'm hungry. I want bread and cold drink."

"Hush, child," I said. "You'll get breakfast later."

We walked up and down the crowded corridors, asking passing nurses if they had heard of Collin. Some stopped and said no, many simply ignored us. At last we ran into a nurse who knew of Collin. "Are you Florah?" the nurse asked me.

"Yes."

"He's been asking for you. Last room on the left." Then she walked on.

A lump rose to my throat as I stepped into the room. Tembi gasped in horror. It was crowded with about thirty cots, and in all of them lay wounded and sick black men. Some wailed with pain. Some reached toward me with contorted fingers, calling for the nurse, mumbling strange names, begging for relief from their agonizing pain. Others were simply lying on their tiny cots, staring at the ceiling with vacant eyes as dangling glass bottles dripped fluids through thin plastic tubing into their veins.

Collin lay below the window at the far end of the room. His eyes were closed. A fly buzzed about his head. His throat was heavily bandaged, and a thin tube disappeared into a small hole at the base of his neck.

Angeline took one look at her father and started screaming. I tried reassuring her that Daddy was all right, but I too began weeping at the sight of my helpless, paralyzed husband. Tembi too was crying.

"Mommy! There's something sticking out of Daddy's throat," said Angeline, pointing. "What is it?"

"That's to help him breathe, darling," I explained between sobs. "It's an oxygen tube."

Angeline's screams awoke Collin. He slowly opened his eyes. A weak smile gradually spread across his tired face.

"You came," he said hoarsely to me, then smiled at his sister.

I could not tell whether the raspy voice had come from his mouth or the hole in his esophagus. Angeline clung to my skirt and cautiously peered around me at her father.

"Who did this to you?" I asked in a voice choked with rage.

Collin stared at me a long time before he answered. "Calvin and I were just sitting outside," he began, with some difficulty. "We were minding our own business and drinking some beer, when this guy walked up to us."

"Who?"

"I don't know him. I'd never seen him before. Calvin seemed to know him, though. The guy sat down beside us and started an idle conversation. He talked mainly to Calvin. I just kept quiet and drank my beer. Then he said, 'Hey, man, it's cold here. Why don't we go across the road and sit in the sun?' He stood up and like fools we followed him across the street to a vacant lot. I assumed the whole time that he was a friend of Calvin's and that everything was cool. They continued their conversation. Suddenly the guy pulled out a gun and blasted Calvin. Just like that. Point blank. I was stunned, but still had enough control of my senses to stand up and attempt to lunge at him. He fired a second shot. The bullet got me right here," he said, pointing to the heavy, blood-stained bandage covering the left side of his throat. "I dropped down and he bolted."

"So you know what he looks like," I said. "You can describe him to the police."

"Don't be naive, Florah. He was probably *hired* by the police."

"But why?"

"I don't know. Maybe Calvin was involved in something illegal and never told me. Now that he's dead I guess we'll never know."

At this time there were rumors that M-K, the ANC's military wing, had infiltrated Alexandra and established one of its best organizations there, from which to launch strikes against government targets. The Pretoria regime, in its determination to defeat M-K, had resorted to hiring assassins. And there had been cases of mistaken identity, where innocent people were murdered.

"Maybe you're right," I said, after reflecting for a moment. "I noticed a change in him over the past few months. He became brutal and nasty. I wondered what came over him."

"He took his secrets to the grave."

"Is there anything I can do to help track down the person who shot you?"

"It might be dangerous to even try. The last place to go is to the police, of course. And if you ask too many questions of the wrong people, you might be next. Just pray for me, Florah, will you, please? Ask your mother to pray for me too, she's so full of God."

"I'll pray for you Collin. And I'll ask my mother to pray too."

"And come and see me often, will you? And always bring little Nonqeba [Angeline's tribal name]. Promise?"

"I will."

"Please forgive me for all the pain I've caused you. Do you forgive me?"

"I forgive you."

Tears started flowing down my cheeks. Despite all he'd put me through, he was still my husband. And he was so young, only twenty-four. The last time I saw him he had been so full of life, and now he was lying helpless in bed, like a vegetable, a paralytic, maybe never to walk again in his life. He still had a special place in my heart, as my first love and the father of my only child. But I wondered if I could ever take him back, now that he was likely to be a cripple. My mind refused to think of it.

"And bring me something good to eat next time you come," he said. "The food here is lousy."

"I will."

"And don't forget my favorite books."

"I won't."

I turned and led Angeline by the hand. She looked back once more at her father with a three-year-old's curiosity, then skipped along beside me, as we headed out to look for some food, while Tembi remained and talked with her brother.

11

GELI

WITCH DOCTOR
UNMASKED

Florah is my second child, and she was born January 6, 1962, while her father Jackson was in prison. He had been arrested the day after New Year's for not having a residential permit allowing him to establish a family in Alexandra. The new yard where we had settled was a haven for illegal immigrants, and the Peri-Urban police constantly targeted it, swooping down unannounced during midnight raids.

In the past, whenever Jackson was arrested for pass-law violations, he would pay a fine and be released. But since he started visiting the witch doctor on Fridays, we seldom had any money left for emergencies, such as bribing the police.

As I wasn't booked at the clinic this time, the nurses didn't come, and my mother and two older women from the neighborhood attended me at childbirth. They were experienced, but it was a somewhat difficult birth, though it was my second child and the womb was now supposed to "know what to do." Florah was born a bit underweight and I bled a lot. Luckily the midwives knew what to do to stop the bleeding.

Relatives gave Florah the tribal name Mkondeleli, meaning "Endurance," "hang in there." It was meant to encourage me to persevere in the face of hardships and in my marriage to an abusive husband, and things would get better. Florah would have been my last child, had there been proper family planning in my days instead of my having to rely on taboos, like the taboo against having sex until the child was two or three.

I also wish children were not regarded as a form of wealth. That way Jackson wouldn't have wanted so many. Two or three would have been enough. But God, for whatever reason, gave me seven, and my life has been one continuous sacrifice to keep them alive and to give them hope.

Jackson was finally released from prison. His Italian employer in Germiston gave him his old job back, which was a miracle in itself. Black men were frequently fired from their jobs for reasons often beyond their control—sickness, arrest, or attending the funerals of their loved ones. One of our neighbors recounted the following exchange he had with his employer the day he was fired after he had taken a week from work to attend the funeral of one of his children, who had died in the homelands.

"What's more important to you," the *baas* (boss) had asked, "working or attending a funeral?"

"Clearly, working, *mei baas*," our neighbor had replied, "but my child died."

"I'm sorry. But the job had to be done, so I had to find somebody else."

There were millions of somebody elses waiting for a chance at the most degrading work paying the most deplorable wages.

Jackson was lucky to have found an employer who cared about him and his family. His employer even gave him old clothing, children's toys, occasional modest raises, a decent bonus of about R15 at the end of the year, and a week's vacation at Christmas.

The landlord increased our rent from 30 to 60 cents a month and we were forced to move to 13th Avenue. I welcomed the move, as I thought it would somehow put an end to Jackson's Friday visits to the witch doctor, but I was mistaken. The nocturnal visits continued even on 13th Avenue.

Florah was seventeen months old when we moved. One Friday after midnight Jackson returned from his visit to the witch doctor all glum and testy and said he was ready to make a confession. He was finally going to reveal the identity of the mysterious witch doctor who had been devouring his wages for so long, who had made me curse the arrival of each Friday and suffer many a sleepless night and beatings.

"I don't really visit a witch doctor on Fridays as I've been telling you," he began.

"I knew that," I said dryly.

"How did you know?" he asked sharply. "Are you a witch doctor too?"

I laughed without meaning to.

"Well," he hemmed and hawed. "Whenever I leave on Friday nights saying I'm going to see a witch doctor, I'm actually headed for a gambling den to play dice."

I was a little relieved. Though the revelation that he was gambling angered me, it was not what I had feared. I had thought he was lavishing his wages on gifts and liquor for mistresses. That's what I thought his brother, Silas, meant by "naughty." Many men had mistresses and used all sorts of ruses to hide the fact. And their wives often pretended not to know because they did not want to deal with the pain, to be beaten if they dared confront their husbands, or to lose whatever little security their marriages provided in terms of support.

"Why do you gamble when you have a family to support?" I asked.

"I'm not paid enough," he said.

"You may not be paid enough," I said, "but if you had saved all the money you've been losing all this time, you'd be a tycoon by now."

He ignored my statement.

"And you're too old to be playing dice with young boys, Jackson," I said.

"I know I'll strike it rich one of these days," he said confidently.

"When? When you're a blind old man and no longer able to see the dice you're rolling?"

"Don't talk to me like that, woman!" he snapped.

"How should I talk to you, when you're being irresponsible? Dice is a game for boys. You're a father and a husband. By playing with children you deserve to be treated like one."

"I said don't talk to me like that, woman," Jackson said, his temper rising.

"Well, what do you want me to do, now that you've told me about this witch doctor that's cast such a spell on you that you've forgotten your duties as a husband and a father?"

"I want you to help me."

I was amazed. As well as I can remember, it was the first and only time he had ever admitted to needing help from anybody. But I soon realized the sort of help he wanted. He wanted me to cheer and pray for him whenever he went gambling so that he'd have good luck.

"The best help for you is to stop gambling," I said.

"My turn to win big is coming, woman," Jackson insisted. "I can feel it in my bones. In fact, I would have made my killing already had it not been for you."

"Me? Don't start blaming me for your gambling addiction."

"Yes, you're to blame. Your evil heart is to blame. I can tell how bitter you are each time I go out Friday night."

"How should I feel? Should I rejoice that my children are being starved and made to wear rags? Should I ululate when you come back having lost and we have to pinch pennies till the next payday? Should I shout hosanna when you beat me and chase me out of the house? I am not that masochistic."

"I don't mean that," Jackson snapped. "I mean stop being so bitter about it. It brings me bad luck. The other men I play with have wives who wish them well, pray for them, and even give them good luck charms."

"Don't expect that from me," I said. "If anything, I should be praying for the police to come close that gambling den and arrest the lot of you."

"You see what I mean? You *are* bitter."

"How should I feel when your gambling causes me such pain? You know something, Jackson? There's no other woman in the world who wants to see you do well more than I do. I want so much to help you succeed. It's true that I wouldn't have married you if the choice had been mine. But now that you've paid *lobola* for me, now that we have children together to care for, I want to be your partner. And I'm prepared to do anything to see us get out of this pit of poverty and prosper as a family."

"Then why don't you stop wishing me bad luck?!" Jackson shouted.

"I do no such thing," I said. "You're the one creating all the bad luck for yourself by shirking your responsibilities. I personally wish you all the good luck in the world because getting money is your only goal in life. And should you win big, as you continue to delude yourself, I don't want a cent of your fortune. I don't want money gained at the expense of other people's miseries and pain. Just as your losses create pain and misery in this house, your win will create pain and misery in other homes."

Jackson's addiction to gambling convinced me that I had to come up with ways to stop relying on him for support. I longed for financial independence and self-reliance. If I no longer had to beg, cajole, and wheedle for a few pennies each Friday, if I could earn my own money, I would no longer have to be scolded, asked to account for every penny spent, and browbeaten about wasting money because I was buying necessities he deemed unnecessary.

I would not have to be constantly living in dread about the future and about whether I would be able to send my children to school when the time came. I would never have to dress them in patched rags, and myself to wear nothing better. I would never have to fear that whatever little money Jackson condescended to give me he could demand back any minute. If I had my own income, I would not care whether or not he gambled or gave me a cent.

But there seemed little I could do to end the abusive dependency. Jobs were scarce. Besides, I had no permit to hunt for piece jobs in the white world, and no education or skills to speak of beyond those of a maid: washing, cleaning, and ironing. But the maids mostly in demand by white *madames* were those willing to sacrifice their families for a pittance of R4 (about $2) a month.

One day, despite the horror stories I heard every day about the impossibility of finding jobs without the proper papers, I joined a group of women from the neighborhood and we went job hunting in the nearby suburbs. All of us were desperate to have our own incomes so as not to depend on our husbands. Since we needed to have a job to get the papers, we hoped that some kind *madames*—we had heard there were a few—would understand our dilemma and have pity on us and agree to register us with the authorities for work permits.

I left my children with my mother. As we couldn't afford the 5-cent bus fare, we simply walked the several miles to the northern suburbs of Sandton, discussing job-seeking strategies as we went. When we reached the entrance to the suburbs, we fanned out, so as not to attract attention from the police. We agreed to rendezvous at the same point of departure by early afternoon. We warned each other to be careful about getting caught by the police, and what to do should that happen.

"If the police come up to me," I said to my friends, "I'll pretend I'm mad. Then they'll just pick me up, as I've seen them do, and drop me in Alexandra."

There were hardly any mental asylums for blacks, despite the high number of mental cases among us. Lunatics roamed the streets, lived in junkyards, and ate out of garbage dumps. There were even stories of mad women being raped.

I timidly knocked at several white people's doors but either found no one in or rude maids who resented my presence, out of fear that I had come to take their job away by offering to work for less than they were being paid. In some places I had to flee for dear life as large dogs chased after me.

Finally, around noon, I came to a huge, mansionlike home, occupying a lot on which two ghetto yards could have easily fit. The difference was that those two yards would normally contain over two hundred people, whereas the mansion was most likely home to just one family.

Madame came to the gate wearing a robe to cover her skimpy bikini, suggesting she might have been sunning herself by the pool. She was sipping some liquid out of a sweaty glass. It was a hot day. She was of middle height, had flowing dark hair, and her skin was deeply tanned, almost like that of a light-skinned black person. She wore tinted glasses.

I was in luck. *Madame* was considering firing her "girl" after catching her with a boyfriend on her property, without permission. I had caught a glimpse of the "girl." She was a full-grown woman, about my age, but all black women—whether teenagers or grey-haired grandmothers—were called "girls" by white *madames*, just as all grown-up black men were referred to as "boys."

"Do you have a boyfriend?" *Madame* asked me in Fanakalo (a pidgin language consisting of a mixture of English and various tribal languages).

I hesitated, pondering how to best answer. After all, the present "girl" was about to be fired because she had dared to have a boyfriend.

"I do have children, *Madame*," I said evasively.

"Can you sleep in?"

Most *madames* preferred "girls" who could sleep in—that is, who were willing to live in an outbuilding in the back of the property. That way, *Madame* would find it easier to get her needs met around the clock. The "girl" could even be summoned in the middle of the night for service. She generally made up beds, cleaned the house, prepared children for school, gave them lunch, washed and ironed laundry, prepared meals, accompanied *Madame* shopping, and so forth.

"No, *Madame*," I said. "I can only work during the day because I have no one to look after my children at night."

Madame shrugged with annoyance at this apparent inconvenience.

"Why don't you send them in the homelands, like other girls do?" *Madame* asked.

"I have no home in the homelands, *Madame*. My husband and I live in the townships."

"So you are married?" *Madame* asked with surprise. Apparently *Madame* was one of those whites who didn't believe that blacks ever married. Black women were promiscuous and bred lots of children, most of them illegitimate, and thus had no need for a normal home life—so said government propaganda as it formulated Influx Control laws designed to break up black families.

"Yes. He's the father of my children. He paid *lobola* for me. And he works very hard but just doesn't make enough. That's why I am looking for a job."

"How much does he make?"

"About R4 a week."

"And that is not enough?" *Madame* exclaimed, incredulous. Her husband probably made two or three hundred times that amount.

"It's enough and not enough, *Madame*," I said quickly, lest she consider me too greedy. "It's enough for food and rent, *Madame*. But then my children need clothes and they will soon be starting school. I need money to pay for their school things."

Madame screwed up her face, as if finding it hard to understand why blacks would be so concerned about school when the apartheid government told her that blacks didn't have any need for education, beyond a smattering to enable them to better serve white people. Perhaps she had been told schooling only made kaffirs more dissatisfied with their lot, and cheeky to whites. Yet her children presumably attended school for free. The government paid for their tuition, books, fees, and lunches, and we had to pay for every penny of our children's education when most of us didn't even earn enough to keep flesh and bone together.

"Can you work weekends?" *Madame* asked.

"No, *Madame*, my husband won't allow it. On weekends I have to do washing, and take care of my own home."

Madame was now exasperated. She said, "Then why are you looking for a job? There's no way I can pay you R6 a month if you can't sleep in or work on weekends."

"I work very hard, *Madame*."

"There are thousands of girls who work very hard too. I need someone who can sleep in or work on weekends."

"I'm willing to work for just R3 a month if I'm not required to sleep in or work on weekends, *Madame*."

Madame showed slight interest in the proposal.

"Can you read?"

"No, *Madame*, I never went to school."

"Not even simple instructions, like how to feed the baby?"

"No, *Madame*, but I know how to take care of babies. I have two of my own."

"I don't mean that. I mean can you take care of white babies?"

I was slightly bewildered. I thought all babies were the same and needed motherly care and love.

"I can learn, *Madame*."

"Are your papers in order? Do you have a permit to work in the suburbs?"

"No, *Madame*."

An expression of incredulity crossed *Madame*'s face.

"Then why in the world are you looking for a job if you don't have the proper papers?"

"I was hoping that if you hired me, *Madame*, you could help me get registered. That's the only way I can get papers."

"Sorry, I don't have the time. I have more important things to do."

Madame had important things to do, like sunbathe, play tennis, go bowling, read, sleep, swim, coif her hair, or entertain her friends. I, on the other hand, had only survival to think about.

12

GRANNY

LIFE AS A
SINGLE MOTHER

My daughter's struggles for independence and self-reliance mirrored my own, showing that little had changed from one generation to another. Women were still having a difficult time making ends meet, especially if they lacked the proper papers to find work or didn't have husbands who supported them.

When I found myself stranded in Alexandra without a husband to rely on, no papers to look for work, I had to find other ways to support myself and my three children. Life as an unemployed single mother was more than trying. It was one of continuous dependency and uncertainty. Custom had taught me to rely totally on a husband, to expect to be taken care of by him in return for my complete devotion. It would take me a long time to overcome such dependency and ways of thinking. What compounded my situation was that as an unemployed, single woman living in the city, I risked being arrested under the Influx Control law and deported to the tribal reserves.

My children and I wandered from place to place, seeking shelter and food. We lived for short spells in various locations around Johannesburg, and with relatives in the homelands.

During that time, partly out of fear of being deported as a single woman, I had my first relationship with a man since John deserted me. His name was Makwakwa. I still mistrusted men and their promises—the pain of betrayal still lingered, the wounds had not yet completely healed. They could never heal. But life had to go on, I had to survive. I had to care for my children, whether or not there was a man in the house.

Apartheid had put so many obstacles in the path of single black women fighting for survival in the cities that we could do practically nothing without men. We needed men to do just about everything concerned with the law. We needed them to get permits to look for jobs, to qualify for housing, to register children in school, to open bank accounts.

Makwakwa was hardworking, sober, single, and he treated me with understanding and respect. He was patient with me and understood the pain I had been through at the hands of John. He never, during the times we were together, raised a finger against me or demeaned me in any way. I had two children by him, Bushy and Piet. He treated my children by John with the same gentle firmness that he used with his own flesh and blood, which was unusual for a man to do. Many men were partial to children they had sired.

But my relationship with Makwakwa didn't result in marriage. He was not yet ready to settle down. Also, his relatives put enormous pressure on him not to marry an older woman who already had children by another man. We parted without acrimony, and when he left me I found myself burdened with having to support five children on my own.

I had no job, and no permit to look for a job. I couldn't pay rent, feed my children, buy them clothes, nor send them to school. I relied on the charity of relatives and strangers. My eldest child, Mphephu, helped from time to time. She and her husband, also a *nganga*, had a thriving practice in Giyane. Every now and then Mphephu would invite me and my children to live with her. We dared not overstay our visits, out of fear that our presence might strain and possibly wreck her marriage. I dreaded the possibility of Mphephu's marriage being wrecked. She was the only woman in my family who had married an understanding man who respected and supported her and never fooled around. And Mphephu's husband had recently taken a second wife, which meant more mouths to feed.

Being husbandless, I was seen by many as a potential home breaker. I even found it hard to rent a shack.

"Are you married?" a landlord would ask.

"No."

"Sorry, this yard is only for women with husbands."

"But it's not my fault that I don't have a husband," I would say.

"That's true," the landlord would say, "but if I rented you a place I would get in trouble with the wives in the yard who are against single women living here. They fear losing their husbands."

Finally I found a landlord without a strict policy against single women, and he rented me a room. But I was immediately made to feel unwelcome, an outcast. Few married women befriended me. Those who did associate with me seldom invited me to their homes, afraid that I might seduce or steal their husbands, whom they jealously guarded and often interrogated.

"Where have you been?" they would demand of their husbands.

"Why were you talking to that unmarried woman?"

"I don't want you drinking at that *shebeen* frequented by that woman without a husband."

Having a husband was seen as a guarantee that a woman would not fool around. Even relatives saw me as a burden. My presence invariably created tensions in the home. My children and I could not be easily absorbed into the family structure, for we created an imbalance. My children, especially the boys, proved difficult to discipline. I had tried hard to keep them in school despite our lack of a permanent home. Reuben was now in Standard Six—eighth grade—and I had hopes that he would soon be able to get a decent job that would alleviate our troubles.

As no yard was hospitable for long, I always found myself returning to the house I least wanted to live in—Matinana's.

One day, after being forced to leave Matinana's place for the umpteenth time—she had the whim, whenever she wanted me to leave, of arbitrarily raising the rent, knowing full well I could not afford to pay it—I found a room the size of a closet, for which the landlord wanted the exorbitant sum of 50 cents a month. Here my three children and I made our home.

For lack of space—the room measured roughly six by ten feet—my daughter Geli, who lived not far away, took in Bushy and Piet, and I remained with Reuben. Jackson did not want Piet and Bushy in his house, but Geli managed to persuade him that it was only for a short time till I found a larger place, that the schooling of Piet and Bushy would be paid for by me, and that they would be helpful with chores and caring for Johannes and Florah.

One day, during a visit to Mphephu, I discussed with her my longing to be able to support myself and my children.

"I'm so tired of hunting for gardening piece jobs in the suburbs," I told her. "They're so hard to find. The work leaves me terribly exhausted and my back on fire with pain from bending all day. And I'm paid so little. The money I've managed to save so far will soon run out. I need to find some way to earn more. Otherwise my children and I will be homeless and without food. Do you have any suggestions?"

"The best way to gain financial security, Mama, is to go into business for yourself," Mphephu said. "That way you don't have to worry about permits. And you don't have to rely on any man or *mali ya mlungu* [crumb wages from a white master]. I'm in business for myself as a *nganga* and doing well."

"What business can I get into, my child?" I said. "I'm not a *nganga*. I have no education, no skills. The only work I have ever done has been with my hands. See how calloused they've become."

I showed her my gnarled hands.

"I know you work hard," Mphephu said. "That's why I believe that if you worked hard for yourself, you would become financially independent in no time."

"But what is there for me to do that would earn me enough money?" I said. "At times I believe that I'm doomed to work forever at menial jobs for white people. I see myself forced to slave that way till old age and have nothing to show for it when I die."

"Well, people rave about the beer you make," she said. "You should start selling some."

In the past I had brewed very small amounts, mainly for myself and friends, and for special occasions like weddings and ceremonies to appease ancestors, purify the house, celebrate the birth of a child, and so forth. People had often praised the quality of my beer, and even suggested that I consider opening a *shebeen*. But I was afraid of the police, of being arrested and leaving my children without anyone to care for them, or worse, of being deported from the city.

"I have considered selling before," I said to Mphephu. "But I abandoned the idea because of the police. Every day, people are being arrested for illegally brewing beer."

"Well, I'll help you take care of the police," Mphephu said.

"How?"

"I can fortify your home with *muti* so that there's less of a chance for the police to arrest you for illegally brewing beer."

"But I have no home. I'm currently living in a closet."

"Oh, I'd forgotten about that."

She gave me some money and said I should return to Alexandra and look for a larger place. She then promised to visit my new home and perform rituals to protect it against police beer raids. She also promised to bring me *muti* that would help me attract and keep customers, especially given the fierce competition among *shebeen* owners.

My *muti* was of a benign sort. It consisted of herbs which I added to the beer during its fermentation, and of some special fat mixture to smear the tins in which I stored the liquor, so they could not be detected by sniffing police dogs when buried underground.

I knew *shebeen* owners who went to criminal ends to gain customers and to prosper. Some were known to kidnap and kill small children for ritual sacrifices so their beer businesses would thrive.

Others were said to keep human skulls in the refrigerators where they stored illegal hootch, as some sort of good luck charm. Still many others indulged in the unsanitary practice of placing old shoes in the fermenting brew, in the hope of making it irresistible to the palate.

Blacks, I believe, resorted to these extreme, criminal, and dangerous measures because selling beer was often the only way most could earn a living under apartheid. Most of us were uneducated, and those who were educated found little work in the white world beyond menial jobs as gardeners, messenger boys, miners, maids, and so forth. Then there were the myriad papers and permits one needed to hunt for jobs in the white world. When we were lucky enough to find work, our wages were deliberately kept low, making it virtually impossible to feed ourselves and care for our own children, let alone our extended families.

So beer selling was often the only option left us, short of becoming criminals. It was easy to set up. One needed no education, and one had an almost inexhaustible pool of customers. Most adults in Alexandra drank, especially the single men in the hostels, who led hard and unnatural lives, separated from their families for entire years at a time. Many found guzzling liquor the perfect anodyne, to make them forget, if only for a while, the hardships of life under apartheid, to numb themselves to the pain of being unable to provide for loved ones and of being constantly degraded and lorded over by whites.

But beer sellers were the fiercest of competitors. Many stopped at nothing to gain customers or to drive their rivals out of business. There were dozens of gangs in Alexandra who were often hired by *shebeen* owners for protection or to harass or murder competitors. Gangs also practiced extortion. Those *shebeen* owners who could not afford to pay the high protection fees gangs charged, or for some reason felt they needed extra protection, resorted to witchcraft. And the *sangomas* (Zulu word for *ngangas*) who dealt in shebeen-protecting *muti*, just as those who dealt in love charms, did a roaring business.

It was generally considered folly for people to open or run a *shebeen* without protecting their investment with the most powerful *muti* they could lay their hands on. In this climate of survival of the fittest, people easily went over the bounds of legality and humanity, becoming corrupt and ruthless.

I guess I could have done the same, given my desperation to earn a living, to provide for my loved ones, to survive. But I have always had what many in the township would have considered a fatal weakness: I wasn't prepared to do anything to get ahead, to stay alive. Yes, I was poorer than dirt. Yes, my children and I were suffering. And yes, every day was a bitter survival struggle. But I wasn't prepared to harm others, to bewitch, to kill in order to keep body and soul together.

Had I done that, I couldn't have lived with myself. And for refusing to act as many others did in the desperate struggle for survival in the ghetto, where most blacks groaned under the dual yoke of poverty and white oppression, I was often the target of evil and malice.

For instance, I could have sought the aid of witchcraft to regain my inheritance, to get my husband back, or to avenge the deaths of my brother and father. I could have lied, cheated, and killed to protect what was mine and those I loved, as many did.

But happiness—if it can even be called that—gained at the cost of my soul would have been as bitter as gall. The spirits of my ancestors would have been ashamed of me. My children would have cursed my repulsive memory when I'd be dead, and those I had harmed would have wreaked their vengeance on my posterity.

As an African, steeped in the humanism that's central to the character of our people, as the daughter and granddaughter of preachers of Christ's gospel, as the proud offspring of the venerable Khosa clan, with ancestors in whose veins flowed the noble blood of chiefs who ruled and gave laws, I believe with all my heart that there is a right and a wrong way to live. Those who do evil will be punished; those who do good will be rewarded. Maybe not in this life, but certainly in the life hereafter. I have attempted to live my life according to this sacred belief, especially during those times—and they were all too frequent—when life in its meanness bared its fangs at me and dared me to fight back in kind.

PART III

13

FLORAH

COLLIN DIES,
WALTER TURNS INTO AN ABUSER

I visited Collin at the hospital regularly at first. The nurses told me he was getting better and would live, but that he would be paralyzed from the waist down for the rest of his life. I still held out hope. I thought the nurses wrong in their prognosis. I continued to believe that by some miracle Collin would be walking by the time he was released from hospital. I had to hold out that hope. I couldn't imagine spending the rest of my life caring for an invalid I no longer completely loved. The thought scared me.

One day when Angeline and I were visiting Collin and were sitting at his bedside, I saw the familiar figure of a woman walking through the door toward us. She was tall, dark, and wore a tight-fitting minidress. It was one of Collin's girlfriends, a woman I had once called a friend. I grew sick with disgust and rage at the sight of her, just as I had when I first found out she and my husband were having an affair. We ignored each other in cool, proud silence. Not a word was exchanged between the two of us as we stared past one another at Collin, the walls, and the other patients. Soon we were joined by yet another of Collin's girlfriends. The three of us stood around his bed like fools.

I still don't understand how women can stand sharing a man. I'd say a very large number of black women in South Africa are forced to share a man at some point in their lives, sometimes for their entire married lives. How I hated Collin's girlfriends! The sight of them filled me with bitterness toward Collin. I vowed never to visit him again. He could die for all I cared.

Weeks passed. People told me that Collin frequently begged to see me. Still I refused to go to the hospital. I sent him a curt note, explaining why I felt uncomfortable visiting him when his other girl-friends might show up at any moment and turn the hospital ward into a harem. He sent back a reply saying that he understood, but added, "Will you come sometimes just to show me little Nonqeba?"

The last time I saw Collin he was looking well. He was sitting up, looking like he used to except for the hole in his throat. I could not believe it when, a few days later, on the 4th of September 1985, I was informed that he was dead. No one thought he would die, least of all myself. The nurses said he would have been a paralytic, but no one said he would *die*. Tembi speculated that Collin had committed sui-cide because he did not want to spend the rest of his life as an invalid.

Collin's death left me stricken with guilt and grief. I was haunted by memories of our painful breakup and regretted that we had never completely forgiven each other.

Widows are supposed to be contaminated with bad luck, so an elderly woman from my mother's tribe had to cleanse me of it. She shaved my head, my armpits, my legs, every bit of hair on my body. I wasn't allowed to shave nor wash myself during the period of mourn-ing; it had to be done by a woman whose husband had died and who knew exactly what to do.

She killed a white-feathered chicken, mixed its blood with *muti*, poured the mixture into a large tin tub filled with water, and told me to strip and get in. She scrubbed me all over, until she was convinced that all the bad luck had been removed from my body.

Because Collin and I didn't have a civil marriage and were separated at the time of his death, I did not have to follow all the rituals of widowhood. I was lucky. I did not, for instance, have to wear black for a year, avoid men, and stay holed up inside my room. It is believed that if a widow visits your house, bad luck will befall you. So if a widow breaks the rules and ventures out and about, she runs the risk of being blamed for all sorts of bad luck incurred by the people with whom she happens to come in contact.

A year after Collin's death we placed a tombstone on his grave. I couldn't control myself at the grave site: I started sobbing uncontrollably. The memories were so heartbreaking. Even now I can't bring myself to visit his grave very often. It's too hard to face the past.

I felt terrible that our marriage hadn't worked out and that we were so distant from each other emotionally at the time of the shooting. I felt terrible for allowing that distance to be there. Sometimes I blamed myself for Collin's death. I thought, Maybe if I had forgiven him one more time and we had stayed together this wouldn't have happened. He wouldn't have been sitting there with Calvin drinking beer. Maybe we would have moved to East Bank and had a nice house. We would have been busy with our lives. There would have been no time for hanging out and being in danger.

But it was too late. Collin was dead. Yet I kept thinking of him, and felt a deep, dull ache inside whenever I recalled the innocence and beauty of our early relationship and the good times we had shared when our love was young. Collin had his bad habits, as I did mine, but he also knew how to treat a woman right when he wanted to. He was one of the most generous persons I have ever met. When we were still together, whenever he bought groceries for his family, he bought some for mine. Whenever any of my siblings needed money for books, lunch, or a school trip, he always gave them. And during my mother's bout with insanity in 1982, when my father neglected the family, Collin stepped in.

And he didn't have a bad temper like Walter. During the five years of our relationship and marriage, he never beat me, never even laid a finger on me.

Soon after Collin died, Walter began treating me differently. He became abusive. He would slap and pummel me with fists for not serving him food in bed, for not handing him a spoon but telling him to go fetch one himself, and for requesting that he occasionally help me with household chores like washing dishes.

"Do you take me for a woman?" he would rant.

He constantly blew up in a rage, prohibited me from having any male friends, and falsely accused me of cheating on him. I remember the first time he struck me. He was annoyed at me for not coming to his place when he had ordered me to come at a particular time. I had held up because Angeline was sick, and I explained this to Walter. He wouldn't listen. He slapped me hard across the face, and I bit my tongue.

"You must do as I tell you, you hear?!" he bellowed at me.

For a while I stood quite still, shocked and motionless.

"Please don't ever do that again," I said slowly, gritting my teeth in anger.

"What did you say?!" Walter bellowed again, and before I knew it, he had punched me in the face and sent me staggering across the room.

Feeling helpless and terrified, I fell silent.

"Don't ever talk like that to me, you hear?!" he demanded, as he raised his hand to strike again. "No woman ever talks like that to me!"

"Yes," I said in a chastened voice. Tears sprang to my eyes, not so much from the pain of the fist—which was excruciating—but from the deeper pain I felt when I thought how desperately I loved him and how that love had been misplaced.

That beating began a very dark and stormy emotional period in my life. I would often flee the shack, fearing for my life, whenever Walter exploded in anger and the beating started. I felt grateful each time his mother, who lived next door, would bang on the wall or door and beg Walter to stop hitting me whenever she heard the thuds, crashes, screams, and slaps of a battery in full progress.

I was constantly on edge. I never knew when something I might say or do would send him into a rage. Sometimes when he looked at me, I could tell he hated me. It terrified me.

And he began taking my love for granted. He stopped saying and doing those little things that more than anything else show a woman that the man she loves truly cares about her: the flowers, the kisses, the compliments, the respect. I now even had to beg Walter to make love.

"What's wrong?" I asked him one night as we lay in bed, after he had once more turned toward the wall without even saying goodnight.

"Nothing's wrong," he snapped.

I was taken aback by the anger in his voice. I felt rejected.

"For three weeks now we haven't made love," I said. "Is anything wrong?"

"Don't ask me about such things," he retorted.

I said no more. But my suspicions that he was having an affair increased. I wondered if he had a mistress whose company he found more enjoyable than mine. I wondered if he had grown tired of me or now thought me ugly.

I believe that Walter changed in part because he no longer had a rival for my love. He felt he could now do anything he wanted to me and I would have no one else to run to. When Collin was still alive and Walter and I had an argument, I would sometimes say, "Remember that at any time I can go back to my husband." Suddenly there was no husband to return to.

I began regretting having fallen in love with Walter. He was really no different from other abusive men, after all. In the two years of our relationship, he had hidden well his true nature. But now that he thought I belonged entirely to him, he had removed his mask. How could I have let myself be so deceived, I wondered.

Walter was always a crafty, smooth operator. I met him through a friend, Thandi ("Beloved"), who lived on my street and dated Walter's friend. I was often with Thandi when her boyfriend would visit.

Thandi and her boyfriend would be together and I preferred keeping to myself in those days, as I was still shaken by the breakup with Collin and overwhelmed with working and caring for a two-year-old child. Also, I had doubts about seeing other men while still married to Collin. One day Thandi, her boyfriend, and Walter showed up in Walter's taxi, and she asked me, "Do you want to go out?"

"Sure," I said.

I left Angeline with my sister Linah, who was good with children. Thandi had a small baby, too, whom her younger sister was caring for.

Walter and Thandi's boyfriend drove us to a take-out joint called "Chicken Lickin." Walter was out to impress me with money, as township men often did when they first met a woman and were interested in her. They would pull out a wad of cash, make sure the girl saw it, watch her eyes bulge in excitement, and then say, "What do you want, my dear? Name anything, and it's yours. I feel like Father Christmas today."

Almost always the girl was impressed. And what she often desired most were clothes, especially the latest fashions and styles from overseas. Young men and women in the ghetto were obsessed with dressing expensively. People were constantly asking each other about the labels on their clothes. If you wore Calvin Klein, Christian Dior, or Gucci, you were held in high esteem and considered rich. Some people even removed the designer labels on the inside of their outfits and sewed them on the front of their outfits, like some sort of badge, to broadcast their expensive tastes. There was also a brisk business in designer labels that one could sew to any cheap garment to make it look expensive.

On the other hand, those who wore plain clothes or clothes bought from a jumble-sale (flea market) were made fun of and considered unimportant. Many people worked hard simply to keep up with the latest fashions. They were often content to live in shacks, and if they had children, they were content to have them wear rags and have little to eat, as long as their insatiable appetite for the latest fashion was satisfied. The irony was that most of these clothes were bought from stores in rich white suburbs, where prices were steep.

This obsession with fancy clothes led to fierce competition among women for men with money. We dressed in high heels, miniskirts, leather skirts and pants, gaudy blouses—you name it, we wore it. We permed, braided, and straightened our hair. We lightened our skins with creams, rouged our cheeks, and painted our lips. We starved ourselves and took laxatives to lose weight—we did all this to gain the perfect figure and look to make us stand out and seductive as we paraded proudly like peacocks in the market for the men to admire and take their pick. What else could we do with our time, when we had been conditioned almost from birth to devote our lives to impressing men and marrying rich?

So when Walter flashed that wad of cash in my face to impress me, I fell for it. I could already see myself decked out as "Walter's lady." We decided to buy something for Angeline and Linah, drop off the food, and then go out, maybe to a disco where couples danced and made out all night to American music, which was preferred by my generation over traditional African music by groups such as Ladysmith Black Mambazo. "That's old-fashioned," we would say. "Only for the old fogies." We adored the likes of Janet Jackson, Madonna, Luther Vandross, Marvin Gaye, Diana Ross, and Michael Jackson (until he began resembling a white girl so much that many in the ghetto thought him ashamed of his blackness and shunned his records).

Walter and I started dating regularly. I would sometimes feel strange when the two of us strolled together down the street, hand in hand. We occasionally ran into people he knew, and they would tease him, saying he had "robbed the cradle." He would retort, "She's no little girl. She has a child and is over twenty-one."

People would be surprised because I looked so small. I didn't look twenty-four at all. I looked fifteen or sixteen. I was petite, and had a fondness for wearing tight jeans that made me appear even younger.

When I told Walter I was married—I did so on our second date—he seemed surprised, and asked who my husband was and where he lived. I told him.

"Do you still love him?" Walter asked.

"I don't know," I said. "But he paid *lobola* for me."

"Why don't you give it back to him? Then you and I can get married."

"I don't have the money," I said. "My father spent it all."

"Why did you leave him?"

"He drinks too much," I said.

Walter remained in a reflective silence. He wasn't drinking at the time, which was quite a relief, because many black men drank, not socially, but to get drunk, to forget their troubles and drown their pain and numb their rage against apartheid.

"I didn't mind the drinking so much," I went on. "What I really hated was the way he slept around with other women. I want a man who will love me and me alone. I can't stand sharing a man with other women."

"But sleeping around is common, isn't it?" Walter said with a laugh.

"It may be common," I said, "but I want no part of it. And if you're into sleeping around, then please, let's not waste each other's time."

"You're quite picky," he said.

"I'm picky because I've been hurt before," I said. "How would you feel if you found out that your girlfriend was sleeping with another man?"

"No girlfriend of mine would ever dare do such a thing," Walter said with deadly seriousness. "I don't like being made a fool."

"I also don't like being made a fool," I said.

14

GELI

SELF-RELIANCE

I could quite relate to my daughter's stories of abuse at the hands of her boyfriend because I was married to an abuser. Jackson and I fought so much during our marriage that our third child, a son, was named Ndwakhulu, which means "Big Wars." His Christian name is George. He was born in 1964, the year Nelson Mandela was sentenced to life imprisonment on Robben Island. Johannes was just over five and Florah a little over two.

My pregnancy with George was a difficult one. I had little to eat and worried a lot as the family suffered through constant police raids and grinding poverty caused in part by apartheid and in part by Jackson's addiction to gambling.

When George was born we were so broke I couldn't even afford diapers and had to use pieces of rags. The week before I had the baby Jackson had lost his entire wage at dice. Our meals were meager. We couldn't afford to buy coal to heat the house in the morning, so my children's teeth chattered in the cold as they went about barefoot and scantily dressed. Sometimes I didn't even have enough milk in my breasts to satisfy the baby. And I couldn't afford to buy the Nestle infant formula, which I had previously used as a substitute for my own milk.

These hardships, and the dreadful foreboding I had that they would only increase unless I did something drastic, made me desperate to find ways of earning an income as soon as George was out of confinement, when his umbilical cord had dried up and fallen off.

My mother, too, was going through the same struggle to be financially independent, so she could support her children and pay rent rather than relying on charity and relatives. I confided in her my plans. She was eager for me to go into the beer-selling business with her.

"I don't have any startup money," I said. "And even if I had the money, I don't think it would be possible to sell liquor with Jackson around. He'd be drinking all the time."

"Then why don't you talk to some of the women in your neighborhood?" my mother said. "I often see them tramping all over Alexandra selling spinach."

"You mean Ma-Xidyoyi [Mother of the Sinner]?" I said. It was customary to call a married woman "Mother of. . . " and then state one of her children's names or nicknames, usually the firstborn's.

"Yes."

Ma-Xidyoyi was an enterprising neighbor in her late thirties. She had been one of the midwives who had attended me during labor. From time to time I went to her for help, and she would lend me cornmeal, tea leaves, candles, or a bottle of paraffin, until Jackson's payday, when I would reimburse her. There was an informal support network among black women united by common problems and abuse. I went to her and told her of my desperation to gain financial independence.

"I think I can help you, Ma-Johannes," she said. "You sure have suffered enough. In fact, I'm surprised you never thought of doing this earlier. So many women are working for themselves nowadays."

"Really," I said. "I didn't know that. I would give anything to stop relying on Jackson. For so long I had placed my trust in him, that he will take care of me and the children. But I have learned a bitter lesson. I need to stand on my own two feet."

"I know what you mean," Ma-Xidyoyi said. "I too have a husband like yours. He drinks too much but fortunately he doesn't gamble. But still he's stingy with money. At first I was upset by this, but then I realized that I wouldn't have to rely on his support if I had my own income. So I went ahead and got my own income."

"How did you do that?"

"Through selling spinach," she said. "Every Monday morning I strap my little girl to my back and walk all the way to Matariani to buy spinach and bring it back to the township to resell." Matariani was the name of a farm owned by a white man on the outskirts of Alexandra.

"Does your husband know?"

"He knows. He's the one that gave me the money to get started. I guess he figured that if I had my own income I would stop hounding him for money."

"My husband wouldn't do that," I said with regret, "reasonable as it sounds."

"Well, you don't need his money to get started."

"I don't?"

"Yes. I know women in your situation who are now supporting themselves through selling spinach."

She named several women, a few of whom I knew.

"How did they get started?"

"Well, Matariani understood their predicament and was willing to let them work in the fields as a way of earning start-up money. He paid them 15 cents a day. By the end of the second week they had earned enough to buy their first supply of spinach."

"Doesn't Matariani ask for work permits?"

"None of the people who work for him has a permit, as far as I know," Ma-Xidyoyi said. "I certainly don't have one. Most of the women have just arrived from the homelands to be with their husbands. And Matariani knows how hard it is for such women to get work permits. All he asks is that if you get caught, don't involve him. It's your own business. But no one has been caught yet, as far as I know. We always have with us clever little boys and girls who play by the roadside while we work. When they see a police van coming, they run back to inform us and we disappear into the fields, falling flat on our faces in the dirt between the rows of spinach and corn."

I was willing to do anything to have my own income. I asked Ma-Xidyoyi if I could accompany her next Monday, and if she would introduce me to Matariani.

"Gladly," she said.

Monday morning came. I woke up early, just after Jackson left for work around 5 A.M. I washed my children and dressed them in neat rags—they had no shoes. For breakfast we ate the previous day's porridge soaked in tea. I packed more porridge with some sugar in a tin to take with me for lunch.

Since our diet was now meager, due to Jackson's heavy gambling, I guarded against our starving outright by begging Jackson each Friday to let me buy necessities such as mealies, sugar, and tea, in big sacks designed to last us more than a week. Even this prudent scheme he acquiesced to with reluctance.

"Don't waste any of my hard-earned money on frivolities," he would say as he gave the R2.

To him, frivolities were things like milk, peanut butter, jungle-oats cereal, and jam.

As for meat, he insisted on being the one to buy it. He would get some each day on his way home from work. For some peculiar reason the meat he brought home always had a funny smell, and at times was downright rotten, leading me to believe that he wasn't actually buying it but digging it out of some garbage dump. Or maybe he bought the spoiled meat sold at giveaway prices by street vendors attempting to maximize their profits. One feature of township life was that nothing was ever wasted. One man's rotten meat was another man's dinner.

The meat Jackson was fond of buying was cattle lungs, in whose airsacks I occasionally found maggots. When I pointed these out to

Jackson, his only reply was, "Wash it good. If it's washed, salted well, and cooked thoroughly, it won't smell."

"But we might get sick," I said.

"I grew up on such meat and never got sick in my life," he said. "Remember, we aren't white people and can't afford to be picky about what we eat."

The children and I never ate any of the stinking stuff. Jackson, on the other hand, ate it with relish. My children and I simply had porridge with *murogo* or fried grasshoppers gathered from a nearby veld.

When I arrived at Ma-Xidyoyi's shack I found about a dozen women assembled. A few were veteran entrepreneurs; most were neophytes like myself. They included pregnant young brides; young mothers with infants strapped to their backs; middle-aged women accompanied by small children with runny noses, pot bellies, and bodies covered with sores; and elderly women who should have been resting their tired bodies after a lifetime of toil but couldn't because there was no social security for blacks—we had to work until we dropped into the grave.

None of the children wore shoes and only one or two was dressed in anything better than rags. The place buzzed with the excitement and expectation of women determined to stand on their own. It was remarkable how similar were the stories of our lives: abusive husbands, too many children, constant work, never for ourselves but always for others, and with nothing to show for it except fatigue, early aging, disease, and scars of physical, emotional, and psychological abuse.

Of the handful of successful spinach sellers in our midst, with the exception of Ma-Xidyoyi and another woman, none had had any money when they started. But now they were netting as much as R3 a day, half the monthly wage for a full-time maid in the suburbs. One woman had even branched off into other businesses, selling chicken intestines, feet, and heads; *muhodu* (cattle lungs); *sonjas*; candy; peanuts; and other items favored by schoolchildren during their lunch break and by migrant workers returning from work at the end of day, with no wives to cook for them.

Money earned from these enterprises was scrupulously saved. Some women used it to improve their shacks and to buy land in the homelands and settle relatives on it to cultivate it. Others spent the money on their children's education. One illiterate woman even had a son attending university.

Many women hid from their husbands the fact that they were working, out of fear that their husbands might start demanding their money, or stop giving them support, or force them to stop working. Others had the approval of their husbands to work, as long as everything they earned belonged to the husband.

After we introduced ourselves to each other, we marched in procession toward Matariani. On the way, we shared the stories of our lives, our hopes for our children, our hardships, and sang songs lamenting our lot. Nearly everyone in the group—young and old—told a story of abuse by their husbands: being beaten for trifles, having to put up with infidelity, perpetual pregnancies, and the hardships of motherhood in general.

All the women were uneducated, more than half were second and third wives, and two were sixth wives. They spoke of the jealousies among the various wives of the polygamist. Some told of rival wives using witchcraft to gain favor with the husband and to thwart the ambitions of the other concubines. Others described the monotony, loneliness, and pain of having to wait in line not so much for affection but for a turn to get pregnant.

It amazed me how easily men bought second, third, fourth, and fifth wives. All they needed was some extra cash to make a *lobola* down payment and they had their pick from dozens of young women to add to their harems. And so many families were desperately poor, so many young women starved for affection and attention, that any down payment—sometimes as little as R1—or promise of down payment was usually enough for a young woman to be sold into a life of misery, drudgery, and abuse.

Matariani, the owner of the farm, turned out to be a benign exploiter of black labor. He hired me without asking questions, at the regular wage of 15 cents a day. It was back-breaking work: I was constantly bending over, tilling and weeding the acres of farmland, under a blazing African sun, most of the time with the infant George strapped to my back. We broke for a fifteen-minute lunch, which I used mainly to feed and suckle George.

Following lunch, it was back to work until 3 P.M. when, achy and tired, we would congratulate each other on a good day's work and march back home, with plans to meet again the next morning at the usual time. I took back home with me several leaves of spinach I had filched to share with the children. Matariani knew that we were stealing a few leaves here and there, but he turned a blind eye. He presumably felt that our petty thievery couldn't possibly bankrupt him, and that we needed at least some nourishment to remain strong enough to work.

I went by my mother's place, picked up my children, gave my mother some spinach, and then went home. I had no time to bathe in the small tin washtub. I needed to make sure that the house was in order, hide any evidence that I had been away for the day, make a fire, and cook before Jackson returned from work around 6 P.M. I hastily prepared a dinner of spinach and porridge, and the children and I had our first decent meal in a long time. I then washed the pots to remove any traces that we had eaten. When Jackson came back with his rotten meat, I cooked it for him and said that the children and I had already eaten at my mother's.

Two weeks later I bought my start-up spinach. I tramped barefoot all over Alexandra selling it, and by late afternoon I had sold it all and netted the kingly sum of R1.20. I was ecstatic. I came back home, bought some rice, a bottle of paraffin for the primus stove, tomatoes and onions, and some liver from the butcher shop two blocks away. I then prepared a sumptuous meal for myself and the children. I even invited my mother and her children to come and share in the feast. We stuffed ourselves until the food was all gone.

Following the meal I began a ritual that became a daily routine of deception. I emptied the paraffin from the primus stove back into a bottle, gathered the leftover ingredients, and took everything to Ma-Xidyoyi to hide for me until the next day, when I would come for them while Jackson was away at work. I then scrubbed the pots clean, filled them with water, and put them on the brazier.

I gathered my children around me and explained to them my plan in a conspiratorial tone.

"You've done a very good job keeping my secret these past two weeks, children," I said. "I don't think your father suspects that I'm working. Now I have another secret for you to keep. Don't reveal to your father that we ate anything special today. He must never find out that I have money to buy the nice food we just ate or he'll beat me and chase us out of the house. You don't want him to beat me, do you?"

"No," my children replied in a chorus.

They faithfully kept my secret for four months.

One day Jackson returned in a foul mood and demanded his dinner. I showed him the empty pots.

"There's nothing to cook, except porridge," I said.

"No meat?" he asked.

"No meat," I replied. "I thought you were going to bring some."

"No, that meat I buy from the corner makes me sick."

"I told you it was no good," I said. "That's why we haven't been having any. And look at those poor children's stomachs." I pointed at Johannes's and Florah's glistening bellies, swollen not from malnutrition but from the delicious food of our secret dinners. And Johannes and Florah were excellent actors. They put on a convincing performance of whining and rolling their languid eyes while clutching their stomachs, to depict hungry children. I guess that wasn't hard to do, as they had known the sort of hunger that drove adults mad.

My spinach business had by now earned me nearly R15. I tied the money in pieces of rags and hid it inside the torn mattress. From time to time I dipped into my savings to take a sick child to the clinic, to buy Piet or Bushy a book, to help my mother pay rent, or to indulge myself with a used dress from a flea market, for wearing to church on Sunday.

I had never felt happier in my life than when my spinach business flourished and I no longer had to rely on Jackson for anything. I prayed every night that he should never find out. I shuddered at what he'd do if he ever found out.

15

GRANNY

NKENSANI

While Geli struggled to become financially independent through selling spinach, I strove to accomplish the same through selling beer. My *shebeen* was a small operation—I sold to three or four people at a time—compared to the large-scale, sophisticated *shebeens* in the neighborhood that attracted scores of customers, selling traditional beer and all kinds of European liquor—vodka, gin, rum, and so on.

Anxious days followed my entering the beer-selling business. I wondered if I had done the right thing, spending the little money I had on brewing beer while my three children still wore rags, went barefoot, ate scanty meals, and attended school depending on whether the beer brought in enough money to pay for their school fees and buy them books, along with meeting our basic needs.

Often it didn't, and it was back to begging and scavenging through garbage dumps for food.

During this period, Nkensani (meaning "Thank You"), the daughter of one of my stepsisters, came to live with me. She was fleeing from her abusive mother, Elsie. Nkensani's running away from home gave me an opportunity to teach my own children an important lesson. They were constantly embarrassed by our poverty, and they envied children of families who had money and could afford to buy them things.

"How I wish I could be adopted by a rich family," Bushy was always saying.

"Just look at Nkensani's situation," I said to her one day. "Her family is rich. Yet she keeps running away because there's no happiness in her home."

"But I thought rich people with nice houses must be very happy," Bushy said.

"That's not always true, my child," I said. "Riches can buy many things but they can't buy happiness. My family didn't have much when I was growing up, but we were very happy. We cared about each other and helped each other. People must have good hearts and love one another, and then they will be happy, even if they don't own lots of things."

Nkensani was the only one of Elizabeth's line of the family close to me. In fact, she worshipped me.

"I love you so very much, Auntie," she would say. "You're so unlike my mother."

She would tell how her mother constantly beat her, deprived her of food, and made her sleep outside in the cold, for the slightest wrongdoing.

Each time Nkensani told me these stories of abuse, I would recall the times when I used to be hard on my own children. I thought the only way to raise them to be responsible adults, to teach them to avoid making the mistakes I had made in life, was to raise them by the hand. My generation fully believed in the adage "Spare the rod and spoil the child."

Then I saw how some parents, in the name of disciplining their children, ended up abusing them. I saw children with hideous scars and welts from being mercilessly whipped; children with gouged eyes, missing teeth, and broken limbs, all sustained from being beaten by their parents with sticks, metal pipes, *sjamboks* (thick black rawhide whips), and fists.

These poor abused children often had nowhere to go. So many simply ran away from home, and started living on their own in junkyards and abandoned buildings, becoming easy recruits for gangs and prostitution rings.

I realized how thin was the line between discipline and abuse, and how easy it was to cross it. I frequently crossed it when my first three children were still young. This happened when I felt too overburdened, too stressed, or was simply drunk. When I was in this state I would take out my frustrations on my children, beating them for trifles, punishing them in ways that were disproportionate to the offense.

I soon learned that children who are constantly beaten never quite learn to do what is expected of them. They grow more defiant, rebellious, stubborn, and disrespectful. Eventually they run away from home. Some children even killed their abusive parents. And many ended up abusing their own children when they became parents. Realizing this, I felt compelled to alter my approach to discipline. I began talking more to my children and whipping them less. Above all, I sought to teach them by example.

"Don't do that," I would say. "It's not right."

I would then explain why it wasn't right, and what consequences the act would lead to.

At other times I disciplined them by making them perform chores as punishment for doing wrong. But occasionally a little whipping was in order. Somehow this new approach, which I used with Piet and Bushy, seemed to work. Most of the time they listened and behaved themselves.

Bushy and Nkensani loved imitating me, and always entreated me to recount stories of my childhood. So at night, after a little beer had loosened my tongue, I would weave story after story, accompanied by dancing and singing while playing a Jew's harp—my favorite instrument and the only one I owned. I would tell stories of my days as a beauty, of my reputation as a skillful and graceful dancer, and of how men vied with each other for my attention.

Nkensani often talked of her intolerable family situation. Her father was uneducated, and my stepsister's domineering had stripped him of his manhood. He did whatever she commanded. Whenever she beat the children and he dared open his mouth to protest, she would tell him to shut up. He would fall silent like a chastened dog. One reason my stepsister had him under her thumb was that he came from a poor family on the farms and had no permit to live and work in Johannesburg, so when he married her—a woman from a rich family—and got a permit through her, he found himself at her mercy.

Nkensani was a sensitive, shrewd, and perceptive child. She would often ask me what I thought of her grandmother, Elizabeth, whom she also detested. I never told her. The memories were too painful and I wished to forget the past. I didn't want her to hate her own grandmother and family over what they did to me. Nkensani didn't even know that her mother and I were half-sisters. For obvious reasons, her mother dared not breathe one word of the truth. Nkensani thought I was some poor, distant relation she loved because I was kind to her and different from her own immediate family. It was only years later, when her mother was on her deathbed and I came to visit and to care for her, that Nkensani finally learned the whole painful truth of my relationship to her family.

During her stay with me, Nkensani became like a daughter and a great help around the house. She and my daughter Bushy cleaned the house, washed laundry, made fire, and helped me hunt for food at the garbage dump on the outskirts of Alexandra. Nkensani and my children didn't mind when we dug up half-eaten sandwiches and half-rotten potatoes, cut out the rotten parts, and made a meal.

Occasionally, when I was lucky, I would, through word of mouth from some of my *shebeen* customers—men who worked at various menial jobs for whites—get a piece job for a day or so in one of the nearby suburbs, weeding massive gardens and flower beds. It was back-breaking work, as I had to stoop for hours in the relentless heat without a sun hat. I wasn't allowed to do the actual gardening because whites considered it a black man's job. I was able to work pulling out weeds because no permit was needed for such jobs, and I was paid from pocket change—R1 (25 cents) a day.

The two meals *Madame* would give me—a peanut-butter-and-jam sandwich with coffee for breakfast and a cold-cut sandwich for lunch—I would save to give to my children. I would also walk to work—a distance that took me several hours to traverse—so I could save the 3-cent bus fare each way and be able to use the money for more pressing needs.

But sometimes there was no piece job and the garbage dump yielded little to eat, and the children and I stilled our pangs of hunger with stale bread soaked in sugared water. The local grocer was willing to sell me stale bread on credit, and a kindly neighbor would sometimes advance me sugar to be repaid when I found another piece job.

Nkensani and my children saw that we were suffering, and they often tried to help. Piet took to gambling at the street corner, playing cards and dice, but I warned him against it, as I knew it would only get him into trouble. Reuben was now old enough to caddy on weekends for whites playing golf on the lovely, perfectly manicured courses of the northern suburbs. The money he earned went mainly to paying rent and school fees. Reuben sometimes lugged those heavy golf bags for seventy-two holes, after arriving at the golf course around five in the morning to stand in a long line filled mostly with grown-up men who could not find jobs elsewhere.

One day Nkensani and Bushy did something bizarre but quite understandable. I had sent them to the garbage dump to forage for food and used coal. Finding none, they were on their way back home when they spotted, not far from the garbage dump, a solitary cow grazing contentedly on stubbles of dried grass. There was no one in sight.

Nkensani had a brilliant idea to get us a meal for dinner. She suggested to Bushy that they get some food from the cow.

"You mean some milk?" Bushy asked.

"No," said Nkensani, "I mean meat."

"Meat? How?" asked a panicky Bushy. "The cow is still alive. You aren't suggesting we kill it, are you?"

"We don't have to kill the cow," said the crafty Nkensani. "We just need to cut out a piece of meat from its side. We'll leave the rest."

"Won't the cow die?"

"No. The meat will grow back."

"How?"

"Don't you know how wounds heal?" said an exasperated Nkensani. "You aren't that stupid, are you?"

"How do we go about cutting the meat?" Bushy asked. "We don't have any knives."

"It's easy," said Nkensani. "Just follow my instructions."

Nkensani got hold of two empty milk bottles from the garbage heap. She broke them on a nearby rock and gave one to an apprehensive Bushy.

"Screw up some courage," Nkensani said as she noticed Bushy's trembling hands clutching the jagged bottle. "You want some meat tonight, don't you?"

"Yes," stammered Bushy. "But I don't want to kill the cow."

"I told you we won't kill it," said Nkensani. "We'll just take a piece of meat and leave the cow alone. The meat will grow back, you'll see."

Bushy was finally reassured. The two girls stalked the cow from behind. The cow kept turning around, bewildered by the sudden attention, wondering what in the world it had done to deserve it. It's huge eyes rolled in their sockets. When the two girls were near enough to the cow's flanks, Nkensani yelled, "Now, attack!"

The two girls pounced upon the cow and began stabbing its flanks. The cow bellowed and started to flee. They chased it, yelling as they drove the broken bottles deep into the cow's body. Nkensani grabbed its tail while she stabbed. Gouts of bright red blood gushed from the moaning cow.

Suddenly, a man emerged from a nearby cluster of shacks, drawn by the cow's terrible bellowing. He was clutching a *sjambok*. He yelled, "Hey, you rascals! What are you doing to my cow?"

Nkensani and Bushy dropped their murderous weapons and bolted. The furious man pursued them, swearing at them. They ran in the direction of a nearby graveyard, across which they hoped to cut and reach home. The man rapidly gained on them, brandishing the *sjambok*.

Nkensani and Bushy leaped over tombstones and dodged around open graves to evade the man's grasp. Up until this time they had been running together, but for some reason they separated, and this gave the irate man an opportunity to go after Nkensani, who was the slower of the two girls.

Ahead of Nkensani loomed a large tombstone. She hesitated whether to attempt to jump over it. The incensed owner of the cow was nearly upon her. She let out a scream as she hurdled pell-mell over the towering tombstone. She barely cleared it, but to her utter dismay, she didn't immediately land on the ground on the other side. Instead, she tumbled straight into the maw of a yawning grave, six feet deep.

The man now had her. He hovered over the open grave, lashing out with the *sjambok* at the helpless, screaming Nkensani, who cowered at the bottom, crawling about on all fours to dodge the blows.

Seeing that Nkensani was in trouble, Bushy attempted to rescue her. But each time she got near, the angry man, frustrated by not being able to land any punishing blows on Nkensani, an artful dodger, would leave her and go after Bushy. This back and forth went on for some minutes, until Bushy spied a group of about eight men coming down the dusty road, noisily singing drinking songs.

Bushy immediately started hollering, "Rape! Rape! This man is trying to rape us!"

The group of men ran to the rescue, chased the man away, and hauled a petrified but grateful Nkensani out of the grave.

"We've heard of people being buried alive before," quipped one of the men, "but this is really something."

When Bushy and Nkensani returned home empty-handed and breathless and related this story, I thanked them for their desire to help, but admonished them about violating other people's property. We were poor, but we weren't thieves. We had to preserve our dignity even in poverty.

16

FLORAH

"I'M STRONG AND HEALTHY.
I CAN NEVER GET AIDS."

I indirectly got confirmation that Walter was cheating on me from his thirteen-year-old boy. The boy's mother was remarried and Walter had custody, as men often did after a breakup when there had been no civil marriage. The boy attended boarding school and came home on weekends and during holidays. He was very fond of me.

Walter and I were sitting around the table one evening eating dinner and talking about his son when he said, "You know, my boy is very funny. Whenever he finds out that the woman in the house is not you, he becomes sullen. He doesn't greet me or talk to me. He just asks me where you are and then leaves the house."

For a moment I was stunned by this revelation.

"So!" I cried. "You mean you bring other women here when I'm away?"

"Oh, I didn't mean that," he said, frantically trying to cover up the slip. He added, rather feebly, "These are just friends I'm talking about."

I knew he was lying. He had inadvertently revealed a secret. I got up, went into the bedroom, and started crying. He came over and tried consoling me by kissing and stroking me, but the damage had already been done. My trust in him had been betrayed. The revelation devastated me.

As a way of punishing him, I went away for two weeks, staying with friends and relatives in Soweto. He pleaded with me to come back. And fool that I was, I did. I half-believed his lies. Like many other women, I didn't want to face up to the truth. I pretended his philandering was but a fleeting problem, and deluded myself into believing that he would soon come to his senses, especially after we were married. I was so madly in love with him that I even considered consulting a *sangoma* (medicine man or woman) to help me keep him faithful.

I had a friend who, fed up with her boyfriend's cheating, went to consult a *sangoma* renowned for love potions.

"My boyfriend keeps falling in love with other women," she told the *sangoma*. "I want him to stop. I want him all to myself."

The *sangoma* gave her some *muti* to insert in her vagina whenever they made love. She did, and the boyfriend stopped seeing other women.

But there were other stories which made me hesitant to take such a drastic step. One woman, claiming to be the jilted wife, went to see a *sangoma* with a similar request. She was given the vagina treatment. Apparently she was in reality the man's mistress trying to win him from his lawful wife. The *sangoma* somehow knew this, and instead of giving her *muti* to bind the man to her, he gave her another type of *muti* that made the man start to despise and eventually leave her. Unlike witch doctors, *sangomas* are bound by the laws of their profession not to break up families or do harm.

I was afraid of getting the vagina treatment. What if Walter already had a wife stashed away somewhere and I turned out to be just a mistress? Maybe that's why he was now evasive whenever I brought up the issue of marriage.

Walter's infidelity evoked painful memories of Collin and his cheating. I started wondering if I might after all have been bewitched by some unknown enemy into never having a faithful partner, into being abused and hurt by men, into never having a home or a family of my own.

Were the women in my family under some sort of .curse? The ordeals endured by my mother, grandmother, sister Maria, Aunt Bushy, and other female relatives who either never married, got involved with abusive men, or were abandoned by men strengthened my belief in such a curse.

The pain I felt from Walter's infidelity came in various forms. One time, as he and I were making love, he called me Tembi, apparently the name of one of his girlfriends.

I was livid.

"Who's Tembi?" I demanded.

"I'm sorry," he said, a hang-dog look on his face.

"Sorry?" I fumed, getting out of bed. "How would you like it if I started having boyfriends?"

"I would kill you," he said icily.

He reached under the mattress and pulled out his gun.

"I would kill you with this," he said, fingering the trigger. I was terrified. He replaced the gun.

Walter's infidelity made me fearful of getting AIDS. The disease was just making its way through the black community. Most blacks were still ignorant of AIDS, even though it was said to be rapidly approaching epidemic proportions because of polygamy, the widespread habit of having mistresses, and the refusal of many men to wear condoms.

One of the myths about AIDS was that it was a disease that only white people, homosexuals, and drug users got. And since blacks were not whites, and homosexuality was frowned upon by Africans, and doing drugs meant smoking marijuana, people thought themselves immune to the disease.

The government regularly ran public service announcements on radio and television, but people made fun of them, dismissing AIDS as a government ploy to keep the black population down. I had paid particular attention to these ads, ever since I found out that Collin, and then Walter, were sleeping around. I knew that AIDS could kill, that it had no known cure, that heterosexuals were not immune to it, and that it was spread primarily through unprotected sex.

My fears increased when, after learning that Walter's girlfriends were promiscuous, I asked Walter to use a condom as a form of birth control and he angrily rejected the idea.

"Only wimps use rubbers," he said. "And don't you want my baby?"

"I do want your baby," I said. "But not now."

"Then you get the birth control."

I didn't know what to do. I wasn't about to go to family planning and get another IUD; besides, it wouldn't protect me against AIDS. Finally I could bear the fears no longer. One night I confronted Walter with my dread of AIDS.

"Aren't you afraid of getting AIDS by sleeping around?"

"Who told you I was sleeping around?"

"No one," I said, holding back, afraid of provoking his wrath.

"And as for this AIDS nonsense," he said laughing, "do I look like a faggot to you?"

"No."

"And did you know that this AIDS thing is just another government scheme to reduce our numbers? We're the majority in this country, you know. And the majority will soon rule."

"But I've seen black men and women with AIDS on TV," I said. "They looked horrible. They were as thin and hollow as *spooks* (ghosts). And they say the disease eventually kills everyone who gets it."

"Don't believe everything you see on TV," he said. "It's controlled by the Boers. Besides, I'm strong and healthy. I can never get AIDS."

"But I tell you AIDS is real," I said. "You may not be afraid of it. But have you ever thought about me? Don't you ever worry that you might get it from one of your girlfriends, especially since they sleep around so much, and give it to me?"

"Oh, I get it now," he said, the expression on his face changing from an amused smile to an ominous scowl. "So you're the one who's been sleeping around. And you're attempting to cover it up by this obsession with AIDS."

"What?" I said, incredulous.

"Yeah, you wouldn't be so worried about AIDS unless you were sleeping with other men."

Suddenly I found myself on the defensive. I began pleading for my innocence, defending my honor, swearing to God that I had never been unfaithful. Walter's irrational anger passed. I resolved never to bring up the topic of AIDS again.

What hurt the most about Walter's infidelity was that I knew most of his mistresses. He never cast his net very far to snare a woman. Most were promiscuous, ugly, and had large behinds and breasts, leading me to believe he wanted them primarily for sex. Eventually he got four of them pregnant.

Many women in the township had no scruples, stealing each other's husbands or boyfriends. Competition for men was so fierce that little solidarity existed among us to stop hurting each other and making it easy for men to abuse us. Through envy and jealousy, we were ever ready to ruin the happiness of those of us who had families and loving husbands and boyfriends. "You don't deserve to be happy," we seemed to say, "while I'm single, lonely, and miserable."

Some of Walter's girlfriends had the nerve to knock on his door in the middle of the night, rouse him out of bed, with me there, and entreat him to come along with them on the pretext that his child was sick and his help was needed.

"How many children does this Casanova have?" I would ask myself. It seemed to be a different woman each night. Whenever Walter would go, I felt deeply hurt, betrayed, misused, miserable, helpless, and worthless. I desperately wanted out of the relationship, but I was afraid. He had the gun and had threatened to kill me if I left him. I kept pondering about safe ways to leave him. There seemed to be none.

One Saturday night a woman came and took Walter away using

the old ruse of a sick baby. Early next morning he knocked and I let him in.

"Why didn't you come back last night?" I asked.

"Do I have to tell you everything I do?" he shouted.

"No."

"Then why do you interrogate me?"

"I was just worried, that's all," I said. "And. . . "

"And what?!" he yelled.

I took a deep breath, searching for courage, and said, "To tell you the truth, I'm bothered and deeply hurt by all these girlfriends of yours coming here at night to get you. They have no respect. . . "

Before I had finished the sentence he had slapped me hard across the face.

"Don't ever talk like that to me, you hear?"

"How am I supposed to feel when strange women come and take you away?" I said, tears flooding my eyes.

He grabbed me and threw me up against the wall. When I saw that familiar, dreadful look of hatred in his eyes I started screaming at the top of my lungs. His mother, who was nearly deaf, heard me from the room next door and came to my aid. She started banging on our door. "Walter, Walter!" she said frantically. "Leave her alone, leave her alone, please!"

Walter opened the door and began swearing at his mother.

"What's wrong, Florah?" Walter's mother asked, ignoring her son's insults. She was used to them.

"Walter didn't come home last night," I said, between sobs. "And he's hitting me because I asked him where he was."

"She insulted me by insinuating I've been with other women," Walter interjected.

"Weren't you?" Walter's mother asked. "Everyone knows that you have too many girlfriends. Florah is right. Why don't you just marry her and stop fooling around?"

"I can't marry her," Walter said. "I don't have the money for *lobola*."

"But I gave you money a few months ago to help you raise the *lobola*," Walter's mother said with surprise. "What did you do with it?"

Walter was tongue-tied. He groped for explanations. He gave the excuse that he had used the money to repair his taxi. This was the first time I had heard that he had been given money for *lobola* but hadn't told me about it. At once I saw that he had no intention of marrying me. I was simply his mistress, one of many.

"I want to go home, please," I said to Walter, feeling deeply hurt. The image of Collin came to my mind and I started weeping. I wished he were alive and that we had never separated.

"Go," Walter said. "No one is stopping you."

I started packing my things.

"Walter, Florah is the best woman for you," Walter's mother said. "Don't make the mistake of letting her go."

"She'll come back," Walter said confidently. "She'll come back because I'm the only man for her. She'll come back if she knows what's good for her."

I continued packing in silence. I then hugged Walter's mother and left.

When I got to my parents' home I found my father alone. My mother, siblings, and Angeline had gone to church. The first thing my father did, as he did every time he saw me, was to ask me when Walter was coming to pay *lobola*.

I was furious that he would ask me about money at a time when I was in so much pain, but I made every effort to contain my rage.

"Collin has just died," I said, with all the calmness I could muster under the circumstances. "It would be wrong for me to remarry so soon. I would be desecrating his memory."

"Well, it's been over a year since he died," my father said. "Besides, he didn't exactly marry you, you know. He hadn't finished paying *lobola*. He had only given me a deposit and made one payment. And you know that if you make a deposit at the store for goods and don't pay the rest, the store repossesses the goods."

"Is that how you see me?" I said, shaking with rage and disgust at being likened to merchandise. "Is that how you regard me, your own daughter? Am I just a piece of merchandise to you, to be sold to the highest bidder? Don't you understand I have feelings? Don't you understand that I can feel pain?"

"I didn't mean that," he said, half apologetically. "I was only giving you an example."

"Giving me an example," I said with a scornful laugh. "What made you change your mind about Walter? If I remember rightly, you hated him. You told me to stop living with him and go back to Collin."

"That was before Collin died," my father said.

"So I'm to be sold to any man regardless of whether or not he's a brute?" I said with vehemence. "Well, let me tell you something. And you get this straight. I'm not going to marry Walter. In fact, I plan never to get married. So you might as well forget about ever receiving any *lobola* for me."

"So you're content to live *vat en set?*" my father said angrily. "You want everyone to call you a *skeberesh?*"

"That's my own business."

"If you don't care about your reputation," my father said with mounting anger, "then I don't want you inside my house. I don't want a daughter who disobeys me and disgraces the family."

"I'm going," I declared, "and I'm never going to set foot in this place again."

I left and went to the home of my cousin Florence, where I stayed for nearly a week. Walter came to my parents' home asking for me but no one knew where I had gone.

One of my aunts had an apartment in a large housing complex in Alexandra. She had occasionally taken me in when I needed a place to stay, whenever my father drove me out or I quarreled with my boyfriend. She and her husband invited me to house-sit while they went out of town. I jumped at the offer, since it would allow me to be near work and near my daughter. I informed my mother and siblings about the temporary move and even brought Angeline to spend the night with me.

A few days later Walter showed up at my door, accompanied by Angeline. It turned out he had bribed her with candy into revealing where I was. I started trembling, painfully aware that I was alone and defenseless.

"You thought I'd never find you, heh?" Walter said, standing by the door, with me gaping at him. He entered, sent Angeline outside to play, and locked the door.

"Leave me alone," I said, backing away from him. "I'm through with you."

"You're through with me, heh?" he said with a sneer. "We'll see about that. Who's your lover now?"

"I have no lover," I said.

"Don't lie to me. Where have you been all this time?"

"I've been staying with relatives."

"You're lying."

"What business is it of yours anyway?" I said. "I don't belong to you. I'm not your wife. You never tell me about any of your other women."

"You don't know me very well, Florah," he said icily. "Today you will." He continued advancing toward me. I felt cornered and grew terrified. There was no way out of the apartment. I was at his mercy.

"Leave me alone or I'll scream."

"You can scream all you want," he said.

I knew he intended to beat me, so I put up a desperate act.

"Please forgive me," I said in a whining voice. "I'll come back to you. I was foolish to run away. You're the only man for me, Walter. I only ran away because you make me so afraid whenever you hit me."

"You call that hitting you?" Walter said, laughing. "You ain't seen nothing yet."

"Please, don't hurt me, Walter, please!" I said frantically.

"You need to be taught a lesson," he said, grabbing me roughly by the arm. "No woman ever leaves Walter, understand?"

The way his face was contorted with rage I thought he was about to kill me. I wanted to scream but somehow my voice failed me. I started weeping piteously, in the hope that he would see how helpless I was and have mercy on me. I remembered all too well the previous beatings I had suffered at his hands. He could be brutal. But apparently Walter was familiar with the tricks I played to avoid a beating and was determined to "teach me a lesson," as he put it.

He started by slapping me hard across the cheeks. Then he punched me with his fists. I covered my face with both arms, as I often did when he beat me because the face is where abuse readily shows. He started punching me in the stomach, on the sides. I balled over and fell to my knees, all the time begging him to stop. A kick to my head sent me sprawling across the floor. He kept going, punching, kicking, stomping, until I was nearly unconscious. The room spun. Blood spurted out of my nose.

Finally he stopped, more from exhaustion than anything else. Through swollen eyes I saw him calmly smooth his ruffled clothes. He then headed for the door. As he was stepping out he turned to me and said, "I want you back at my place by tonight, you hear?"

I made no reply. My mouth was swollen. My clothes were bloody. Several of my teeth were loose. Every part of my body ached. The slightest movement was torture. I crawled to the bathroom, where I painfully raised myself to the level of the mirror to look at my disfigured face. All the time I thought I was dreaming. I wondered what I had done to end up in a relationship with a jealous madman. I wiped my face with cold water, gingerly dabbing the cuts on my mouth and nose. I took a couple of aspirins, went into the bedroom, and lay down on my stomach, weeping silently, dreading sunset.

That evening I went back to Walter. Now terror, more than anything else, kept me with him. I never told anyone of the extent of the abuse. Fortunately my face was not permanently disfigured, and the swelling on my lip and black eye went down after a few days. My limbs ached for days and I walked with difficulty. I missed several days of work.

My family knew that something was wrong when they heard I was living with Walter again. Yet there was nothing they could do. My father still expected *lobola*. My mother and siblings were terrified of Walter because of his reputation as a *tsotsi*.

Walter continued to abuse me. He would beat me and I would leave, only to come back. One time he chased me screaming down the street in the middle of the night, and I only escaped a savage beating by barricading myself inside a stranger's house. Friends and relatives did not understand why I stayed with him. I stayed with him purely out of fear. He had a gun and had threatened to kill me. Also, I was very good at hiding the truth, even from myself. One day he beat me after accusing me of flirting with other men at a disco we had gone to together. Again I left and went to stay with Florence. Again she advised me to leave him.

"You must leave him," Florence said. "This can't go on. Look how thin and haggard you've grown."

"But he's threatened to kill me," I said.

"That's a chance you'll have to take," Florence said. "It's better to die at once from a bullet than to be battered slowly to death."

"I don't know if I have the strength to leave him," I confessed.

"You must do it," Florence said. "You can't go on living like this. And why do you refuse to report him to the police?"

"That's a sure way of getting killed, Florence," I said. "You know how the police are. They care very little about black problems, especially domestic ones. All they'll do is send him a letter. At best, they'll arrest him and release him in a month or so. And where does that leave me once he comes out? You know all those stories about women trying to stop abuse by reporting their husbands and boyfriends to the police? What happens to these women? Many are killed by their abusers as soon as they get out of jail. I don't want to end up dead."

"Well, I still think the best thing to do is to leave him," Florence said.

Reluctantly, I decided to follow Florence's advice. I hoped that by staying with her I could muster the courage to leave Walter. My mother knew where I was and kept my secret. But everyday I lived in fear, wondering when Walter would show up and what he would do to me. I had recurrent nightmares of being murdered by him. I would wake up screaming, drenched in sweat, my heart pounding, still picturing Walter riddling my body with bullets or chopping me to pieces with an axe. And the fact that I knew of several women who were killed by their abusers only added to my anxieties.

One such woman had lived on the same street as my family. She worked as a domestic in the suburbs. Her white employers went away for the Christmas holidays and left her in care of the house. She lived in an outbuilding in the backyard, and one Sunday—her day off—she hosted an outdoor party, inviting her friends and boyfriend from the township. Amid the feasting, dancing, and drinking, one of her male guests started flirting innocently with her. Her boyfriend, who was the possessive and jealous type and accustomed to beating her, was enraged. When she got up to fetch something from her room, he followed her there, an argument ensued, he stabbed her in the chest with a knife, and left her to bleed to death. He leaped over the fence and ran away. He was caught when he went to work on Monday, and by then his girlfriend was dead.

17

GELI

JACKSON HAS
AN AFFAIR

One day on his way to work Jackson was arrested for a permit viola-
tion. A neighbor who had been arrested with him and later released
after paying a fine brought me word that Jackson, too, had been
fined the usual R2. Jackson wanted me to borrow the money from
the landlord and come bail him out. He still didn't know I was working.

I went to the landlord but he said he had no money. "Your husband has yet to pay me the R3 he owes me from three weeks ago," he
said.

I showed up in court the day of Jackson's sentencing. I had R5 of
my own money tied in a piece of cloth around my waist. There were
no trials for pass-law violations. Those arrested were considered
guilty as charged and appeared in court only to be sentenced or to
pay fines and be released. The place thronged with prisoners—
mostly men—and their relatives. Arrests for pass and permit viola-

tions were so routine that on a given day there was sure to be more than a hundred cases processed. And the processing of each case took less than two minutes.

Jackson appeared in the dock and was asked, "Are you guilty as charged?"

"Yes, my lord," he replied through a black interpreter.

The judge sentenced Jackson to fourteen days in jail or a fine of R2.

"Can you pay the fine?" the black interpreter asked Jackson.

Jackson looked expectantly in my direction.

For a moment, as he stood there helpless in the dock, gazing at me like a whimpering puppy, I was overcome with pity and wanted to untie the rag around my waist, get out the R5, and bail him out. But something told me not to do it. So I left him there.

I wasn't going to use any of my hard-earned money to get him released from jail. Get him out to do what? To continue his abuse and starve me and my children? To resume his gambling? Maybe prison will teach him a lesson, I told myself. I felt no remorse. I had suffered enough. I was prepared to be a dutiful wife and helpmate, but only to a responsible husband, one who cared about his family and provided for them.

I wasn't asking that Jackson love me. I now knew that that was an impossible request to make of a man who seemed incapable of loving anyone else but himself. I was simply asking that he respect me, my feelings, and the sanctity of our marriage, and to stop making my life a living hell.

Jackson was released two weeks later. He came back even thinner and more embittered than after his previous arrests. His Italian employer once more gave him his old job back. To my surprise, the first Friday back on the job, he brought home his entire wage. He said he was giving up gambling. He gave me most of it, saying I should buy groceries and save a portion for a rainy day.

"I learned important lessons while in prison," he said. "I need to save money instead of wasting it. One never knows when trouble will strike."

"I'm glad to hear you say that," I said, puzzled by his changed attitude.

"I want our children to have a better life," he said. "They shouldn't be ashamed to have me for a father."

"Yes, my husband," I said. I never thought I would live to hear Jackson say these words. My heart overflowed with joy at the thought that maybe Jackson had finally grown up.

Yet I wondered if Jackson's changed attitude was for real. If it was real, what had brought it about? He had been arrested before and came back the same, if not worse. But I chose not to dwell on possible motives. I was simply glad that life promised to improve.

Jackson's new attitude made me start feeling tinges of guilt at having left him in jail for fourteen days of hard labor. Had I known that he was on the verge of this miraculous transformation, I would most likely have bailed him out. On the other hand, he had admitted that time in jail had taught him a lesson.

Jackson even allowed me to buy fresh meat for dinner. Every meal now seemed a feast of chicken intestines, heads, feet, wings, and his favorite delicacy, "Smiley," the cooked head of a sheep, so called because the sheep's teeth seem to be grinning at you after being cooked. Jackson even resumed a habit he had abandoned a long time ago, that of bringing the children fish and chips every Friday. Their dread of his presence diminished. The youngest now ran up to him whenever he came home, especially on Fridays, lisping, "Daddy, daddy! You're home! Did you bring us fish and chips today?"

Jackson also agreed that we help out my mother by taking in my siblings, Piet and Bushy. They became a great help around the house, as they cleaned, cared for the children, and ran errands. As if all these miracles were not enough, Jackson even promised that we would soon go get married before the magistrate, which would qualify us for a family permit and low-income housing in Tembisa, where the government was relocating blacks as it proceeded with plans to demolish Alexandra.

The ghetto had been declared a "black spot," which meant that it had to cease accommodating families. Instead, single-sex hostels were being built for men and women who would provide labor to the suburbs and the city.

In the past, Jackson had adamantly opposed any move from the one-room shack we lived in, which had been partitioned by pieces of wood and cardboard into a "bedroom" and a "kitchen." Bushy, Piet, Florah, Johannes, and George slept on the floor in the "kitchen," and Jackson and I shared a twin bed propped up by bricks in the "bedroom."

Jackson's changed behavior made me wonder if I should reveal to him that I was working and proudly show him my savings.

"I have a confession to make, Jackson," I said to him one evening as we lay in bed.

"What do you have to confess?" he asked suspiciously.

"I have some money of my own," I said.

His suspicion grew. "Where did you get it? Do you have *shigangus* [lovers]?"

"No," I laughed. "What makes you think that?"

"Where does a woman who doesn't work usually get money?"

"I'll tell you in a minute where I got it," I said. "Don't you first want to know how much I've got?"

"How much?"

"I have R40."

"Forty what?" he exclaimed, raising himself from the bed.

"You heard me, R40."

"Where is it? Where is it?" he asked excitedly.

"Get off the bed and I'll show you," I said.

He jumped off the bed in his ragged pajamas, wild with excitement. I removed the blanket and faded sheets, reached into the torn mattress, and pulled out three tied rags containing wads of wrinkled rand notes.

Jackson's eyes bulged with disbelief as I counted the money.

"Woman," he said after a while, "where on earth did you get that kind of money? It would take me almost half a year to make that much."

"I've been saving it bit by bit since I started working."

"You've been working?" he said incredulously.

"Yes."

"Where?"

I explained how I got started selling spinach. I didn't include the part about eating secretly. "Your behavior forced me not to tell you I was working," I said. "I feared you wouldn't approve. Oh, it's such a relief to finally tell you these things. They've been weighing on my conscience. You aren't angry with me, are you?"

"Not in the least," Jackson said, "though you should have told me about this a long time ago." He then paused for a moment, and turned to me with a quizzical look.

"Did you have this money when I was in jail?" he said.

"No I didn't," I said. I wasn't such a fool.

"Well woman, I don't know what to say. This is too much money to leave lying around here. Let me keep it."

"No," I said, taking the money back. "I'll keep it. But know that if you continue bringing me your wage every week, this money is available for both of us and for the children."

He continued giving me his wages. We left our shack for a larger, two-room place in the same yard. That Christmas our children got new clothes and shoes. No longer did I have to lock them inside the house while their friends paraded in the streets, out of fear that they would be mocked for the rags they wore. We also had a big Christmas celebration, where we drank Kool-Aid and ate chicken and rice, beetroot, custard pudding, and scones I baked in a secondhand stove I bought. Jackson liked the scones, but grumbled about the expense of the secondhand stove.

"Wasn't the *mbawula* [brazier] adequate?" he asked. "Why did you waste money on a stove?"

"You know *mbawulas* are dangerous, Jackson," I said. "Remember how the children almost died because one night I forgot to take the burnt coal outside before we went to sleep? And with a stove I'm also able to bake. I couldn't bake with a *mbawula*."

"Oh, I see," he said with mild irritation. "We are into baking now. We are quickly becoming like *white* people."

Any major improvement in our way of life Jackson often resisted on the grounds we were imitating white people.

"Not just white people bake, Jackson," I said. "Most of our neighbors have stoves and bake. They bake cakes, bread, puddings, and many other foods which save them money. I can also bake cookies to sell to schoolchildren as a way of earning more money."

"I just don't like seeing money wasted, that's all," he said.

The argument over the stove blew over, and for nearly half a year from the time I revealed to Jackson I was working, our household knew peace and some measure of happiness. Jackson had stopped gambling, we seldom fought, the children had enough to eat, and I could afford to buy them an occasional toy to substitute for the tins and stones with which they were accustomed to playing. Johannes and Florah now looked forward to school, as they no longer feared being punished for not paying school fees or not having the proper books and uniforms.

My mother's situation, too, had stabilized. Her beer-brewing business was bringing her a small income, enough to live on anyway, and I was helping her pay for the education of Reuben, Piet, and Bushy.

But this happiness proved short-lived. Deep in my heart I knew it couldn't last. I knew that something was bound to come along, as in the past, and ruin everything, bringing back the horrors I had grown accustomed to and almost considered a normal way of life: abuse, hunger, fear, uncertainty, misery, and hopelessness.

I don't exactly know what caused Jackson to lapse back into his former behavior. I can only speculate, and point to things which make sense to me but may not to others. The obvious cause of the change was witchcraft. Some people out there simply didn't want to see me and my family happy.

There were some among our neighbors who were jealous and spiteful. One *shebeen* owner, a woman, kept complaining that she preferred the old Jackson, as he had been one of her best customers. Another woman complained that the moment Jackson quit gambling, her husband had resumed beating her as he no longer won as much as when Jackson was playing and losing heavily. Other people resented the fact that I had bought an old stove and that my children now wore decent clothes while theirs ran around in rags.

Then one day I learned that Jackson was having an affair with a Mosotho woman in the neighborhood who had three children by different men. This woman had no husband and was known as a home breaker. Previously she had considered Jackson unworthy of attention because he had no money, but now she was constantly fawning over him.

She started inviting him to parties at her house, with people who only drank "white people's liquor": gin, rum, and vodka. I found out that she even cooked him meals, which led me to wonder what sort of *muti* she was putting in the food. Obviously she was slipping some love potions into his food because Jackson started spending more time with her than with me. He would stumble home drunk late at night, even during the week.

One morning I marched over to the Mosotho woman's house to have it out with her. I pounded on the door. She opened it, looking haggard and cotton-mouthed from a hangover.

"Jackson has been coming a lot to your place lately," I said as I hovered by the door. "I want him to stop, you hear?"

"Oh, you must be one of the wives," the Mosotho woman said with a laugh. "Your husband comes here on his own free will, woman. You haven't seen me dragging him on a leash from your house. So he can stop coming any time he wants to."

"You know that Jackson has a family, don't you?" I said. "He has children to care for."

"I too have children to care for, woman," she said. "And as I said before, your husband comes here of his own free will. It's your husband you should talk to, not me."

Though Jackson had been eager for us to get a marriage license so we could move to Tembisa, where the government was resettling qualified black families, he now opposed the idea. In Tembisa we would have had more space—four tiny rooms—and amenities we never dreamed of—electricity, plumbing, and flushing toilets.

"This isn't such a bad house," Jackson said of the overcrowded, crumbling shack when I reminded him of the Tembisa homes.

"I think we should leave as you promised we would," I said. "I don't like what's happening to you."

"What's happening to me?" he retorted.

"I don't like the fact that you're drinking again," I said. "Remember, you're a married man and a father."

"Who are you to tell me what I can and cannot do?" Jackson shouted. "Have you forgotten who's the man in this house?"

"No, I haven't forgotten," I said. "But you aren't acting responsibly. And as for your daily visits to this Mosotho woman, people are talking."

"Talking about what?"

"Talking about you and her. I don't want to get into details."

"What details?"

"You know what I mean," I said.

"Listen, woman," Jackson said. "You've forgotten your place. I wear the pants in this house. I am lord. I can do as I please. And I don't have to answer to you or to anyone else for it."

I dropped the subject. I pondered about what to do. Though I was convinced he was having an affair—practically everyone in the neighborhood knew—there was little I could do. We weren't legally married and I therefore couldn't sue for divorce. Also, I didn't believe in divorce. I had been raised to respect the sanctity of the family, and to do whatever I could to keep it together. There had been little if any love between Jackson and me, but I was bound to him by our children. If we were to separate, under the *lobola* custom he would keep the children, and I sure didn't want to lose them.

I sought to ease my own pain by telling myself over and over again that Jackson's infidelity wasn't anything unusual. Almost every married woman I knew complained of her husband's unfaithfulness and had made her peace with it, feeling that men will be men and that as long as she got support and had a roof over her head and her children's she could overlook or minimize the issue. I did the same.

18

GRANNY

MY SON IS ARRESTED
FOR ARMED ROBBERY

Growing up without a father was hard on my son Reuben. He was also bitter at having been cheated out of his inheritance. He constantly worried about the hardships we were enduring and the pressures on me to find food for us each day, somehow, somewhere.

I did my best to keep him in school. As he was my eldest son, I had pinned my hopes on him. The little money I made from selling beer and working piece jobs as a gardener I spent on books, school uniforms, and school fees for him and his siblings. We frequently went to sleep on empty stomachs and I was always behind in rent payments. But somehow we managed to get by.

Our suffering deeply affected Reuben. He and I often discussed the bleak future. He wanted to leave school so he could help me but I strongly urged him not to, telling him he could best help the family by getting an education. I constantly told him that only educated blacks got decent-paying jobs.

One day he said to me, "Mother, I know you want me to stay in school. But I can't take your suffering anymore. I'm planning to quit and start working."

"There's no need to do that," I said. "We're managing. I'm making enough to keep us going. We often have something to eat and a roof over our heads. And you and your siblings are in school. That's a lot to be thankful for. Think of all those hungry and homeless children who cannot go to school."

"I know you're doing your best, Mama," Reuben said. "But we're still poor. And we'll remain poor unless I do something about it. And it troubles me that you're constantly being arrested for brewing beer."

I had been arrested several times, because the beer I brewed, *skokiani* and *mbamba* ("catch me"), was considered illegal. Yet customers unanimously preferred it to the tasteless government beer. Each time I was arrested I avoided doing time, thanks to Mphephu's *muti*, by bribing the arresting officers with cash or free drinks when they were off duty. The police were easy to bribe. Most of them were poor and desperate for a little extra cash. And often, like the rest of us, they sought solace for their miseries in liquor.

"What would you do if you left school?" I asked Reuben.

"I'll look for work," he said.

"What kind of job will you get, my child, if you left school now, being so young?"

"There are many jobs," he said. "There are factories opening up all around Alexandra and they need workers. I've just *got* to help you, Mama."

"Remember the promise you made your grandfather Lazarus shortly before he died?" I said. "You told him that you loved school and wanted to go on to university and become a teacher. Remember how proud he was to hear you say that?"

He was silent. He remembered.

"And that's why you were his favorite after my brother, Shibalu, died," I said. "That's why he wanted to leave you some property and money, so you could go to university."

"And where's that inheritance now?" Reuben said bitterly. "Elizabeth and her children have it. And look at us, struggling everyday to scratch a few pennies together so we can survive."

"I'm aware of the injustice they've done us, my child," I said, "but let that be a thing of the past. God will make them pay for their evil deeds. Just keep your grandfather's promise to become a teacher, and you'll defeat our enemies. They've robbed us of everything and we are poor. But if you get educated you can lift us out of poverty, my child. You can do your grandfather's spirit proud."

"Okay, Mama," Reuben said with a heavy sigh. "I'll try."

And Reuben tried his best. He entered secondary school and was aiming for his J-C certificate (the equivalent of a high school diploma). But there was no money to keep him in school long enough to graduate. So he dropped out in his final year. Luckily, his ability to read and write landed him a job as a clerk at the Peri-Urban administration offices in Alexandra.

Our lives were instantly transformed by Reuben's new job. We moved out of the shack into a decent two-room place in a yard controlled by Peri-Urban, which was not subjected to constant police raids. Because my son now worked for the municipality, we even got a permit legalizing our residency in Alexandra. With his first paycheck we bought a table, an extra bed, and boxes of groceries. We now had more than enough to eat and treated ourselves to weekend feasts of chicken and rice.

Gone were the days of digging in garbage dumps for food, eating rotten potatoes, chasing grasshoppers across the veld, and boiling cattle blood to make soup.

Bushy and Piet became normal schoolchildren. They could now afford books, school fees, and uniforms. They no longer returned home in tears from being beaten with canes by teachers for not wearing the proper uniform or not having the right books. They now accompanied their classmates on field trips to the Johannesburg Zoo and to the planetarium. All because my Reuben now earned R40 a month, about $13.

But our newfound financial security was all too brief. The curse of witchcraft soon returned to ruin our happiness. I point to witchcraft because there is no other way I can explain why the son I had raised so well, the son I loved, could throw away so much that was good and embark on a life of self-destruction.

Reuben's fall began when he started drinking. He became dissatisfied with his job and salary as a clerk. He came under the powerful influence of *tsotsis*, gangsters. I don't know exactly how he got mixed up with them. He never told me the complete story. I think it had something to do with his starting to drink, gamble, and stay out late at *shebeens* among bad company.

Like many young men of his generation, Reuben became enamored of the fast lane, the dangerous but exciting life of criminals—their easy money, flashy clothes, fancy cars, and loose women.

At the time Reuben was growing up in Alexandra the township was infested with gangsters of all descriptions. There were the Msomi gang, the Spoilers, the Berlin gang, the Black Koreans, the Mau-Mau, the Young Americans, and Zorro's Fighting Legion. They practically ruled the township. They were into racketeering, extortion, robbery, numbers games, and were implicated in most acts of murder and violence. Their depredations had earned Alexandra names such as Dark City, Slaagpaal ("Slaughterhouse"), Hell's Kitchen, Little Chicago, and Terror Township.

I knew of gangs because almost everyone in Alexandra sought their protection, especially those of us who were into some sort of business for ourselves. The grocer, the *shebeen* owner, the taxi driver, the soccer player—all sought protection by paying a weekly or monthly fee to gangs. Those who didn't pay were roughed up, knifed, or put out of business. Even ordinary workers were not immune from the terror of gangs. Many of my *shebeen* clients constantly complained, whenever they were behind in their payments of drinking debts, that they were paying too much "cost of living money," the name for payments to gangs. Maids and garden boys paid for the right to be allowed to go to work in the suburbs. Those who didn't make these payments became targets for robbery, assault, and even murder. Friday night, payday, was notorious for the number of murders committed and people knifed.

The police did nothing to stop gang activity. In fact, many police-men were informants for various gangs. So people dared not openly complain about gangs, or report them to the police, because they might end up dead.

A gang member often made in a day as much as ten times what the average worker made in a month. It's therefore easy to see how my son, once he was bewitched by someone who just didn't want to see us improve our lives, could have been attracted to such a destruc-tive way of life.

I began suspecting something was wrong when, after quitting his job, Reuben began dressing in expensive zoot suits and giving me money with generous abandon. Sometimes he would give me R50, which was more than he used to earn as a clerk.

"Where did you get this money, child?" I asked.

"Oh, I just found it lying on the roadside and picked it up," he said, laughing.

"Picked it up! Stop trying to fool me now, child. Where did you get it?"

"I'm not fooling you, Mama. I recently got me some *muti* which makes me smell out wads of money people have lost or buried for safekeeping. This way of making money sure beats working for a gov-ernment that oppresses our people, won't you say?" He spoke in a swaggering, boastful, cavalier way that was new to him.

"I know you're lying to me, child," I said. "I'm worried about you. You've changed somehow."

"Don't fret, Mama. I can take care of myself."

At other times Reuben would say he had won the money gambling at dice, horses, or *fahfee* (a numbers game). One day he gave me R40 and said he had just found an easy job working half a day for Indians who owned several stores at Alexandra's main shopping center.

"What sort of Indians pay you that much?" I said, incredulous. "I know Indians and they can never pay a black person the sort of money you've given me, unless they're mad. You remember how hard your own sister Geli slaved for that large Indian family for only 50 cents a week."

"That was a long time ago," Reuben said. "The Indians I work for are different." All the time we were speaking Reuben wasn't looking me in the eye, which told me he was obviously hiding something from me.

Reuben realized that his attempts to hoodwink me weren't working, so he said, "Listen, Mama, I can take care of myself, okay. I'm a grown man now. You need money, don't you?"

"Yes," I said, "but I don't need money that you've lied, cheated, and possibly killed for."

I could no longer play dumb. I had to tell my boy about my suspicions. I knew about gangs—everyone did—and how they ensnared young men.

"What makes you say that?" Reuben said sharply.

"I already suspect the worst, my son," I said. "So why don't you go ahead and tell me the whole truth."

"You want to know the truth?" Reuben said, his voice changing to a tone that told me he was now serious. "Yes, I do work for a gang. But we don't kill people. We simply protect them from other gangs who kill. I work for Bra-Modise."

"Who in the world is Bra what-you-may-call-it?"

"B-R-A MO-DI-SE," he said slowly. "He owns a *shebeen* on 14th Avenue."

"What do you do for him that he gives you this kind of money?"

"We protect his interests."

"What interests?"

"You wouldn't understand, Mama," Reuben said. "Just trust me. I'm not doing anything bad."

I trusted him but nevertheless worried every day and night about him. I was torn. The money he gave me kept us alive. It prevented us from tumbling back into the dark pit of poverty, suffering, and desperation. It made me stop relying on relatives like my half-sister Matinana, and burdening my daughters Geli and Mphephu with my problems. It made us stop living like animals. It gave our miserable lives a little dignity.

Reuben sometimes would disappear for weeks. I would never know where he was or what he was doing. At each knock on the door I jumped, expecting the worst, news that my dear son was in prison, in hospital, or lying stabbed to death in some *donga* somewhere.

I started hearing rumors that Reuben was a notorious *tsotsi* who went about the township, armed with a knife and a tomahawk, robbing people. Complete strangers accosted me in the street and spat at me. Some warned me that my son's days were numbered. I began hearing that the police, too, were looking for him, and that members of other gangs were also after him, determined to turn him into a cripple or a corpse because he was infringing on their business.

The day I had dreaded finally came. A friend of Reuben's brought me the news that he had been arrested for armed robbery. He and a friend had broken into a house in the suburbs and been caught. They were carrying guns. As black men they could get the death penalty for robbing a white home.

My daughter Geli and I were present at his trial and sentencing. Reuben pleaded for mercy, and since it was his first recorded crime, the judge was lenient and sentenced him to three and a half years hard labor, without parole. He could have been hung. I wanted to tell the judge that my Reuben was not a bad boy, that he had been led astray, that he was my only hope, that he should not be imprisoned for so long because prison made men not better but hard and mean, that I, his mother, was to blame for not providing him with a father and a stable home, and that I should be the one sent to jail. But I never got the chance to say all this. And I doubt if the judge would have understood.

My only hope and support was gone. Poverty, with its thousand terrors, returned. There was hunger. There was the struggle to meet rent payments. Soon we were evicted and returned to a one-room shack in a yard that was subject to constant police raids. Because I could no longer pay the fees, the schooling of Bushy and Piet became sporadic. I feared losing my only remaining son to the streets.

What had I done to deserve such pain, such persecution? Where were my ancestors and their protection? Where was God and his mercy? Hadn't I already suffered enough? I never felt so helpless and lost in my life. I began drinking heavily. I would be depressed for weeks on end. Many nights I cried myself to sleep, thinking of my dead mother, brother, and father, wondering how different life would have been if they were still alive, if all of us were together.

I thought fondly of death as a release from all the heartache and pain. More than once I considered taking my life, but each time I would remember my children. Now more than ever they needed me. I had to live for them.

PART IV

19

FLORAH

I FINALLY
LEAVE WALTER

I continued to live in fear that Walter might someday discover my hiding places, which kept changing from week to week as I stayed with relatives and friends. I had made up my mind to leave him for good. I had steeled myself against anything that might happen because of my decision. If Walter carried out his threat to kill me, then that would be my fate. I was simply tired of being battered.

Weeks went by without my running into Walter or hearing from him. Then one afternoon he surprised me by showing up at the place where I worked. I was leaving the building and heading for the bus stop when he emerged out of a corner where he had been hiding and blocked my way. Anxiety seized me. I told myself not to panic.

"How are you?" he said in a calm, almost gentle voice.

"Fine," I said without emotion.

"Where have you been?"

"I've been around."

"Why haven't you been to my place?"

"There was no need."

"There was no need?" he asked.

"Yes," I said, "no need."

"I want you back," he said.

"No way am I coming back to you," I said, masking my fear with anger. "I'm through with you. And I mean it this time."

"No woman ever dumps me, you know that?" he said in a hard voice.

I tried to go past him but he kept barring my way.

"No woman," he repeated, twisting his mouth.

"I didn't dump you," I said. "I'm just tired of being beaten, that's all. I'm tired of pain. I was wrong in thinking we belonged together. If you loved me you wouldn't treat me the way you've been treating me."

He remained silent a while, gazing at me. I didn't like the expression that was working on his face. It was hostile, menacing. I had seen it before when he was about to explode. I started walking quickly, anxious to reach the bus stop about seventy yards or so away, which was crowded with people. Once there, I knew that it would be difficult for Walter to assault me.

He must have read my mind, for he grabbed my hand tightly and said, "Not so fast. My car is the other way. Come with me quietly. If you resist I'll kill you."

"Let go of me!" I said, struggling to wrench free. "You're hurting me."

"I won't hurt you if you do as I say," he said. There was a deadly coldness in his eyes. "Now let's go."

He turned me sharply and we headed for his car a distance away.

"I'm not getting into your car," I said.

"I'd get into it if I were you," he said ominously. "You know I have a gun. I'm not afraid to use it. Even here, in the middle of the street, in front of everybody."

"Okay," I said, trembling. "I'll do as you say. Just let go of my arm. You're hurting me."

He released my arm from his tight grip but kept close to me, ready to grab me again should I try to flee. We had come to an intersection. His car was parked about fifty yards down the street. There was a white traffic cop standing in the middle of the intersection. The traffic lights were broken and he was directing traffic. In an instant I had bounded into the middle of the intersection and stood right next to the cop.

"Go on, move, get out of here," the cop said, as cars roared past us on either side.

"No, I'm not going," I shouted over the traffic. "That man over there wants to kill me."

"What! I can't hear you!"

"That man over there wants to kill me!" I repeated, shouting louder.

"What man?"

"That one over there in the loose red shirt." I pointed at a bewildered Walter, who was beginning to slink away. "He's got a gun. He wants to shoot me."

A police car happened to come along. The traffic cop signaled for it to stop. Two white police officers jumped out and came over to where we stood. When Walter saw them he turned and ran, disappearing behind a corner. I explained to the cops what had happened. They told me to get into the back of their car and they drove me to the white police station, where I told the whole story of abuse and death threats. They promised to open a file on Walter.

"Aren't you going to arrest him?" I asked one of the officers who was ushering me out.

"We can't arrest him without sufficient evidence, Miss," he said.

"But I told you what he's done to me," I said. "He's beaten me many times. And he's threatened to kill me. Track him down and lock him away and don't ever let him out."

"I know how you must feel, Miss," the officer said. "But many people make threats they don't intend to carry out."

"But he'll carry his out," I said. "He has a gun."

"Many people have guns, Miss."

"What should I do?" I said, exasperated. "I can't go back home to Alexandra. He'll come after me. He'll kill me. Especially after I called the police on him."

"The best advice I can give you is for you to inform your local police. They'll take care of the matter."

"But we no longer have a police force in Alexandra," I said.

Most Peri-Urban cops had resigned after many of them were killed by the Comrades, using necklacing, the popular method of killing suspected "Uncle Toms," informers and others accused of collaborating with the apartheid system. One cop near our shack on 13th Avenue was cornered inside his house one afternoon and burnt alive while a mob celebrated. Ironically, the man, mild-mannered, helpful, and devoted to his family, had been a good neighbor and was liked by many people, but the SAP (South African Police) uniform he wore branded him a traitor and collaborator and he was killed. Many of the black policemen who dared remain on the force, largely because police work was their only source of income and they had extended families to support, had fled the township with their families and taken refuge in tents and police barracks in the white suburbs.

The white officer in charge was perplexed when he heard that the police had fled from Alexandra, fearing for their lives. He was apparently unfamiliar with the anarchy reigning in the ghettos. I wasn't too surprised. Most whites were simply out of it. They were hopeless prisoners of a false sense of tranquility and security. In many instances, whites were forbidden by segregation laws from entering black ghettos; in cases where such laws were not strictly enforced, whites were merely afraid to venture into such worlds out of guilt and fear. Therefore, most of what they knew about black life and the conditions in the ghettos they had gleaned from the heavily censored media, seen on state-controlled television, or heard as gossip from their servants.

As far as most whites were concerned, blacks might as well have been aliens living on remote planets in outer space. One reason why it was so easy for successive apartheid governments to find overwhelming support for their racist policies among white voters was that most whites simply didn't know the atrocities being perpetrated on the black community in their name, or they chose not to know.

The white officer and I were now standing on the doorsteps. He went back into the station and consulted with his superior, a tall, burly man who looked Afrikaner, about the strange news that there was no police force in Alexandra. The burly man came over and said to me, almost gloating, "Well, Miss, I sympathize with your problem, but there's nothing we can do here. This is a white police station. Your case can only be handled by a black police station. But you people are killing all the policemen, and now you need them. I honestly can't help you with that one, Miss. Maybe you should take your case to the Comrades, heh. Maybe they can solve it in the People's Courts." He chuckled as he and his colleague went back into the white police station.

The People's Courts the officer was referring to were tribunals haphazardly organized by Comrades to replace white power structures. They dispensed street justice. While a few People's Courts had done some good in terms of settling minor disputes between neighbors, closing down sheheens, and reducing crime by dealing harshly with tsotsis, many were little more than Kangaroo courts. Most of the people who sat on them knew nothing about the law. Many were prone to favoritism and easily bribed. There were cases of people getting favorable verdicts after giving members of the court cases of beer, cigarettes, and money. And men predominated in these courts.

What chance did I have appearing against Walter before a People's Court, especially if one was held in his neighborhood, where he was certain to have friends and even relatives sitting in judgment of my case against him?

I left the police station distraught and in utter despair. I went directly to my cousin Florence's place. She was, as always, my last refuge. I told her what I had done and she was pleased. She gave me her total support.

"If the bastard shows his black ass here," Florence said, "I'll kill him. I have a long butcher knife in the house and I won't hesitate to plunge it into his filthy heart."

Walter didn't show up. I stayed with Florence several weeks and then returned home. By then I had gained the strength to face anything.

20

GELI

FIGHT WITH
JACKSON'S MISTRESS

Despite the pain of having an unfaithful husband, I took comfort in the fact that I now had my own life. I was earning my own money and taking care of my own children. I didn't have to rely on an unreliable husband for anything.

But a shock awaited me. One day I discovered that the money I had been saving under the mattress—the only savings I had in the world—was gone. I was in a panic. I asked Bushy, Piet, Johannes, and Florah, and none of them had seen the money.

"Where could it be?!" I kept saying as I ransacked the house. I was beside myself.

"Maybe Papa has it," Johannes said. He, Piet, and Bushy were helping me scour for it. It was a Saturday, and Jackson had left that morning with a group of his friends.

That evening he staggered back home drunk. I feared the worst. As soon as he came through the door, reeking alcohol, he demanded food. But I was in no mood to obey him. This was no time to be a dutiful wife. I got straight to the point, as he sat slumped in a chair by the table, waiting to be served dinner by his slave.

"Where is my money?" I demanded.

"What money?" he mumbled drunkenly. "Why are you talking about money when I'm hungry? Hurry up and give me my dinner."

"Dinner can wait," I said. "I want to know what happened to my money."

"What money, woman?" Jackson said irritably. My confrontational tone had sobered him up a bit.

"The money I keep under the mattress," I said. "I looked for it all day. It's gone."

"Oh, that," he said. "I have it. I'm keeping it. It's a man's responsibility to keep the money in the house, so I took it."

"Took my money!" I cried. "You had no right to do that. I worked hard for that money. It's mine."

"What's yours is mine," he said.

"Give me back my money, Jackson," I said. "I'm tired of arguing with you."

"I don't have it on me," he said, standing up and emptying his pockets. "You see? I'm keeping it in a safe place."

"Where?"

"If I told you it wouldn't be a safe place, would it?" he said, laughing.

I was beside myself with exasperation and anger. But there was nothing I could do. He had my money and only he knew what had happened to it. It had been there the last time I checked two days ago, so he had taken it recently.

"I hope you haven't spent my money on liquor," I said, "or gambled it away."

"I told you, woman, that I'm keeping it in a safe place," he said. "I no longer gamble."

"But why do you do this to me?"

"Do what?!" he retorted. "This is my house and I can do what I please in it."

"I sure pray to God that my money, wherever you're keeping it, is safe," I said. "You know that I'll soon stop selling spinach. The season is almost over."

I badly needed the money because I had just found out that I was pregnant with my fourth child. The news meant it would be over a year before I could resume selling spinach. How would I survive in the coming months? Where would I get the money to book myself at the clinic, to buy diapers and baby food when the baby arrived, to pay for my children's schooling, to buy food and pay rent whenever Jackson refused to? Where would I get the money to help my mother and siblings?

My mother had taken my brother's imprisonment hard. Her depression and heavy drinking made it difficult for her to go out hunting for piece jobs. I had been helping her with rent and food from my earnings selling spinach. But now that money had disappeared.

Several days passed. Jackson offered no clues as to what he had done with my money, except that he now took it upon himself to buy the groceries. He started spending an inordinate amount of time away from home, even during the week after leaving work. I wondered why.

Then the devastating news reached me. I found out through some of my friends that Jackson had given my money to his Mosotho mistress! I couldn't believe the news at first. But then the pieces of the puzzle fell into place. This Mosotho woman couldn't have agreed to become Jackson's mistress if he didn't have money. And his measly wage of R8 a week was obviously not enough to impress and satisfy her. But my savings of over R40, well, that was another matter. For that amount she would do anything, including wreck a home.

This was the last straw. I marched over to the Mosotho woman's shack. I planned to have it out with her once and for all. She could keep Jackson for all I cared. But I'd be damned if she was going to enjoy life on my sweat and toil.

It was no time for formalities. As soon as I burst through the door of her shack I said, "I came to get my money, woman."

"What are you talking about?" the Mosotho woman exclaimed. She was short, slim, and fond of lightening her skin with Ambi cream. In fact, when I walked in, her face was still covered with the white cream. She was sitting by the table, a bottle of beer in front of her. Two of her youngest children—a boy three years old and girl who was five—were playing some game on a dirty floor. The room was a mess, as became the homes of women of her sort.

"I'm talking about my money," I said. "I'm talking about the R40 my husband gave you for both of you to enjoy behind my back."

"You're mistaken, Musadi," she said. "Your husband gave me no money." There was a hint of fear in her tremulous voice. That was confirmation enough for me that she had the money.

"Don't lie to me, you whore," I said. "Now give it to me."

"I didn't ask your husband to come here," the Mosotho woman said. We were now standing face to face, about a few feet apart.

"My money," I said insistently, moving closer to her. "I want it now. I'll be damned if I'll let you and Jackson have a nice time with money I've slaved so hard to earn. You can have a nice time with his money, not mine. Now cough it up!"

"I don't know what you're talking about," the Mosotho woman said evasively. All the time we were talking, she had been inching slowly toward the door, in the hope of running away. But I read her intent and moved between her and the door.

"Okay, let me jog your memory," I said. I grabbed the half-empty beer bottle that was standing on the table and smashed it against her head.

She hollered with pain.

"Now do you remember where my money is? Are you going to give it to me or do you want another reminder?"

"What are you doing, Musadi?" she cried.

I replied by grabbing her by the shoulders and butting her face with my head.

"Let me go, let me go!" she yelled.

"Not until you give me my money," I said. I forced her head down and then drove my left knee into one of her eyes. She howled with pain. We both fell to the floor. She clawed at my face with her long painted fingernails. I ignored the pain and clung to her. I continued landing blows all over her body while she hollered. I was determined to teach her a lesson. I knew how to fight another woman. I had learned it in the streets growing up.

Finally Jackson's mistress could take no more.

"Stop, please, stop!" she cried. "I'll give you your money. I'll give you your money!"

"Where is it, bitch?" I demanded. "Where is it!"

"It's in the drawer over there." She pointed.

I let her go. We rose together, and I followed her to the drawer, watching her every move like a hawk. She opened it, took out a gaudy black purse, and emptied its contents on the table. There were several crumpled R5 and R1 notes, along with some loose change. I counted the money. It came to R33.

"Where's the rest?" I demanded.

"Your husband has been buying beers with it," she said.

"Consider yourself lucky," I said as I picked up the money and prepared to leave. "Other women won't be as lenient as I've been. They wouldn't hesitate to kill you for breaking up their homes. I would stop this sort of life if I were you."

The Mosotho woman said nothing. But she was clearly shaken. Her contrite look told me she would never mess with me again. I went back home exhausted, a bit achy but triumphant. Jackson was out so I was able to clean myself up. I rested a bit, and then went about my household chores.

Late that evening Jackson returned earlier than usual. He was livid with rage. He stormed through the door and came straight at me. I was by the stove cooking dinner, George tied to my back. Piet and Bushy were helping Johannes and Florah with their homework. They all stopped and crowded fearfully in the far corner as soon as they saw the angry look on Jackson's face as he walked in. They knew his moods.

"Why did you do what you did this afternoon?" He fired at me.

"What did I do?"

"What right do you have to interfere in my life?"

"Am I not your wife?"

He didn't answer. I could see he was gingerly dancing around the issue. He didn't want to mention his mistress in front of the children or be forced to answer unpleasant questions. Yet he was itching to confront me over the beating I gave his mistress and the fact that I had reclaimed my money.

"I see nothing wrong in taking back what is mine," I said.

"Why did you beat that poor woman up?"

"Poor woman indeed!" I said with a sarcastic laugh. "What was your so-called poor woman doing with my money?"

"I gave it to her."

"Gave her my money!" I said. "What for?"

"For safekeeping," he said. "It wasn't safe in this house."

"Do you really expect me to believe that?" I said. "You must think me a bloody fool. Wasn't the money safe all these months that it's been under the mattress? What suddenly made it unsafe?"

He had no answer.

"Jackson," I said. "You can choose to be unfaithful to me. That's your own business. It's your own life. You're old enough to take responsibility for what you do. You have to answer to God for committing adultery. But I'll be damned if I'll allow my own hard-earned money to support your philandering."

"Who do you call a philanderer!" Jackson screamed as he lunged at me and grabbed me by the throat. His eyes blazed with rage as he tightened his grip. I gasped for breath. The children started screaming. Piet and Bushy instantly came over and started pulling Jackson by the legs and beating him in an effort to pry him off me.

"Get away, damn you," he railed at them. "Get away or I'll kill you too."

"Leave our sister alone," Piet and Bushy cried.

Their interference was enough distraction for Jackson. He loosened his grip on my throat. With a mighty effort I was able to wrench free. I fled outside. The children followed. Jackson attempted

to come after me. But the children and I began running. Jackson
didn't follow, as he knew I would outrun him, even with an infant
tied to my back. The children and I ran through the dark streets all
the way to my mother's place, where I told her what had happened.

The following day my mother and a neighbor went over to see
Jackson and attempt to mediate our dispute. Jackson was ready with
lies. He didn't admit to having a mistress. Instead, he accused me of
insubordination and said I had attacked an innocent woman out of a
fit of jealousy. As for the money found at his mistress's place, he said
he had given it to her for temporary safekeeping, until he could open
an account at the bank. He wanted me to go apologize to the woman,
and to give her back the money. If I refused to carry out these
demands, he didn't want me back in his house.

After my mother had related what Jackson had said, I replied, "He
must be mad to think I will give her back my money and apologize to
that bitch."

"What are you going to do, then?" my mother said.

"I'm going to leave him," I said.

"What about the children?"

"I'll take care of them myself, as I have been doing all these years."

"What if Jackson comes here and forcibly takes you back, as he's
sure to do? Your brother Reuben is in prison. There's no man in the
house to protect you."

"I'll go to my father then."

My father now lived in Diepkloof with his third wife, Melinda, and
my stepsiblings. Though my mother wanted to have little to do with
him, she nonetheless allowed me and my siblings to visit him from
time to time, saying that he was still our father despite how he had
treated her.

The following day, while Jackson was at work, I went over to the
house. I found the door locked, but I had a spare key tied on a string
around my waist. I took my scanty belongings and the children's,
packed them in two worn-out suitcases, and then left with my three
children for Diepkloof, a section of Soweto.

Melinda was unlike Elizabeth. She didn't mind contact between my father and his children by his first wife, in part because she no longer saw my mother as a threat. There was no possibility of reconciliation between my parents. Too much water had already flowed under the bridge.

I was my father's favorite. He had had no girls with his other wives, only sons.

"Jackson is clearly not fit to be your husband," my father said as we discussed my marital problems. "You should leave him permanently."

"What will happen to the children?" I asked, recalling the hard life we had led after we had been left fatherless.

"I'll help you take care of them," he said.

"I'll think about it," I said.

We stayed with my father nearly a month. Though Jackson feared my father, a ruggedly strong man, he came to Diepkloof several times seeking a reconciliation. But he was afraid to enter the house, unwilling to risk my father's wrath. Instead he ended up roaming the streets and peering at the house through the bushes, in the hope of catching me alone. Occasionally he would send a neighborhood youngster to come get me, but I refused to go talk to him. Frustrated by his attempts to talk to me without first meeting with my father, he returned to Alexandra and sent several of his relatives to plead his case. Through them he apologized for his behavior, promised to mend his ways, and assured my father that he would start behaving responsibly, as a husband and father should.

My father listened but was unconvinced.

"He always says he'll change just to get you back," my father said. He then asked what I wanted to do.

I thought hard about the matter. My fourth child was on the way and I didn't want to have it in Diepkloof, away from my mother. And Melinda had been understanding of my situation, but I wondered how differently she would feel when my children and I became a permanent part of her household. I feared she would start feeling the way Elizabeth had felt about my mother and her children.

Also, I longed for the familiarity of my own home, imperfect though that home was. I decided to give Jackson another chance. My children and I returned to Alexandra. When my fourth child, Maria, was born, I gave her the tribal name, Azwidovi—"Never Again." Never again would I let myself be abused.

21

GRANNY

BUSHY IS

RAPED

After my daughter Geli fled her abusive husband and went to Diep-kloof, Piet and Bushy came back to live with me in the crammed one-room shack. When Geli returned she wanted them to come live with her and Jackson again, but I decided against it. I didn't want to burden her fragile marriage with my problems and provide Jackson with yet another excuse to resume his abuse.

Jackson had never liked my family. He thought us intrusive and parasitic, and often accused Geli of spending his money on our needs.

"I'm poor because of your relatives," he would say. "Remember, I married you, alone. Not your entire family. You never see any of my family members coming here to stay with us or asking for help."

After I helped deliver Geli's fourth child, I knew there was no way I could let my children live there. They would simply be two more mouths for Geli and her husband to feed, and two more bodies to find room for in their already overcrowded two-room shack.

So when Matinana approached me and asked that my daughter

Bushy come live with her, promising to pay for her schooling and support her in return for her help with chores, I agreed to the request, despite some misgivings.

I spoke to Bushy, who had just turned sixteen, about the offer. She was ecstatic. It meant she could live in a big house, with her own room and enough food to eat. She could go to school regularly, and be near her friend Nkensani, whose parents lived not far away from Matinana's.

Bushy's attitude toward Matinana's family was full of innocence, trust, and love. She was impressed by their riches and proud to have them as kin, despite their looking down on us. Neither she nor Piet had the bitterness of my son Reuben.

I didn't want my children to grow up full of hatred and bitterness. I didn't want them to be prisoners of the past, especially a painful one. That's why I seldom talked to them about the pain of my life, the suffering I had undergone. I always looked to the future. I always told them, "We're all right, we're together, we're a family, and we'll survive. God knows and will judge everything in the end."

Part of this refusal to dwell on the past is for self-protection. I think I would die if I ever sat down and thought about all the pain I have endured in my life. So I try to forget, which is why I never really hated my stepsiblings. If I had hated them I would have fought back in kind. I would have left no stone unturned to make them suffer the way I had suffered. I would have used witchcraft against them, and even sought ways to kill them. I wouldn't have visited them when they were sick, eager to nurse them back to health.

I was ever eager to extend a hand of friendship to them, to trust them, to think no evil of them. They had the comfortable life and I had poverty. But in the end what makes life worth living are not things like money or property, which cannot make us happy if our hearts are not good, and which we cannot take along to the afterlife. What makes life worth living is love, caring, giving, sharing, and family.

And Matinana and her siblings were still family, despite what they had done to me. I was brought up to believe that family members must take care of each other. Not to do so imperiled the family unit, by leaving it vulnerable to outside forces bent on its destruction. If, as part of the same family, we didn't take care of each other, especially in times of need, there could be no future for posterity, no survival in the long run.

That's why I had expected from my stepsiblings the same unconditional love I gave them. After all, they came from the same seed as Shibalu and me. This was not naivete, as many people later told me. It was a sacred belief, which for thousands of years had enabled my people to survive. They took care of each other.

Shortly after Bushy moved in with Matinana, it became apparent that Matinana had no intention of keeping her promises. She merely wanted a slave. She made Bushy clean the huge house alone, wash clothes for Matinana and her children, and cook. And her payment? My poor Bushy was sent to school barefoot and without lunch money. She would occasionally come by my shack during lunch break to eat whatever little food I had, usually yesterday's porridge with tea. At other times Nkensani shared her lunch with her. Nkensani was given plenty of pocket money by her mother each day, along with a lunch box of peanut-butter-and-jam sandwiches.

"Do you want to come back home?" I asked Bushy during one lunch break when she came home.

"No, Mama," she said. "Things are not that bad at Aunt Matinana's as they seem to you. I do get enough to eat and I have my own bed. And I am near my friend Nkensani."

"Anytime you want to come home, child," I said, "please do. I don't have much. But the little I have we'll all share."

"Thanks, Mama," Bushy said. "I think this arrangement works best because now you only have Piet to look after. And Aunt Matinana isn't all that bad, honestly. She has a temper, yes, but she treats her own children the same. And she does sometimes appreciate the work I do. Why, just last week she bought me a pretty secondhand dress."

Months went by. I found piece jobs weeding white people's gardens in various suburbs, and on those days when I wasn't working I baby-sat children from the neighborhood. My daughter Geli came to visit me often. Her baby was still nursing, and Jackson forbade her to work. Yet the money he gave her each Friday was not enough to meet their ever-growing needs. He was against her working not so much because he didn't need her extra income but mainly out of spite. He wanted her to know that he had control over her life. His main argument against Geli working was derived from tribal tradition, which stated that as long as a man was working and supporting the family, the woman's place was in the home, looking after the house and raising children.

Jackson and Geli still fought from time to time, but Geli, aware of my own problems and wishing me not to worry too much about her, would minimize the abuse. One time she knocked at my door in the middle of the night. When I unlocked it I saw her standing there with her four children, who were shivering in the cold night air.

"What happened?" I asked, as I led them into the shack.

"Nothing serious," she said. "Jackson and I just had a little quarrel, that's all. He was drunk and started making noise. And I wanted some peace. So I took the children and came here."

"In the middle of the night?" I said, not believing her explanation. "Don't you know it's dangerous? You could be raped or killed by tsotsis."

"Don't worry, Mama," she said. "I can take care of myself. And I have Johannes with me," she added with a smile, looking in the direction of her sleepy, thin, nine-year-old son. "He's now strong enough to take care of his Mama. Aren't you child?"

Johannes nodded sheepishly.

"You should see how fiercely he defends me against Jackson," Geli said.

The next morning I accompanied her home. When we got there I found, to my horror, that there had been more than a mere quarrel between her and Jackson. The windows of the shack were shattered, smashed pots and plates lay strewn outside the house, and the bed was turned upside down.

"So this is nothing serious, heh?" I said to Geli, pointing to the chaos. "Now tell me what happened."

"Oh, the usual," Geli said indifferently. "He gave me some money for groceries and then demanded it back. I wouldn't give it to him because I knew he would squander it all on dice. You know he's gambling again. I had to save some money for food and for the children's school needs. Johannes and Florah have been coming home with welts after being beaten by their teachers with canes for not having books and the proper uniform."

"That Venda bastard," I said angrily. "If only my Reuben were here he would teach him a lesson."

"Don't worry about me, Mama," Geli said. "I can take care of myself. I'm able to fight back now. And as soon as the baby is grown, I'll start searching for piece jobs so I can again be independent."

"But the ogre doesn't want you to work," I said.

"I know he doesn't," I said. "But if I find a job, I'll take it. We'll see what he'll do then."

Lobola or no lobola, tradition or no tradition, my daughter was determined to get a job as soon as the baby was old enough to be left in my care. Daily she went out with groups of women to canvass for jobs at the Indian place, where it would be easy for them to work without a need for the various work permits, which were almost impossible to get.

Geli finally found a job working for a large Indian family. She told Jackson about it. He huffed and puffed but she was determined to take the job.

"If you take that job," Jackson threatened, "neither you nor the children will get any money from me."

"That's fine," Geli said. "I'll support my own children, as I've always done."

Jackson carried out his threat to stop giving Geli money. But at least he still paid rent. Geli toiled almost seven days a week at the Indian place to earn enough to buy groceries and meet all her children's school needs. I looked after those of her children not attending school while she was away at work. I also cleaned her house and made the fire so that when she came back in the evening, always exhausted, she didn't have much left to do but cook. This also blunted Jackson's objections to her working: that she would neglect her duties and children.

From her job at the Indian place she brought home bags of leftover food: curried rice, chicken, and other Indian delicacies. She took none of the food to the home she shared with Jackson, but instead she brought it to me, knowing that her children spent most of the day with me.

"I'll be damned if I ever let that man eat or have anything I've earned," she vowed.

The little comfort and happiness I now knew—derived mainly from seeing my grandchildren often, playing with them, and having decent leftovers to feed them—didn't last long. It was shattered by one of the most horrible events in the life of my family, an event that made me, for the first time in my life, hate enough to want to kill. My daughter Bushy was raped.

When my daughter went to live with Matinana, the latter had a neighbor, a man in his forties who lived alone. He was old enough to be Matinana's husband. Matinana used to cook for this man, under some strange boarding arrangement that few people understood.

Matinana would send Bushy to take this strange man his food, always alone and always at night. Bushy, unsuspecting, did as she was told. I still don't understand why Matinana would send a young woman, a virgin at that, alone to the home of a strange man at night.

And she was raped. But my poor Bushy didn't tell anyone of the awful experience. She was afraid and ashamed. She simply withdrew into herself, confused and terrified. She thought she was somehow to blame for what had happened. The trauma Bushy suffered from the rape was so great that to this day she has trouble discussing it. All I know is that the man threatened to kill her if she told anyone. And she dared not tell Matinana, out of fear that she would be driven away. So she clammed up, suffering in silence, tormented by fear, and hoping against hope that someday her recurrent nightmares would stop, that no one would ever find out if she never told. And poor Bushy didn't even know a thing about sex and pregnancy. She didn't know that in a few months the whole world would know her terrible secret. She was only sixteen.

Abortion was illegal in South Africa and frowned upon culturally. She would have had to have one performed in a back alley, by old hags using hangers, laxatives, and strange *muti*, endangering her life. Many women who had back-alley abortions died. I don't even know if I could have taken her to a back-alley abortionist had I know soon enough that she was pregnant. I simply don't know.

But it was too late by the time I found out. Her tummy had started to show. Everyone was shocked. Matinana called my daughter a slut and drove her away. Bushy returned home in tears, humiliated and degraded. She wanted to die. I wanted to die too. But I had to live for her. I had to be strong so I could help her through her enormous pain.

"I love you very much, my daughter," I said. "It wasn't your fault in the least. You were deliberately put in harm's way by one of the most evil persons I have ever known, my own stepsister."

"What will happen to me now, Mama?" Bushy asked.

"You'll have the baby," I said. "Then I want you to go back to school. I'll help you take care of the child."

"But what will people say?"

At this my heart broke and I wept. I knew of the stigma that attached to rape and illegitimacy. Pregnant students were expelled from school.

"They'll say many horrible things," I said. "Be prepared for that. But always remember I love you. Remember you did nothing wrong. God knows that."

"Will I ever be able to get a husband?" Bushy asked.

"Yes, my child," I said. "There are some men who will understand and not blame you for what happened. But let's not talk about husbands now. We have to take care of you and prepare for the baby."

Bushy had a difficult pregnancy. We didn't have enough food and lived under the constant threat of eviction, as I wasn't able to find regular work. But in the end my daughter and I made it. I helped her deliver a baby boy. We were so poor when he arrived that we had no money for diapers and had to borrow old ones that Geli had used with her fourth child and was saving for her fifth.

The poor thing must have sensed the suffering, hardship, and cruelty of the world he was born into, for a month or so later he died from *nhlokwani*. We simply couldn't afford to take him to a *nganga* to treat the small opening on top of his skull that newborn infants have. Under tribal custom it was imperative to smear it with special *muti* to prevent the infant from getting sick while the opening closed, as the newborn grew and gathered strength. But we had no money to afford a visit to a *nganga*. So one day the heartbeat stopped and Bushy's baby boy died. The year was 1970.

22

FLORAH

RITUAL SCHOOL

I have often wondered why the women in my family suffered so much pain at the hands of men, why many ended up in relationships or marriages with abusive men and found it hard to leave.

Granny clung to the belief that her husband would not abandon her even when it was perfectly clear to everyone else that he had long ceased to care about her and in fact had already married another woman.

My mother was forced to marry the man she abhorred. She constantly suffered terrible physical and mental abuse from him, and many times spoke of leaving him—and each time she meant it—yet she always changed her mind and stayed.

And then there is my sister Maria, six years younger than me. A star athlete and top student, she was forced to drop out of school in 1981, after she became pregnant at age fifteen. Because throughout the 1980s black schools were shut down by boycotts and violence most of the time, youngsters often roamed the streets with little to do. They were left vulnerable to experimenting with sex. Before she was twenty-five Maria had had three children by different men. All of the men proved abusive.

Even though Maria's first two boyfriends hadn't paid *lobola* for her, it was difficult for her to extricate herself from the relationships. She was only able to escape from one abuser by falling in love with another. The father of her third child did offer to pay *lobola* for her. My father wanted R2,000 because, he said, the price included Maria's two sons, whom he claimed to have raised, though he had done nothing of the kind. But I told Maria's husband not to pay the extravagant amount.

"Spend it on Maria and the children instead," I said to him. "Don't give it to my father. He likes money too much. Build your family a future with it."

Maria's husband was called Wayne. He had the potential to become a good husband. He was more mature than Maria's other boyfriends had been. He was hardworking, quiet, respectful, and always attentive to Maria's needs as a woman—that is, while they were still dating.

But as soon as Wayne had paid *lobola* for her, and Maria officially became his wife, he changed dramatically. He became jealous and possessive. He forbade Maria to work, to go to the store, and even to go draw water from the communal tap. Paranoid that some man might lure her away from him if she even so much as stepped out in public, he sought to confine her in the house most of the time. This drove Maria nuts. She rebelled by sneaking out and going to *shebeens*, where she would drink and party with her friends. Whenever she returned home, he would accuse her of sleeping around and beat her with his fists.

One time, while she was still nursing their baby son, he beat her so badly he broke her arm. This battery took place in the presence of his mother, who did nothing to intervene, except to tell Maria after it was over that if she behaved herself, there would be no need for her son to "discipline" her.

Maria left Wayne and returned home, but my father refused to let her stay. He told her she was a disgrace to the family for leaving her husband. He kept reminding her that *lobola* had been paid for her and that she had an obligation to remain with Wayne. So Maria went back to her torturer.

When I consider the lives of Maria, my mother, and Granny and the other women in my extended family, I come to the conclusion that part of our problems with men, aside from the abuses of *lobola*, is that we were brought up to see our lives as incomplete without them. We were taught to consider men as our superiors, the absolute rulers not only of the home but of our lives too. Custom and tradition told us it was normal for men to cheat and lie, to abuse and domineer, in the course of a marriage. On the other hand, we women were told we were duty-bound to remain steadfast and faithful to our husbands no matter what they did to us or how undeserving of our affections they were.

Growing up in the city—where I saw many women, from my own tribe and others, demand to be treated by men with respect, as individuals and not as property—led me to challenge this view. It helped me acquire the strength to go against deeply held traditions and prejudices. The sight of Winnie Mandela defying apartheid, asserting her presence and legitimacy as a woman and a leader, and exhorting crowds to fight without flinching against white power, was most inspiring and empowering. I never thought a woman could be like that. And there were hundreds of Winnie Mandelas, from all walks of life, whose actions and words spoke eloquently for women's rights and liberation, and who everyday fought and never gave up.

Even my mother and Granny, in their own ways, old-fashioned and uneducated as they were, challenged and defied custom and the status quo. They had something of Winnie's fire smoldering in them. Yet there was with them, as with many women bred under tribalism and apartheid, always a limit to their defiance. Something held them back, some sort of invisible chain, riveted deep in the psyche, in their very being. It was as if a powerful fear had been instilled in them, drummed in, a fear which told them that to be anything other than a dutiful wife, obedient of her husband's will and forgetful of her own, was abnormal, unwomanly, a mortal sin, and would be visited by all sorts of calamities and punishment.

This potent, nameless fear, this way of thinking about ourselves as women, this transforming of our nature into something that catered to men's desires, found strong enforcement in the initiation most women in my family underwent: ritual school. The chief purpose of ritual school, as it was explained to me during initiation, was to kill a young girl's self-will so she could be remolded into a mature and complete woman: self-sacrificing, obedient, capable of assuming the role of wife, and thus appealing to men as the perfect complement to their desires, wishes, and whims.

I attended ritual school in 1976, at age fifteen, before I had my first boyfriend and shortly after the June riots. I was totally unprepared for the experience, which I can never forget for as long as I live. I describe it here with some trepidation, at the peril of my sanity, because those of us who were initiated into its mysteries were warned never to breathe a word about them to the outside world and the uninitiated, lest we go mad.

Only girls who had had their first period were drafted into ritual school. I didn't know what a period was until my friend Joyce explained it to me. It was taboo for my mother to speak to me about sex and ritual school.

Joyce, on the other hand, was from a different tribe, which didn't adhere strictly to the custom of ritual school, nor prohibited mothers from discussing sex with their daughters. So Joyce, though she was my age, knew all about the birds and the bees before I did. She even knew what an abortion was. One day I saw blood on her panties and said, horrified, "Are you sick? Are you dying?"

"No, silly," she said with calm sophistication. "Don't you know what this is? I'm having my period."

"What's a period?"

She explained, and I understood, somewhat.

When I related Joyce's explanation of a period to my mother, she reluctantly said to me, "Joyce knows a lot of things she shouldn't know at her age. And it's all because of her mother, who has little respect for taboos. The blood you see on your panties shouldn't alarm you. It only means *wa kula*, you are growing up." That was the extent of the sex education lesson, which left me more confused than informed.

Ritual school was supposed to end all my naivete about sexual matters. I had just started junior high school when I went. Few girls, especially those living in the townships, willingly attended ritual school, because of the many horror stories they heard from hearsay about what went on there: that girls were beaten, starved, and forced to go around naked. Either their parents had to force them to attend, or they were lured there by subterfuge, as I was. My mother and grandmother laid out an elaborate plan of deception to take me there during June, when schools were closed for the midwinter holidays.

One afternoon I was invited to visit a relative's home for dinner. When I got there, I found one of my mother's cousins, together with four or five other Tsonga women. They asked me to take them to Granny's house. I was surprised at this.

"But I thought you knew where Granny lives," I said.

"We do," said my cousin. "But we want you to come along. That's where we'll have our dinner. There's something important we want to show you."

I sensed something was fishy, but decided to take them there anyway. During our walk to Granny's shack the group of women cracked jokes and talked volubly with me about a variety of trivial matters, as if seeking to allay my suspicions and prevent me from asking too many questions. We finally arrived at Granny's. When I stepped across the threshold, I had no idea I would not be allowed to leave the place for the next four weeks.

We had a regular dinner of porridge and meat, sitting cross-legged on the floor. Afterwards, I got up and said, "I have to go now. It's getting dark and I have to walk alone all the way to 13th Avenue."

"You can't leave," one of my cousins said.

"Why not?" I asked, perplexed.

"Because you're now a *khomba*," she said.

"But I want to go home," I said in desperation, realizing what she meant.

"You're not permitted to leave," she said. "You'll go home in a month."

"But I want to go home now," I insisted.

"If you leave now you'll go crazy," she said ominously. "No one leaves a *khomba* house before it ends. But if you want to leave, there's the door"—she pointed. "But remember, you'll go stark-raving mad if you do."

I was afraid, and curious, so I stayed.

Ritual school officially began the following day, in a rather festive atmosphere. I was joined by four other Tsonga girls, all of school-going age, sent by their mothers to be turned into women. There was a big dinner, where we ate *semp*—a ricelike grain—mixed with brown beans and peanuts, and drank soft drinks. The women who were to be our teachers drank beer and danced for us in traditional tribal dress, their dozens of colorful bracelets jangling rhythmically like percussion instruments.

No men were allowed. It was taboo for them to even enter the house anytime ritual school was in session. Because I was my mother's oldest daughter, she too was not allowed to be present. But Granny and Aunt Bushy were there. Over the next four weeks they and various women teachers came and taught me something about men, about what it meant to be a woman, about the importance of respect, and the crucial role women play in family life.

Most of the lessons, though, boiled down to knowing how to be an obedient, subservient, compliant, and man-pleasing woman.

The room where we were holed up was bare. There was no furniture. We wore nothing but a burlap thong, wrapped around our pelvises like diapers. Our naked legs, arms, breasts, and stomachs were exposed to the raw cold. We sat all day huddled in a corner, in the same posture, our legs folded, with our backs turned away from the door and from our teachers. Meals were cooked in a huge pot. We were served incredible amounts of porridge on big plates, with small portions of chicken feet or intestines. We ate in pairs, with our fingers, and were required to eat everything on the plate. We were told we were being fattened up so we could become nice, plump, and womanly, and thus attractive to prospective husbands.

Once, I dared to say I could eat no more.

"Eat!" one woman barked. "Eat or you'll be thrashed. No man wants to marry a reed!"

I forced down the remaining porridge and felt nauseous.

"I'm going to vomit," I said, clutching my stomach.

"If you vomit, you'll have to eat your vomit," the woman said severely.

I tried hard to keep the food down. Luckily, I didn't vomit. Some girls who refused to eat more were beaten.

Our daily routine inside this house of torture we were forbidden to leave included singing special tribal songs with dirty lyrics, listening to stories, and doing gymnastic-like exercises. These exercises involved mainly stretching. Our teachers told us that a complete woman had to be fully limbered so as to be ready for love making, pregnancy, and childbirth. The exercises loosen your limbs and make your inner vaginal muscles tight, which is supposed to make you fantastic in bed and therefore irresistible to men.

The tradition of ritual school grew partly out of the old African custom of marrying off young girls to older men. The school prepared the girls for sex long before experience could teach them anything, as they married while virgins and often in their teens.

We also memorized erotic poems which we recited in the presence of our teachers, whom we called "Mothers." If you made a mistake when reciting it, your Mother beat you for being "stubborn." We practiced them all day, reciting them to each other, trying to perfect our recitation so we wouldn't be punished. If you didn't do a task right, or if you had an attitude, your Mother scolded or thrashed you. One form of punishment favored by the Mothers involved pinning the offender's hands in a vice made of pieces of wood and squeezing until the offender howled with pain. As this torture was being inflicted, the other initiates would loudly play drums to drown out the screams and give outsiders the impression that we were having a wonderful time.

There was no escape from this chamber of horrors. There were stories of girls who couldn't endure the punishment and pain and tried escaping by crawling through windows, but they were soon brought back by their parents, and their punishment was multiplied. One reason many parents wanted their daughters initiated was that a lot of men preferred women who have been to ritual school.

Every day, our Mothers—who had none of the motherly milk of human kindness about them but were as harsh and cruel as slave drivers—drummed lessons, admonitions, taboos, and threats into our heads.

"By the time you leave here, we will have beaten out all the stubbornness in you."

"You must become meek, obedient, and subservient to men. These are the characteristics most of them—the ones who've been to mountain school, that is, and are fit to be called men—look for in the perfect woman."

The mountain school was the male equivalent of *tikhomba*. When a young man reached the age of fifteen or sixteen, he was taken there, to learn how to fight, to hunt, to endure pain, to accept responsibility, to be brave, to suppress his feelings, and always to keep a woman in her place.

Boys often returned from mountain school circumcised and truncated into sexist tyrants. They were expected to domineer and command women, including their own mothers. In the mountain school, they were taught that women were created to satisfy, to please and serve men, and that all insubordination, sauciness, or "cheek" should be lashed out of them.

"Living in the city has given you the wrong impression of what it means to be a woman," our Mothers told us. "A true woman doesn't shout at her husband. A true woman doesn't refuse her husband anything. A true woman doesn't contradict his counsels. A true woman respects her husband as ruler of the house. She obeys and supports him in everything. She helps him accomplish his duties of providing and protecting the home."

The Mothers would add that a girl's will had to be broken before she could assume her rightful place next to her man. Strong wills were said to make women too wayward and independent. We were there to be transformed from selfish little girls into self-sacrificing women who lived only for our husbands and children. We were never explicitly taught about sex or how to make love, but the clever ones among us quickly learned by inference.

Our group was lucky to be attending ritual school in the township. In the homelands, *tikhomba* went on for several months and conditions were even harsher. At the end of the four weeks we were allowed to dress and were given special *doeks* to wear on our heads, signifying that we were now mature, complete women.

Two weeks later, after our release from this sexist, prison boot camp, a big celebration was held to welcome us back into the community. It was a coming-out party of sorts. Goats were slaughtered and beer brewed. The family of each girl contributed equally to the catering. Since I didn't eat goat's meat, my family provided a sheep. I received many presents, mostly from men, and we wore colorful *doeks* and *muchekas* as marks of our new status.

Dressing this way easily identified us to men. They competed for our attention because they knew that we, fresh from ritual school, would make ideal wives—after all, our wills had been broken. Boys who had been to mountain school and were circumcised had the right to stop us in the streets and demand that we recite certain poems, about which they had been told during their own initiation. If you recited it perfectly, they gave you money as a reward. If you fouled up, they had the right to beat you with a stick. And whenever you met them during this two-week period, and they recited a certain bawdy poem, you were supposed to drop down on your knees right there in the middle of the street, in front of everyone, and curl up in a fetal position, and lie on your side at their feet, almost groveling, in recognition and respect of their superiority.

Despite the important role ritual school played in the life of the family and the village—by teaching women about their role in traditional society—essentially the practice, especially in the twentieth century, only reinforced the inferior status of women in society. It taught us to accept polygamy in men, to obey them unconditionally, to see our lives as consisting primarily of sacrifice and self-denial, and to be obsessed with petty rivalries and jealousies to gain and keep the attention of men.

This unconditional obedience to the will of men and their whims was something against which many women instinctively rebelled, despite having been through ritual school. But that rebellion had an enormous cost. I found that out first with my father, then in my relationship with Collin, and later with Walter. Yet I was prepared to bear the cost, if the price I paid resulted in my becoming the strong and independent woman I knew I could be, and longed to become. I yearned to be a liberated woman who needed a man only for the right reasons—reasons of friendship, mutual respect and support, trust, reciprocal dependence, and love, which, in going beyond mere sex and childbearing, encompassed the feelings and the soul. I knew I had the potential to become such a woman, despite what I had been through and the world in which I lived.

23

GELI

I BECOME
A DRUNKARD

When Jackson slid back into his old pattern of alcoholism, gambling, and abuse, I felt myself slipping too. I simply couldn't cope. I was overwhelmed by the hard work of keeping the family together. I no longer had the strength to bear the suffering and the pain. I started drinking heavily. I sought in liquor escape from the miserable life I led, an anodyne to numb me from the pain of Jackson's infidelity and beatings.

Unknowingly, I was repeating the same pattern of my mother, who had taken to drinking after my father had left her and she was overwhelmed with raising five children alone.

Most women in the ghetto became alcoholics because of the hardships and pressure of black life under apartheid. They constantly worried about the future of their children; about getting work permits and finding jobs paying enough to enable them to feed and take care of their families. Then there was the stress and pain of seeing their men emasculated by apartheid, turning abusive and becoming unfaithful, and seeing the family flounder in a quagmire of poverty and hopelessness, without a future.

I had been a social drinker in the past. It was common for women in the cities and homelands to drink socially, mainly traditional beer made of malt and yeast. Drinking was an integral part of African life. But now I drank to get drunk. I drank not only traditional beer but mostly the white man's liquor, a bottle of which was more intoxicating than entire drums of traditional brew.

And when I was drunk I cared about nothing in the world except my next drinking binge. And without a job, I had all the time in the world to get drunk.

Daily I visited *shebeens* after leaving my two youngest children at home with Johannes and Florah or with my mother. I often went in the company of a group of women from the neighborhood who were also seeking an escape from misery and abuse in liquor. We would spend the whole day drinking and swapping stories about our miserable lives and abusive husbands. Somehow being able to laugh about our condition eased the pain and suffering.

Drinking made me neglect and start abusing my children. I would shout at them and beat them at the slightest provocation or for no reason at all. At first this filled me with guilt. But the guilt was soon replaced by despair and then by indifference. I couldn't have cared less whether or not my older children, Johannes and Florah, went to school. If they did, they usually left with no lunch money and wearing dirty uniforms. They often came back from school crying, saying the teachers had punished them for being unkempt, for not doing their homework, for not paying school fees, and for neglecting a host of other things which a caring parent would have attended to.

They began staying away from school, afraid of being beaten for my mistakes and neglect. In the past I had been strict about their attending school and doing their homework, but now I no longer cared. I began treating Johannes and Florah, who were nine and seven years old, respectively, as adults. Knowing they would be home all day, I would leave for the *shebeens* quite early in the morning, after giving them instructions to clean the house and care for George, five, and Maria, three. I took Mirriam, one year old, with me to the *shebeen*, strapped to my back.

I frequently abandoned my children with nothing to eat. In those sodden days, which passed away in a haze, there was little to eat in the house because of Jackson's gambling and drinking. My children were lucky to have crusts of stale bread to dip in sugared water. Whenever I left, I always promised them that I would bring some food back with me. But of course in my drunken state I would forget. Whenever I returned and found the shack dirty and my children whining from hunger, I would shout at them and beat them.

They came to fear me, just as they feared their father. And whenever Jackson and I fought they would cower in the corner, crying, whimpering, confused, terrified. Jackson and I now fought almost daily. I no longer cared about his battering me. Drink numbed the pain of his blows and loosened my tongue so I at least had the courage to defend myself verbally.

But sometimes when I was sober I would realize that my drinking was traumatizing my children. I would feel terribly guilty and vow never to touch the bottle again. For a week or two I would stay away from liquor. But then a drinking buddy would stop by and coax me to join her, or the powerful urge would seize me, and I would be off again to the *shebeen*, and the whole vicious cycle would begin again.

"Stop this drinking, my child," my mother said one day. She had come to my place and found me so drunk I couldn't do a thing. I was sprawled on the bed, the house was in filthy disarray, the children were unfed and neglected, and Mirriam was wearing a soiled diaper. "You're only hurting the children and yourself."

"I don't care," I muttered, battling a splitting headache.

"This drinking makes you no different from that good-for-nothing husband of yours," my mother said. "In fact it makes you worse. The children need you more than they need him. And look at them. They're worse than orphans."

"I don't care," I said, turning toward the wall and trying to block out my mother's words. "And leave me alone."

"There's a better way to deal with your problems, my child," my mother said.

"Is that so?" I said, laughing. "I thought this was the best way. I remember you drank to try and forget your pain after Papa left us."

"But it didn't work."

"Well, it works for me," I said. "I forget everything I want to forget."

"Including the welfare of your children?"

"They aren't my children," I said. "They are *his* children. He doesn't care for them, so why should I? I'm tired out, Mama, I can't take it anymore. I just can't. So please leave me alone."

My mother kept pleading with me to stop drinking. In my sober moments I agreed, but I was addicted. I seemingly couldn't let go of the bottle.

One of my favorite drinking buddies was Ma-Mahafa ("Mother of the Mad One"). She was so called because one of her sons was a wild one. Ma-Mahafa had a reputation for having lovers who showered her with presents and money. It was easy for women to have lovers because they seldom worked, and when they did they earned little. Yet they had enormous responsibilities that required money.

Ma-Mahafa was a distant cousin with five children and a sweet but passive husband, a menial laborer whom she and her youngest son bossed around. Ma-Mahafa was sophisticated and shrewd, and she loved fancy clothes. Whenever we were together, she always paid for our drinks.

One day, while we were sitting in a *shebeen* drinking, she said to me, "You never have any money on you. Don't you want to have more than enough to take care of your children and your needs?"

"Yes, I do," I said eagerly. "Can you find me a job?"

Ma-Mahafa had the distinction of having a permit allowing her to work as a maid in the suburbs.

"I can find you something better than a job," she said. "Something you'd enjoy doing."

"Just tell me what it is and I'll do it," I said.

"You know," she said, "you aren't bad looking for twenty-nine.

Even with five kids. Of course you aren't a beauty like me, but you have your appeal. Just this moment I see a man across the room who's been staring at you each time we've come here. Can't you tell when a man is interested in you, girl?"

I became apprehensive. What was she leading to? I scanned the throng of drinkers in the *shebeen*. Most of them were women, as most men were away at work. The handful of men present were either unemployed or had the day off. They worked mostly as kitchen boys and gardeners in the suburbs and regularly came to the township on their day off to visit friends and relatives and to drink. Most of these men had left their wives in the homelands so they could qualify for work in the city. They were often lonely and constantly having affairs.

"With all these men always coming here," Ma-Mahafa said, "their pockets full of money, have you ever thought about getting yourself a lover or two?"

"Oh!" I said, covering my open mouth.

"That way you don't have to rely on that deadbeat, two-timing husband of yours," she said.

"But Ma-Mahafa," I said, shocked, "that would be wrong."

"Wrong!" she retorted. "Why wrong? You have no husband but in name only. He doesn't support you. He beats you. And he has mistresses."

"He may do all that," I said. "But that's no reason for me to start sleeping around with other men."

"Wake up, girl," Ma-Mahafa said. "You're still living the old way, back in the tribal reserves. We're now living in the city, t-h-e c-i-t-y. Women are sleeping around left and right. You have to do what's best for you. You have to think about yourself for once. This is survival."

"But I was taught that sleeping with other men when you had a husband is wrong, terribly wrong," I said. "Even the Bible says adultery is a sin."

"And doesn't the Bible also say it's wrong for a man to sleep with other women when he's already married?"

"Yes, it does. But two wrongs don't make a right."

"Who do you think you are? Are you Jesus' mother? The Virgin Mary?"

"No."

"Then why do you talk like her?"

"I just won't feel comfortable cheating on my husband," I said, "even if he's rotten."

Ma-Mahafa laughed. "Girl, you've got a hell of a lot to learn about men. You've got so many hangups that you should have been a nun. Well, don't say I didn't offer to help. Men have had the upper hand for way too long, girl. They've enjoyed the nice time while we've slaved and scratched. It's time we women also had a nice time. And that's what I'm having. The time of my life."

"What about my children?" I asked. "They're growing up. They're already old enough to be ashamed of me for drinking. I don't want to give them reason to hate me like they hate their father."

"Children are children," Ma-Mahafa said. "And you will be discreet of course. You won't be doing it in front of them."

"No, thank you," I said. "I understand what you're saying. But I just couldn't."

I started keeping my distance from Ma-Mahafa. I felt awkward in her presence, particularly when different men would come up to her in a *shebeen* and I would have to watch her flirting with them. Occasionally some man would ask about me, saying he had a friend, and Ma-Mahafa would say, "Don't waste your time on her. She's so married she always has her chastity belt on."

One day something happened to make me stop going to *shebeens*. I had left my children unattended as usual. In my absence they got hungry, and Johannes attempted to make them porridge with the little mealie meal that was left. He poured some water in a pot and lit a primus stove to boil it. The rest of the children crowded around the primus stove in anticipation of food and for warmth. It was the middle of winter. There was no heat in the house. In their eagerness to get warm one of them accidentally tipped over the primus stove, spilling the scalding water all over the floor and the children. Fortunately no one was seriously burned. As the children screamed from pain and shock, no one noticed that the newspapers covering the table as a makeshift tablecloth had caught fire. Soon the table itself was ablaze.

The children rushed outside, with Johannes and Florah shouting, "Fire! Fire! Help! Help! Our house is on fire!"

Neighbors heard their cries and rushed into the shack. They managed to douse the flames in the nick of time, before the fire was out of control and would have engulfed not only our shack but the adjacent ones as well.

When I got back and heard what had happened, I heaved a great sigh of relief that a tragedy had been averted. I knew well the stories of shacks going up in flames and children being burned alive or badly maimed. Jackson came back from work that evening and heard what had happened. We had a major fight. I escaped being battered by fleeing to my mother's. I stayed with her a couple days, until Jackson's rage cooled and my mother and a neighbor went to him and negotiated a reconciliation. I felt terribly ashamed of myself. I kept telling myself over and over again that my children could have died and I would have been to blame, all because I loved liquor and neglected their welfare.

Over the next few months I fought one of the toughest battles of my life—that of weaning myself from alcohol. I didn't have the benefit of drugs or therapy—those aids were either unknown or unavailable to most black alcoholics because of apartheid. I had to rely on sheer will power and prayer. Many times I felt such a craving for alcohol that I thought I would go mad, but I resisted picking up the bottle again. I felt I owed it to my children and to myself to quit.

My mother was a great supporter. She urged me to rejoin the church, where I soon formed a new circle of friends. I began spending most of my time with them, and I sought their help in finding work so I could care for my children. By the grace of God I became sober, thus ending a two-year, nightmarish, vicious downward spiral into full-blown alcoholism.

At the Full Gospel Church of God I daily prayed for miracles. I begged God to make Jackson stop drinking and gambling, so we could be a whole family again. It was his drinking that had made it easy for me to become an alcoholic. I also prayed for God to help me find a job so I could take care of myself and my children. God denied me the first miracle but granted me the second.

I found a job working for a large Indian family—cleaning the house, washing and ironing laundry for over twenty family members, and caring for hordes of children. I was paid R10 ($3) for working ten hours a day, seven days a week. It was back-breaking work, but I expected it. It was my third time working for an Indian family.

The first job I ever held was working for an Indian family of twelve. I was about nine years old at the time. My mother, my siblings, and I were stuck in Alexandra with no means of support when my stepsiblings kicked us out of my grandfather's house after he died. My mother was working as a gardener earning 10 cents a day. I was making a little more than that, about 80 cents a week, mainly because I worked full-time, including weekends.

My mother knew I was too young to work, but the family was suffering and everyone had to pitch in. We were so poor we had to use burlap sacks for blankets and wore mealie sacks for clothes, tied to the waist by a string to hold them on our slight frames. I wasn't the only child working. There were hundreds of children all over Alexandra, as young as seven, who were toiling to help support their families.

The Indian family I worked for was good to me, despite the many chores I had to do. They used to let me take home leftover food, and with the salary I earned they allowed me to buy from them used blankets, a bed, and some secondhand cooking pots. I worked there for over a year, stopping when my older sister Mphephu, who was soon to marry and move to the homelands, asked my mother if I could live with her. It was a tradition that a bride's younger sister or niece must live with the new *makoti* for some time to help her with chores.

Working for Indians at age thirty was harder. I now had five children and a sixth was on the way. Jackson was still opposed to my working, primarily because I refused to give him any of my earnings.

But he relented when I told him I would only stop working when he stopped drinking and gambling and started bringing home his entire wages.

In the past, he would have beaten me for making such a demand. But now he was afraid to lay a hand on me because my brother Reuben had just been released from prison. Jackson knew he could no longer abuse me with impunity or my brother, hardened by hard labor on the chain gang, would not hesitate to come around and trounce him.

ughter and mother: Geli (left) and Granny (right).
ty Van Lith

)ther and daughter: Florah and Angeline.
Mathabane

Florah and her husband, Sipho.
Gail Mathabane

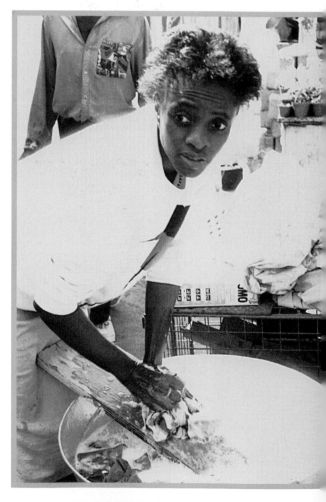

Florah washing laundry
in the tub, which is
also used for bathing.
Gail Mathabane

A Shangaan witch doctor in Granny's time, carrying the paraphernalia of his profession, along with shield and spears.
Johannesburg Africana Museum

Geli in front of her shack on 13th Avenue.
Gail Mathabane

Bushy flanked by her two daughters, Fikile ("She Has Arrived") on the left and Nkensani ("Thank You") on the right.
Gail Mathabane

Nkensani and her husband, Glen.
Gail Mathabane

...ldren outside their home in Alexandra.
Mathabane

...n outside Phuthadichaba feeding center.
...d Mathabane

Lines of people waiting to be fed at the Phuthadichaba soup kitchen.
Gail Mathabane

An initiation ceremony for *ngangas* (tribal healers) in Alexandra. The front three are holding *chovos* in their right hands, which are partly used to scatter *muti*.
Gail Mathabane

Maria's son Tsepo ("Faith"), who was born premature.
Gail Mathabane

How village maidens
dressed in Granny's time.
*Johannesburg Africana
Museum*

Granny,
her children,
and their children.
Gail Mathabane

A cluster of shacks in
Alexandra that sprang up
in an alley.
Gail Mathabane

Linda Twala, directo
Phuthadichaba, with
Community Builde
the Year awa
Phuthadich

phans waiting in line for their daily slice of bread at one of Linda's four feeding centers.
ny children lost their parents to factional violence and live in abandoned buildings and
yards.
Mathabane

white soldier in a *casper* truck, nicknamed "Mello Yello" by blacks, with its gun turrets.
Mathabane

Granny's father, Lazarus Khosa.
Khosa family

Granny in Giyane, outside daughter Mphephu's h
The Mabaso fa

Shangaan women in Granny's time, drawing water from the river in calabashes.
Johannesburg Africana Museum

...oman cooking in front of a traditional Shangaan hut and chicken coop.
...nnesburg *Africana Museum*

...y outside row of latrines, picking up empty tin cans to resell for food money.
Mathabane

Nkensani and Granny in 1992.
Gail Mathabane

Reuben, Florah, Piet, and Angeline gathered in the shack that Piet inherited from Geli and Jackson.
Gail Mathabane

...men and children at the Twelve Apostles Church of God. Geli is in first row, far left.
Mathabane

...a-Mahafa and Geli, former drinking buddies, now ardent church members. Mahafa's son, Herman, was burned alive.
Gail Mathabane

Granny's grandchildren and great-grandchildren. Back row, left to right: Tsepo (Maria's), Given (Maria's), Angeline (Florah's); front row, left to right: Khensani (Piet's), Vutshilo (Maria's), Sibusiso (Mirriam's).
Gail Mathabane

Geli and Jackson in Alexandra after thirty-five years of marriage.
Stedman Graham

24

GRANNY

AN EX-CONVICT
BECOMES A CHRISTIAN

When Reuben was released from prison it took him some time to readjust to society. Luckily Bushy was now working. After the rape and the death of her baby son she lost all enthusiasm for school. Also, there was no money to keep her there. It had been a struggle to get her to complete at least Standard Six (junior high). I had paid for her schooling with money I earned toiling as a gardener and selling beer on the side.

But I was so overwhelmed with the basic demands of survival that I could no longer afford the cost of books, school fees, and uniforms. So Bushy quit without ever finishing high school.

The only option left her was to look for work. Again it was a struggle to obtain all the necessary permits. Fortunately Bushy had a birth certificate showing that she had been born in Alexandra, and while Reuben was working as a clerk he had made sure we got a residential permit.

Once Bushy had her working papers she aggressively looked for work. She tramped all over the suburbs begging for jobs as a maid, and was willing to work for practically anything. After months of searching, she finally found a job as a sleep-in maid in Sandton, and her salary of R20 a month, meager though it was, helped pay the rent and Piet's school fees and provided Reuben with daily bus fare to go hunt for jobs.

For a long time Reuben had no luck finding a white employer willing to hire an ex-convict, for it was stated in his passbook that he had served time for armed robbery. Already in his thirties, Reuben was reduced to joining long lines of teenagers at the golf course waiting to caddy for white people. He thought the work degrading for someone his age, but he did it anyway.

He grew so increasingly frustrated at his inability to find a decent job that I feared he would soon yield to the temptation—which was everywhere—to take up with *tsotsis* again, commit crimes, and get sent back to prison. I didn't know what to do to prevent his yielding to the temptation. He was saved by the church.

Around this time my daughter Geli had left her old church and found a new one, the Twelve Apostles Church of God. She told me that the priests in her new church worked miracles. They were getting people jobs, permits, saving them from eviction, transforming husbands from deadbeats and abusers into responsible family men, and transforming prostitutes into self-respecting women and wives— all through the power of faith and prayer.

One day Geli came to my shack and told a skeptical Reuben about her new church.

"This is unlike any other church I've attended," she said with excitement. "And I've been to many. These are truly men and women of God. They're filled with the holy spirit. They have such a love for Christ that many of their prayers are promptly answered."

"I don't want to have anything to do with churches, sister," Reuben said. "There's no God. If there was a God why is mother suffering? Why have our lives been so miserable?"

"But God lives, Reuben," Geli said emphatically. "I doubted the fact myself until I discovered I'd been looking for Him in all the wrong places. I had been like the children of Israel wandering forty years in the desert. I went to countless false churches. Most of them wanted only money or had bizarre covenants. You remember the Donkey Church, the Seven Wives Church, and the Hundred Rand Net Worth Church?"

Reuben nodded.

"But the Twelve Apostles Church is different," Geli said. "They don't want your money. They give you money."

"How?" Reuben asked, sarcastically. "Do they own a bank?"

"They have something better than a bank, my dear brother," said Geli. "They can get you a job. They can help you reclaim your dignity and pride. You know the troubles I've had with the police? I was constantly being arrested because I had no proper permit and no job. And without a job I couldn't support my children and had to rely on Jackson, who squandered his wages every week gambling and drinking. Those troubles are now all but over. I now have a permit, and have lined up well-paying part-time jobs as a maid in white suburbs all over Johannesburg. I've so many job offers that I can't possibly fill them all, and have had to give some of them to neighbors. All because of the Twelve Apostles Church of God. Even Jackson's problems would end in a minute if only he became converted and believed. The brothers at the church plan to work on him, though. They're praying for him and intend to start visiting him in the hope of getting him to start coming to church."

"Good luck in reforming that *Mbvesha*," Reuben said, "let alone getting him to set foot in a church. He's the very Devil himself. Even if God were to appear before him he would never change his ways."

"Just you wait and see," Geli said with conviction. "This church is no ordinary church. The Lord says nothing is impossible for those who believe."

"Tell him how you came by this church of miracles, my child," I interjected. I had been listening eagerly to my daughter expounding the virtues of her church. Though I wasn't a regular church-goer, I was so anxious to see my son turn a new leaf that I was willing for him to try anything.

"That's a miracle in itself," Geli said. "You know Ma-Mahafa? She's a distant cousin."

"The one with the bad reputation?"

"Yes, the very one," Geli said. "Well, she was the first to tell me about the church. She took me there for my first visit. She no longer fools around with men, you know. She's now a staunch church member. And she no longer drinks. It's a miracle if you consider the sort of life she used to lead."

My daughter, having whipped herself into a frenzy of faith, went on to relate how she had come to know of the Twelve Apostles Church. The church was located in the yard next door to where she lived on 13th Avenue.

"But Satan was so bent on torturing me that I didn't even pay attention to this Rock of Salvation next door, waiting for me to come lean on it," she said. "I had heard of the church, but I had dismissed it as just another one of those black churches where Sunday collection was used as a measure of devotion. If you gave money, you were considered a good Christian. If you didn't or couldn't because you were poor, you were made to feel guilty."

"And you know where all that collection money goes," Reuben said. "It lines the pockets of the ministers and enriches the white men who started these churches in the townships."

"I don't know if that's true," Geli said. "But I've often wondered why some ministers live in fancy houses when they don't have regular jobs. Anyway, I became so frustrated with these kinds of churches that I stopped attending. The last one I attended was the Full Gospel Assembly of God. In the beginning everything was fine. They helped me stop drinking and one of the members helped me get a job.

"The job wasn't much, I worked three times cleaning toilets at the women's hostels. I made about R6 a week. But as soon as the minister heard I was working, he started demanding that I pay half my meager wages as a tithe. I told the minister that I couldn't do that because I desperately needed the money for survival. 'Other people need money too,' he said, 'but they give because it's their sacred duty to God.' I wanted to give but I couldn't. Then the minister began obliquely criticizing me during sermons. He called those who didn't tithe greedy and selfish and anathematized them as sinners. He predicted that they would be barred from entering the kingdom of heaven and their souls would roast in hell. I knew he was referring to people like me. So I stopped going. Then I found Christ's true church."

Geli told how she would often hear the Twelve Apostles Choir singing hymns while she was in the communal latrine. Their music—sung a cappella in various tribal languages—was sweet and comforting, and her spirit soared and thirsted for more. But still she never made any attempts to investigate the church.

One Wednesday afternoon Ma-Mahafa—whom she hadn't seen in a long time, since their drinking days—paid her a visit, accompanied by a group of four or five women. Geli happened to be off work that day, and the children were away at school. At first, Geli, remembering the old Ma-Mahafa, thought they were a drinking party come to pick her up to go to a *shebeen*. The women were from various tribes and included two Coloreds.

They greeted her as "Sister," and their faces radiated smiles and love. Geli welcomed them into her home and apologized for the house still being a mess. She served them tea.

Ma-Mahafa introduced the group, and while Geli fed Mirriam, her infant child, each of the women started testifying, telling her the good news about the Lord.

"In the beginning was the Word, and the Word was with God, . . . " began Ma-Mahafa, reciting verses from the first book of Genesis before launching into a testimonial on how she had met the Lord. She spoke eloquently about His Goodness and Mercy, and about the miracles He had wrought in her life once she believed in Him as her Savior and Lord.

"You know the sort of sinful life I used to lead," Ma-Mahafa said to Geli. "Drinking, sleeping around, fighting, swearing, and all those unclean things the devil made me do. They are now a thing of the past. I've been saved. I'm now a child of Christ. I'm a new person. Jesus has made me whole. I've found in Him the perfect lover and friend."

Each of the women gave similar testimonials about the sinful roads they had traveled before reaching the true church, and about being saved from eternal damnation by faith in Christ. They always began their testimonials with, "In the beginning was the Word, and the Word was with God. . . ."

The women testified and sang hymns praising God for about an hour, at the end of which they invited Geli to visit their church on Sunday.

"I'll think about it," Geli said.

"God loves you," Ma-Mahafa said. "He wants you to become His bride. With Him by your side you'll never know fear or despair. He'll work such wonderful miracles in your life that your past life will seem like a bad dream. All you have to do is open your heart to Him and let Him come into your life."

Sunday arrived. Ma-Mahafa was at Geli's door before she awoke from sleep.

"She helped me wash and dress the children," Geli told Reuben. "I hadn't informed Jackson about my intentions to go to church. He came into the kitchen in his pajamas and asked what was going on. I let Ma-Mahafa deal with him. She had a feisty temper and was a match for any man. But I wasn't prepared for the tactics she used. I had expected a shouting match, a battle of wills."

"What is all this hustle and bustle for?" Jackson demanded. "Where are you taking my wife and children?"

"We're all going to a party," Ma-Mahafa said, a smile on her face. "Do you want to come? You too are invited."

"What party?" Jackson asked.

"A wedding feast unlike any you've ever been too."

"Will there be drinks at this party?" asked Jackson. He was familiar with the old Ma-Mahafa, and knew that wherever she went there was bound to be great quantities of liquor.

"More than you can drink," said Ma-Mahafa. "And it's the best liquor you've ever tasted in your life. It will make you feel soooo gooood you'll never want to stop drinking it."

Jackson was more than interested. He must have thought he was about to stumble upon a spigot endlessly pouring forth ambrosia. He inquired where the party was being held so he could come as soon as he had washed up.

"It's just next door," said Ma-Mahafa. "There's no need to come alone, we'll wait for you. And don't forget to wear a coat and tie."

"What do I need a coat and tie for?" Jackson asked suspiciously. "I never wear coat and tie when I go drinking."

"Only people who look sharp are invited to this party," said Ma-Mahafa.

"Jackson donned a jacket and tie and off he went with Ma-Mahafa, the children, and me," Geli said, laughing. "You can imagine his astonishment and disgust when he found out that the special liquor he had hoped to feast on was the Word of God. He would have instantly stormed out of church had he not thought of the shame it would bring him. During the service, as he sat in the men's section, he felt most uncomfortable and was constantly fidgeting. Midway through the service he got up, saying he was going to the latrines. He never came back.

"He never forgave Ma-Mahafa for what he called 'making a fool of me,' but the miracle is that though he never went back to church himself, he didn't interfere when I and the children started attending regularly, as long as I remembered to do my household duties."

Geli completed the story of her conversion to Christ. Reuben was most intrigued and touched. He had always respected his sister and was desperate to improve his life. So he agreed to accompany Geli the following Sunday to see if Christ could work a few miracles in his life, as he badly needed one or two.

PART V

25

FLORAH

MY FATHER BURNS
OUR SCHOOL UNIFORMS

My mother's sobriety and her job at the Indian place brought us immediate relief. My siblings and I now had enough to eat, wore clothes better than rags, and were no longer ashamed to play with other children or to go to school.

I almost didn't go to school. Like many other African men of his generation who were raised in the homelands, received no education, and had been emasculated by apartheid, my father thought school a waste of time. He had beaten my mother for taking my brother there against his wishes, and for spending food money on school fees and books. So when it was my turn to go to school, he gave her another hard time.

Nursing her fifth child—my sister Mirriam—and unable to work, my mother approached my father for money to pay my school fees so I could be allowed to register. My father would have nothing to do with it.

"If you want them to go to school," he said, "you pay for their education. I have no money to waste. I'm struggling as it is to pay rent and feed the lot of you."

So my mother secretly went to the landlord and borrowed money to pay my school fees and buy me a slate and a primer. She paid the money back as soon as she resumed working.

I grew up fearing my father. I didn't understand him at all. The very sound of his voice set me trembling and crying. As a child I would sometimes urinate in my panties whenever he threatened to beat me for something I had done wrong.

There were, however, moments when he would reveal glimpses of kindness, like when he brought us children fish and chips on Fridays, or bought us cheap outfits for Christmas. But these moments were rare.

There is one enduring moment of his cruelty, a moment that forever etched his character in my heart and led me to hate him with an intensity that even frightened me. It happened when I had just proudly completed my third year of school, against great odds.

Many students had already dropped out by this time, for a variety of reasons: they had no money for school fees, books, or uniforms; or their families were being deported back to the homelands because they had no permits to live in the city; or their parents had lost their menial jobs; or they had to stay home baby-sitting younger siblings because their mothers needed to work.

It was a few weeks before Christmas 1973. My mother had been working for the large Indian family as a maid for a couple of months. Every day she would rise before dawn and set off for work on foot, only to return at sunset, exhausted but miraculously still able to do her household chores and tell us stories, which were a perfect substitute for the books we couldn't afford.

She had painstakingly saved her wages for a big Christmas surprise for my brother and me, in recognition of our fine work at school. My brother had again come out number one, and I was among the top five students in my class.

My mother returned home Friday and, as usual, my father gave her no money. Instead he went out gambling and came back flat broke, without a penny to his name. Having lost his week's wage, he was of course in a very bad mood. It was nearly midnight, but Johannes and I were awake on our bed of cardboards on the kitchen floor. On Fridays we often stayed awake until our father returned from his nocturnal gambling trips and banged on the door to be let in.

Now we heard him arguing with my mother in the bedroom.

"Why are you asking me for money?!" my father was shouting. "You're working, aren't you? You can start buying food and paying rent."

"But I'm saving my money to pay the children's school fees and buy them books," my mother said.

"Damn the bloody school," my father said. "Didn't I tell you not to send them to school? And you not only defied me once but twice. How did you think we'd pay for their schooling?"

"That's why I went to work."

"So you think I let you resume working so you can waste money on this school nonsense?"

"Who's wasting money?" my mother shot back. "What did you do with your wages tonight? Did you save them? Are they in the bank? Or have they gone to enrich those little boys you gamble with? They must be laughing at you each time you lose money you're supposed to be supporting a family with."

"Shut up," my father said. "What I do with my own money is my own damn business."

"What I do with my own money is my own business too."

"Just remember," my father threatened. "I warned you. If you spend money on frivolities, I'll put an end to your working."

The following day, Saturday, my mother took my brother and me to Seedat, an Indian store on 1st Avenue which specialized in school paraphernalia. Before we reached the store, she went behind a clump of bushes and unstrapped my little sister, Linah, one year old, from her back, and handed her to me. She then took off her faded dress, untied a rag around her waist, and removed from it several crumpled bills. She counted them and then beamed with satisfaction, saying, "It's all here."

"What's that money for, Mama?" I asked. I was with my mother behind the bush, and my brother was standing guard in front of the clump of bushes to warn my mother if any stranger approached while she dressed and strapped Linah onto her back.

"To buy you uniforms, my dear," she said. "This rag tied around my waist has been my bank for months."

"Uniforms!" I shouted excitedly. "Oh, thank you Mama! Thank you very much." I hugged her. I badly wanted a new uniform. The old one was now ragged and I always felt ashamed wearing it.

My mother and I emerged from the bush and I shared the wonderful news of new uniforms with my brother, who was thrilled. He too needed a pair of black shorts to replace the old patched ones. Then I remembered why my mother kept her money in a rag tied to her waist. It was the perfect hiding place because my father, whenever he had lost his wages and wanted my mother's money, would ransack the whole house searching for it, after he had chased my mother out of the house.

At Seedat my mother looked on proudly as I was outfitted in a new black gym dress, a white shirt, and brand new black shoes. My brother got a new pair of black shorts, a white shirt, and a school tie. The clothes were of the cheapest material, but to us they were gold. She even bought us notebooks, reading primers, pens, rulers, crayons, and smooth brown paper and plastic with which to cover our books.

It was the rule in our school that students cover their books rather than leave them naked. This was supposed to make the books appear pretty, but preserve them too. Teachers regularly conducted inspections on book covers, and those students found with uncovered books were whipped.

My brother and I were so happy and proud of our mother for all the purchases. Now we would look like normal schoolchildren, instead of constantly being punished for not having school things, and being laughed at by fellow students for being poor.

The clothes and school paraphernalia cost a fortune, much more than my mother had saved, so she made a down payment and got everything on layaway. On the way home she bought some mealies and chicken intestines for dinner, and we also stopped at Granny's to pick up George, Maria, and Mirriam, whom we had left there on the way to Seedat.

Granny was worried about my father's reaction to my mother's spending spree, but my mother told her that there was nothing he could do except curse her and threaten to beat her up, "punishment" she had become inured to.

We reached home at dusk. There was no sign of my father. My mother unpacked the bags and spread our clothes on the bed in the hope of having us try them on in front of our father when he came back.

"Don't show them to him, Mama," I said. "He won't like it."

"Oh, you know how your father is," she said. "He's only angry on Fridays. But today is Saturday and he's calmer. He'll realize his mistake when he sees how handsome you two look in your new uniforms. After all, when people see you, they'll remark, 'My, my! There goes the Mathabane's children to school. Look how sharp they are. Their daddy must love them to buy them new clothes.'"

My father came back.

"Where's dinner?" he demanded as soon as he entered through the door.

"It's cooking," my mother said, hurrying to the stove and inspecting the pots. "It shouldn't take long. I have a surprise for you, Jackson."

"What surprise?" Jackson said. "Where have you been all day?"

"I took the children shopping."

"Shopping for what?"

"That's my surprise," my mother said, as she pointed at the uniforms and school items spread on the bed.

"What the hell!" my father raged as he saw the items. "Didn't I tell you not to waste money on useless things? Why did you disobey me?"

"Come now, Jackson," my mother said in a placating voice. "These things are for your children, your own flesh and blood. They've been

wearing rags to school. What does that say about their father? With
these new uniforms people will now see that these children have a
father and that he loves them."

"I don't care what people say," said my father. "Now you march
right back to that store with those uniforms and things and get the
money back."

My mother was defiant.

"I won't do it, Jackson," she said. "Those children need to start
looking decent. They need to be like other children. I worked hard
to save enough money to buy them uniforms. And I'm not even done
paying for them."

"I say take them back," roared my father.

"I won't."

"Well," said my father with deadly intent. "We'll see if they'll get
to wear them."

At this he stood up, gathered the uniforms from the bed, grabbed
the primus stove, and stepped outside.

For a minute or so I was at an utter loss as to what he planned to
do. Only when I saw him dump the uniforms on the ground, open
the primus stove spout, and start pouring paraffin on the uniforms
did I realize his malevolent aim—he meant to burn them.

Even then I stood frozen where I was, along with my mother and
siblings, dazed and uncomprehending. My own father would not do
what this strange ogre was about to do, I thought, it must all be some
hideous dream.

But it was no dream. My father deliberately lit a match and flames
leaped up from the heap on the ground. My mother, brother, and I
snapped out of our trances too late to prevent him.

"You bastard! I hate you! I'll kill you! I hate you! I'll kill you! I
hate you!" my mother screamed, flinging herself at my father. She
had Linah tied to her back but was heedless of safety. He shoved her
away, and stood guarding the bonfire with cruel eyes. In desperation
my brother and I tried to distract him so that my mother could grab
the burning uniforms and stamp out the fire. We clutched at his legs

but he kicked us away. We pelted him with stones, with everything we could lay our hands on, but it made no difference.

Finally, when he knew that the uniforms were scorched beyond salvage, he slowly and silently walked away, back into the shack. By the door he turned his head toward my wailing mother, with whom we were standing in tears and grief around the smoldering heap.

"That should teach you never to disobey me."

At that moment, ten years old, I so hated my father I wished him dead.

My mother gathered us children and we trudged forlornly all the way to Granny's, where she related what had happened. Granny cried, so did Aunt Bushy, as they comforted my mother, Johannes, and me. Uncle Reuben and Uncle Piet were out caddying. When they returned and heard about the uniforms they were so mad they wanted to go beat my father.

"It's time we taught this *Mbvesha* a lesson he'll never forget," Uncle Reuben said. "He could get away with abusing you while I was still in jail. But no more."

"No, no!" my mother said. "Please leave him alone. He doesn't know what he's doing. He's a sick man."

I couldn't believe my ears. How could my mother be preventing justice from being done? Had she forgiven my father, and so quickly? I hadn't. I could never ever forgive him.

"Beat him, Uncle Reuben," I said lustily. "Beat him good. He's not my father. He's a bad man."

"Don't say that, child," my mother said. "Your father is a very sick man. That's why he burned those uniforms."

"He's not sick," said Uncle Reuben. "He knows exactly what he's doing. He thinks he can get away with it because you're a woman."

"Please don't hurt him," my mother pleaded. "He's very confused and troubled. He meant no harm. The children and I are fine, and that's what matters most, isn't it?"

"Why are you defending the bastard?" asked Uncle Reuben. "Hasn't he abused you enough? Are the horrible stories about what he's been doing to you and the children while I was in jail untrue!"

"They're true," my mother said. "But he didn't mean any harm. Whatever wrong he's done God has already punished him for. I pray for him every day. He'll change."

"He'll never change," Granny said.

"He will. We must have faith. God will help him change. He's suffered so much under apartheid. He gets no respect anywhere, so he takes it out on me and the children. Yes, he's to blame for his actions, but also apartheid is to blame for what it's daily doing to him, what it's doing to our men. It denies them jobs and it turns around and arrests them for being unemployed. Do you know how many times Jackson has been arrested for not having a job?" (My father had been arrested over a dozen times.) "And the few men with jobs get so little pay they start gambling to try to make ends meet. When they lose, as they often do, they drink to forget their pain and their impotence. I've seen this happening to Jackson over the years. Yes, he's to blame for what he does, but he needs help. You should know this better than I, Reuben. Look at what apartheid did to you. It denied you opportunities so you turned to crime. It's even more so with Jackson because he never went to school and continues to cling to tribal ways. I'm not defending him. He's hurt me a great deal. And I feel a deep pain in my heart over what he did tonight. But I want you to understand that Jackson is a sick man and needs help, not punishment. He's already suffered enough."

There was a long pause after my mother's lengthy and perplexing speech defending my father's actions. I thought my mother was mad. I didn't understand her attitude until years later when I was more mature. Then I saw that my mother was not only perceptive of the plight of black men under apartheid, but her actions were consistent with her nonviolent nature and her faith as a Christian. She abhorred violence of any kind. And since joining the Twelve Apostles Church she increasingly saw my father as a victim, more sinned against than sinning. She believed that he was not entirely to blame for his actions, that they were caused by the devil and the apartheid system, which to her were in cahoots.

Her faith made her determined to rescue my father from the clutches of these evil forces. Thus her daily attendance at church, her constant prayers, her tithing, her proselytizing, her attempts to share the gospel with my father—which he always rudely rebuffed. The more my father rejected any attempts to help him, the more my mother tried. She showed this same forgiveness and understanding toward all who did her harm. Many people thought her naive and even crazy, but she staunchly believed she was doing the bidding of her God. She explained her strange attitude by saying that Christ had told His disciples to love those who persecuted them, and when slapped on one cheek, to offer the other one rather than strike back.

Uncle Reuben broke the long silence by saying, "All right. I won't thrash him. But he must be told that this abuse has got to stop."

Uncle Reuben and Uncle Piet left together to go see my father. It was late at night. As they told the story later, they found my father in no mood to listen to reason. He hurled insults at Uncle Reuben and Uncle Piet, and demanded that his *lobola* be returned so he could get himself a better wife, one who was more obedient to his will and didn't regard herself as man of the house.

"So you refuse to change your ways?" Uncle Reuben asked him.

"I will change my ways for no one," my father said stubbornly. "Least of all a woman."

"You mean that if my sister came back you'll keep doing what you did this evening?" Uncle Reuben asked.

"This is my house," my father said. "And I paid *lobola* for your sister. She needs to learn to behave like a woman should. It's clear your mother didn't do a good job teaching her manners. Either her daughter starts obeying me or she stays out of my house."

"Has it ever occurred to you that you're the one to learn to behave? The one to stay out of this house?" Uncle Reuben said.

"This is my house," my father insisted.

"It's my sister's house too," said Uncle Reuben. "She's earned the right to live here by slaving for you all these years and bearing you children."

"Those are her duties," my father said. "I paid *lobola* for her, didn't I?"

"Don't tell me that rubbish about *lobola*," Uncle Reuben said angrily. "Paying *lobola* doesn't give you the right to abuse her. You can go to jail for that, you know."

"Who are you to talk like a policeman? You jailbird," my father said scornfully.

That was too much for Uncle Reuben. He grabbed my father by the collar with one hand and punched him in the face with the other. My father tried fighting back but he was no match for Uncle Reuben, who kept pummeling him until neighbors, drawn by Jackson's yells for help, came to his rescue.

"My sister is going nowhere," Uncle Reuben shouted at my father as the two were forcibly separated. "This is as much her house as yours. If you don't like it, pack your things and leave. My sister can take care of herself and the children just fine. If I ever hear that you've touched as much as one hair on her head, I'll be back. And next time you won't be this lucky, *Mbvesha*. Remember, I went to jail for a reason. And I won't blink an eye to kill a dog like you. They don't send people to prison for ridding society of the likes of you."

26

GELI

BATTLE OF
THE MATCHMAKERS

After being beaten by my brother Reuben, Jackson stopped physically abusing me. He still made threats, swore at me in front of the children, opposed every sensible suggestion or plan I made to improve our lives, denied me money to book myself at the clinic when I was pregnant with my seventh child, and bought the children nothing for school or Christmas. He did all this as a way of punishing me for what he called "insubordination unbecoming the woman he had bought." But this sort of treatment I could live with. I now had my own income, and no longer had to hide the fact that I was working.

I left the Indian place after my seventh child, Diana, was born in 1975. She was given the tribal name Mangalani ("Surprise"), because her pregnancy was a complete surprise, as I no longer wanted any more babies. After Diana was born, some friends told me that if I wanted no more babies, I could go to the clinic and get my tubes tied. I immediately jumped at the opportunity, and I told Jackson about it. He was against my having the procedure, but I went ahead and had it anyway. With all those children to feed and to keep in school, I wanted no more babies to interfere with my working.

I was now working as a maid for various white households in suburbs around Johannesburg. Four of my children were now in school, and even though I still earned little—I was paid R2.50 a day for washing laundry, ironing, and cleaning the house—I was able to pay for their schooling.

The Twelve Apostles Church became the center of my life. I attended services practically every day. I went to choir practice, visited the sick, went testifying door-to-door to win new converts for Christ, took my dreams to the priest to decipher their meaning, and punctually paid a tenth of my earnings each month as a tithe. I didn't mind tithing this time. In fact I did so heartily because the Lord had blessed me with so many miracles in return.

One of these miracles was my brother Reuben joining the church and rapidly becoming strong in the faith. He gave up liquor and gambling, and even stopped visiting *shebeens*. A few weeks after he began attending church he found a full-time job through one of the members, working at a Jewish bakery.

As a former thief, drunkard, womanizer, gambler, and smoker of *dagga* (marijuana), his testimony on how he came to embrace Christ was most powerful. He brought many converts for the church. People predicted that he would rise quickly in the church, and might easily be made deacon and perhaps priest.

But there was one obstacle in the path of his ambition. He needed a wife. The Twelve Apostles Church was a family-oriented church. Single men and women were encouraged to get married, preferably to other members of the church, brothers and sisters in Christ. Since single women outnumbered men, there was great competition for eligible bachelors, and matchmaking factions were constantly forming within the church.

One day Reuben came up to me and said that he needed my help in finding a suitable wife.

"You should have little trouble finding a wife," I said. "You have a job and are educated. You should be able to get any woman you want."

"I don't want just any woman, sister," Reuben said. "I want someone I can be proud to call my wife. I need a helper and a friend."

"I'm glad to hear you say that," I said. "Most men just need a slave. You see the sort of man I ended up with. I sure wouldn't want you to treat another woman's daughter the way Jackson treats me. I know you won't, but I'm just saying it. No man has a right to treat a woman like rubbish, even if he's paid *lobola* for her."

"But I still want to pay *lobola* for my wife," Reuben said. "I know men often abuse women because of it, but it's not so much because *lobola* is wrong. It's how men misuse their power."

"I agree *lobola* may serve a good purpose," I said. "It's part of our way of life. But I still believe it's easy for men to abuse it. That's why I want you to marry the right woman, so that whether or not you pay *lobola* for her, you'll still respect her and treat her right."

I knew that finding a woman for Reuben would be easy, but finding a good woman would be a major undertaking. Many women had been reduced to desperation in the search for spouses. They stopped at nothing to get a man. They had bags full of all sorts of tricks to snare an unsuspecting man. I sought to use my experience to protect Reuben from their traps and wiles.

For several months after this talk with Reuben I scrutinized single women in our congregation. As soon as word got out that Reuben was looking for a wife, factions broke out in the church for various candidates. Single women got their mothers and friends to lobby me hard. Each time I went to church, whether for choir practice or worship, or when I went testifying with a group of women, I was sure to be cornered and told that so-and-so would make the perfect wife for my brother.

Some women were recommended for their youth, as being most likely to bear my brother many robust children. Other women showcased their experience and maturity. Still others supported their cause by pointing to the fact that they were working, or that they already owned shacks into which Reuben could move instead of having to go through the arduous and uncertain process of applying for a permit and hunting for a place in an overcrowded ghetto.

My mother was in favor of an older, mature woman, preferably one from our own tribe.

"A Shangaan woman will provide him with stability," my mother said. "And she'll be familiar with our customs."

"But what if she's too old to bear children?" I asked.

"Of course, she shouldn't be too old to have any," my mother said. "I just meant she should be serious and mature. I don't want Reuben to marry one of those frivolous materialistic township girls. Remember what happened to my brother, Shibalu? I don't want the same to happen to Reuben. He's my oldest son. I want him to have a good family and to carry on the family tradition."

My mother, too, was approached by representatives of various women aspiring to be my brother's wife. As the competition among those desperate to get married intensified, animosities sprang up between various factions. Accusations flew back and forth about underhanded dealings. People started vilifying each other for resorting to witchcraft to win Reuben. I was indignantly told by some women that I had no right to exclude them as potential wives for my brother simply because they were older and had children.

Finally, realizing that the longer this process dragged on the greater the hard feelings it would produce within the church, I decided to inform my brother of my preference.

"I've been most impressed with Ruth, the daughter of Mangaso," I said to Reuben. "I've checked her background thoroughly. She's not yet twenty and has no children. She's been to ritual school, doesn't drink or smoke, and comes from a good family. And the *lobola* being asked for her is reasonable. I think she has the potential to make you a very good wife and to bear you as many children as both of you want and can support."

"I know the girl you're talking about," Reuben said. "She's caught my eye too."

"Do you want me to formally speak to her parents?"

"Let me think it over first, and get to know her a little," Reuben said. "But I approve of your choice, sister."

Reuben spent several weeks courting Ruth. They seemed to hit it off well, and I began eagerly anticipating having to lead a delegation of my relatives to Ruth's family to formally make a proposal of marriage. In no time the entire church was buzzing with the news of Reuben's potential choice of a wife.

I had assumed this news would put an end to all the bickering and name-calling, so that people could get back to worshipping in the true Christian spirit. But that was not to be. The factions that stood to lose out if Reuben married Ruth started spreading vicious rumors about me. They accused me of hating their favorites, of having maligned the reputation of older single women to reduce their chances, and of having long made up my mind to give my brother to Ruth.

One particular faction supported the claims of an older woman named Rachel, who already had had five children, two of whom had died. When Rachel's faction heard that Reuben was getting advice from me, they pushed harder than ever to bring him and Rachel together at every available opportunity. They thought that by so doing they would blunt my influence. Rachel asked Reuben to escort her to choir practice at night. She invited him to tea and to dinner, ostensibly to share the Word with him, but I knew her true motive. I don't know what exactly happened when the two were alone, but the results soon became clear.

The several weeks Reuben had requested to make up his mind about Ruth passed. Still he was undecided. Then one day he came to me and said, "Sister, I know you won't like this. But I think I've found the perfect wife. And it's not going to be Ruth."

"Who is it?" I asked, masking my disappointment.

"It's Rachel."

"Rachel!" I cried out in shock. "Why Rachel?"

"I know how you feel about her," Reuben said. "But I'm sure she's the wife for me."

"But isn't she a bit too old for you?" I said. "And she has all those children. Do you think she can still bear more? And will you be able to support them?"

"She's told me that she's fertile."

"And do you believe her?"

"Yes, I believe her," Reuben said. "Sister, you may be prejudiced toward Rachel because she's older and has three young children. But she's a good woman. She's suffered so much. The men she's been with abused her."

"Is that why you plan to marry her?" I asked. "Because you pity her?"

"No."

"Why is she your favorite then?"

"She's just so mature," Reuben said. "She knows how to treat a man. I like Ruth too but I'm afraid she's still too young."

"And aren't you bothered by the fact that Rachel is from another tribe, a Mosotho?"

"No. She's willing to learn our customs."

"Have you told Mama about this?" I asked.

"Not yet. I wanted you to tell her for me."

"Why?"

"Oh, you know the reason. She doesn't like Mosotho women. She still remembers that one of them made father abandon us. She blames them for our suffering."

"How do you yourself feel about marrying a Mosotho?"

"I have no problems with it," Reuben said. "Rachel should not be judged because of what some other Mosotho woman has done. She should be judged on who she is."

"Of course she should be judged on who she is," I said. "And I'm not saying she's not fit to be your wife just because she is a Mosotho, or because she's older. I'm saying she's not the wife for you because of the sort of woman I think she is."

"What sort of woman is she?"

"I've known Rachel since I joined the church," I said. "Don't be deceived by her meek exterior. She's the kind of woman who'll do and say anything to get what she wants. She wants you badly, that's obvious to everyone. And she's prepared to do anything to get you. But it's your life, my brother, and you're responsible for it. I can only advise you. Whatever you decide I'll go along with. If it's to be Rachel, then it will be Rachel."

"Will you still be my go-between then?"

"Of course, I'll be your go-between," I said. "I'm still your sister, after all, despite my disappointment at your choice. But I won't lie to you and say it won't be awkward. Rachel knows that I don't favor her to be your wife. But I'm prepared to forget the past and move forward. I hope she is."

"I know she is. I'll let her people know."

Reuben paid R60 *lobola* for Rachel. Her family wanted more, contending that Rachel's three sons constituted wealth for my brother as they would soon be old enough to work for him. But I pointed out that the boys would have to be supported, sent to school, and most likely would leave home to start their own families when they were grown.

And as for Rachel's value, there was no guarantee that she would bear Reuben any children. Thus, there was some risk for my brother in marrying her. I drove a hard bargain and so incurred the enmity of Rachel and her entire family, but they did their best to hide their resentment. They badly wanted the marriage to take place. Yet I felt compelled to speak my mind, even at the risk of being detested for it. One of my weaknesses is that I can never knowingly wear a mask to give people a false impression of my feeling and thinking, even if diplomacy calls for it.

It finally remained to inform Ruth that she was not to be the bride after all. It was a heartbreaking thing to do, as Ruth, though young, was passionately in love with Reuben and anticipated marriage.

"You're still young," I consoled her after breaking the news. "You'll find another good man to marry you."

"But I thought Reuben was in love with me," Ruth said, a look of pain in her eyes. "I gave my heart to him. I have a foreboding that I'll never marry after this."

"Don't say such things, dear child," I said. "Of course you'll marry. And you will find a good man. And you'll be happy."

I thought of my own long-lost love, David, and understood the pain Ruth was feeling. I remembered the torment I experienced during years of being married to a man I didn't love, a man who abused me, and I wondered if the same fate lay in store for poor Ruth. Tears came to my eyes at the thought. I silently prayed to God that Ruth would find happiness.

When Rachel and her family started making elaborate preparations for the wedding, Reuben suddenly developed cold feet. He confided in me that he was not sure that marrying Rachel was the right thing to do after all. As soon as word got around that the impending marriage between Rachel and Reuben was in jeopardy due to last-minute doubts on the part of Reuben, church matchmaking factions again resumed their intrigues. Reuben began courting a daughter of an underdeacon named ManGubeni, and even saw Ruth from time to time.

Rachel and her supporters blamed me for Reuben's vacillation. I protested that I had nothing to do with how Reuben felt about women. I admitted that I had made my preference known, but Reuben was a grown man and made his own decisions.

Rachel was more calculating, shrewd, and experienced with men than her two younger rivals. They were no match for her craftiness. Soon she had Reuben eating out of her palm again, and once more headed for the altar, albeit reluctantly.

A week or so after Rachel and Reuben were married, I ran into Ruth on the street. She stopped me to ask, in a tone of cheerful curiosity, how Reuben was doing. She doesn't yet know the bad news, I said to myself. When I told her that Reuben and Rachel were now married, and that he was about to move into her shack, a look of shock, followed by a look of pained disappointment, swept across Ruth's face. For a while she stood there without uttering a word.

"Is anything wrong, child?" I asked.

"Oh, nothing," Ruth said with a heavy sigh. "I wish him well, that's all. Tell him I'll always remember him. At least I have something I'll always remember him by."

"What do you mean?" I asked.

"I'm pregnant," said Ruth, dropping her eyes and staring at the ground.

"You're what?"

"I'm pregnant," she said. "And it's Reuben's child."

"Oh, my God," I exclaimed. "When did you find out?"

"Just recently."

"And you're sure Reuben is the father?"

"I'm positive," she said, apparently hurt by the question. "He's the only man I've known."

"Oh, my poor child," I said, hugging her. "Does your mother know?"

"Not yet," Ruth said. "I'm afraid to tell her. She's still very upset that Reuben hasn't married me yet. She thinks it's somehow my fault."

"Of course it's not your fault, dear," I said. "How could it be your fault? I'll talk to your mother. Should I tell Reuben about the baby?"

"Will it make any difference?" asked Ruth. "I guess it's too late now. But he's the father. At least he's got the right to know that."

I spoke with Ruth's mother about the painful dilemma her daughter was in. Her reaction was somewhat strange. She seemed quite pleased that Ruth was pregnant, and appeared confident that Reuben would leave Rachel and marry her daughter.

"That woman is as barren as the Kalahari desert," Ruth's mother said of Rachel. "Reuben wants children. And my daughter is about to give him one."

"But Reuben is already married to Rachel," I said.

"That doesn't mean anything," Ruth's mother said. "A woman who can't bear children is not fit to be wife. Reuben has the right to leave her and demand his *lobola* back."

"But we don't know yet if Rachel is infertile," I said.

"I know it," she said emphatically.

"I think I need to talk to Reuben about the whole matter."

I told Reuben the news that he had fathered a child. At first he was incredulous, then happy, then confused, and finally he didn't know what to do.

"You think I can get my *lobola* back from Rachel's family?" he asked.

"I don't know if that's possible," I said. "And how would that look? You made her a promise and you should keep it. If you left her she'd be the wronged party. You have to think of your reputation, especially in the church."

"So what should I do?"

"Whatever you do," I said, "you must support your child with Ruth."

"Should I tell Rachel about it?"

"I guess you have to."

"I don't think I should," Reuben said. "She'll be mad at me."

"But she's bound to find out," I said. "Ruth's mother will make sure everyone knows. Just do what you can to reassure Rachel that even though you have a son by another woman, she's still your wife. Hopefully she'll understand. I sure wish you'd married Ruth, though," I said with sadness and regret. "I have a feeling you would have been very happy with her. You'd even have a child already."

"It's too late now," Reuben murmured under his breath.

27

GRANNY

BUSHY IS HAUNTED
BY THE PAST

I wish my son had married Ruth. But he didn't, and much evil followed from his bad judgment. After Rachel married Reuben, off came the mask of fawning over him. She now ran his life, chose his friends, watched his every move, and even tried driving a wedge between him and Geli.

"I don't want that sister of yours in my house," she said to Reuben. "And I don't want you to help her in any way. She has a husband who should be taking care of her."

"But she's been so good to me."

"She may have been," Rachel said, "but you now have a family of your own to look after."

Rachel so disliked Geli that when Geli asked Reuben for help with paying Johannes's fees to attend secondary school, after he had obtained a first-class pass in his Standard Six examinations, Rachel said no. Fortunately Johannes's sterling academic achievements won him a government bursary, which paid for his school fees and books.

Time passed. It soon became clear that Rachel was indeed barren, as Geli had warned.

As for Ruth, she gave birth to a baby boy. Reuben, as the father, was duly informed. He was thrilled and promised to support the baby. He even began talking of possibly having Ruth as a second wife. Rachel would have none of it.

"I'm your only wife," she said. "If you ever marry that girl I'll kill you both."

Reuben abandoned the idea of a second wife. Ruth's poor little baby died a few months after he was born. Her grief knew no bounds. She was never quite the same afterwards. Eventually she went mad, and her mother, now an alcoholic who never stopped blaming Ruth for letting Reuben slip through her fingers, began abusing her, often beating her up with metal pipes.

Reuben felt terrible guilt over the loss of his son and about what had happened to Ruth, but there was nothing he could do. It seemed as if Rachel had cast a spell on him. Many times he spoke of leaving her, but he seemed unable to summon up the strength to do so.

My daughter Bushy had grown into a fine lady. She now had a steady job and dressed well. She began attracting the attention of suitors. She seemed to have overcome the trauma of the rape and the death of her baby, and looked forward with eagerness to the prospects of a married life. She was still living with me, having transformed the house into something we were immensely proud of. She bought a kitchen cabinet, a stove, a dining table with four chairs, a bed, and there was even linoleum on the kitchen floor. And she kept the three rooms spotlessly clean.

But her enormous help wasn't confined to her immediate family. From time to time she assisted her sister Geli in keeping her children in school. She was particularly fond of Johannes, who was now in high school. She regularly gave him money for books, lunch, and school trips to the segregated Johannesburg Zoo.

I was thrilled when Bushy fell in love with Mr. Brown, a bus driver who lived in Geli's yard on 13th Avenue. Mr. Brown was a self-made man who had quit school after a few grades to go to work. He had a passion for learning, and bought the newspaper every day. He hired Johannes to teach him to improve his reading and writing skills. He was taking correspondence courses toward earning his high school diploma and came to rely heavily on Johannes's help.

Bushy would tell me how each time she was with Mr. Brown, he would rave about Johannes's abilities as a teacher, going on and on about how they had done arithmetic, English assignments, and crossword puzzles together.

I had a sneaky suspicion that one reason Mr. Brown liked Bushy so much was because of Johannes. Soon Mr. Brown made it known that he planned to marry Bushy as soon as he had saved enough money for *lobola*. He already had a wife in the Venda homeland, but he assured Bushy that she would be her equal instead of being a junior wife. He planned to purchase a place in Alexandra for Bushy, so as to prevent any conflicts between her and his other wife. At first Bushy was uneasy about such an arrangement, and she talked to me about it.

"I don't know if I can share a man with another woman, Mama," she said.

"Granted it's not the ideal arrangement," I said, "but you love Mr. Brown, don't you?"

"Yes I do," she said. "Very much. He treats me very well. I would marry him in a second if it weren't for his other wife."

"I know from bitter experience that it's hard to share a man," I said. "Especially for the older woman. But women do it all the time. It's part of our customs. We have to because good men are hard to find. Most men who are the least bit successful have several wives, as you know. What's important is that the wives get along, and that your rights are protected. How does he propose to wed you? Does he plan to give you a ring?"

Giving a woman a ring meant having a civil marriage, in which case the woman had some rights. The traditional marriage of just paying *lobola* gave the woman no rights whatsoever, as I had bitterly found out.

"He says he wants to pay *lobola* but that we'll also have a civil marriage, if that's what I want," Bushy said. "His first wife was only *lobola*."

"That ring is very important," I said. "I'm speaking from experience. I didn't have it. So another woman with a ring took my husband away and there was nothing I could do about it. I was stuck with three children and no means of support."

"I'll insist on the ring," Bushy said. "And Brown says I can continue working even after we're married because he believes a woman ought to have her own income."

"That's a sensible man for you," I said. "My advice would be to marry Mr. Brown if you love him."

"I told him I needed some time to think it over," Bushy said. "He said I should take as much time as I want."

Word of Mr. Brown's proposal of marriage to Bushy spread quickly among neighbors and members of the Twelve Apostles Church, despite the family's attempts to keep the news a secret until things were firmed up. Many were happy for my daughter, but others were envious. They knew Mr. Brown was well to do, and they had daughters of their own they wanted to see married to such a man. They set to work to sabotage the marriage. Because there are so many single women in the ghetto desperate to get married, and so few eligible men, people were known to use witchcraft to ruin impending marriages.

I don't know exactly how my enemies, whomever they were, accomplished their evil design, but one afternoon Bushy came to me crying.

"My life is ruined," she sobbed. "There won't be any marriage for me."

"What do you mean?"

"Mr. Brown has called the whole thing off," said Bushy. "He says he's sorry to have led me on but that under the circumstances he can't marry me."

"Under what circumstances?"

"Someone told him about the rape and the baby," Bushy said.

"Oh, my God," I said in shock. "Who told him?"

"He said some woman—he won't reveal the name—came up to him and told him he'd be making a terrible mistake if he married a girl like me. She said I was a whore, that I had been pregnant several times, by different men, and each time killed the baby."

"Oh, my God," I cried. "How could people be so evil? Didn't you tell Mr. Brown the truth?"

"I tried telling him," Bushy said. "And he listened. But you know how it is when a lie has a grain of truth in it. I had to confess to him about the rape and my poor baby. He said that though he believed me, he could not go ahead with plans to marry me."

"I wish I could lay my hands on the witch who did this to you, my poor child," I said. "I would strangle her."

"But that's not all, Mama," Bushy said, sobbing even harder. "I just found out I'm pregnant."

"Please God!" I cried, as my heart was torn to pieces by pain. "What have I done that my poor daughter should be punished like this? Why not take my life and leave her alone?"

Bushy and I wept as we clung to each other. For a long time neither of us spoke.

I used my *mucheka* to wipe away tears from her face and mine, and I finally said, "What are you going to do about the baby?"

"Brown says he'll support his child," Bushy said.

"Do you think he'll keep his word?"

"I don't know. Whoever told him about my past has also been trying to convince him that I have lovers and it's not his child. You know the old man Maluleka, who owns a store on 7th Avenue and occasionally gives me rides to work?"

"Yes," I said.

"They told Brown that he was my lover."

"Did they?"

"Yes. Even though he's old enough to be my grandfather."

I was completely devastated. For a while I could say nothing, except to curse the witches who had done this to my daughter.

Finally, I spoke. "Well, both of us are working. We'll take care of the baby if Brown doesn't keep his word."

"Will I ever get married, Mama?" Bushy asked, in a voice full of doubt. "Will any man ever want me because of my past? Or will I forever remain damaged goods?"

"You *will* get married, my child," I said. "There must be a good, honorable man out there who won't hold the past against you, especially because you did nothing wrong. That wicked man took advantage of you."

I never found out the identity of the woman or women who had told Mr. Brown all those lies about my daughter.

Bushy lost her job when she took time off to have the baby. There was no such thing as maternity leave for maids like her. Bushy gave birth to a baby girl, whom we christened Fikile ("She Has Arrived") Adelaide. Without Bushy working, we were plunged back into poverty, and to make ends meet, we had to pawn most of the furniture Bushy had so proudly bought.

Our poverty led my youngest child, Piet, to quit school and join gangs. He never finished high school. Each day on my way home from a gardening job I would be met with news that his gang had been involved in a bloody street battle with other gangs, and that several boys had been knifed. Unlike in Reuben's day, gangs in the 1970s were younger, more violent, and fought over such things as turf and girls. They had names such as the Dirty Dozen, the Mongols, and the Gladiators. They often fought pitched battles in the streets with knives, tomahawks, and slingshots.

Knowing that Piet was into gangs brought back the nightmare days of Reuben's involvement with gangsters. Daily I begged Piet to quit gangs, but he responded by saying that they gave him something to do, a sense of pride, a place to belong. Nothing in our shack could compete with the powerful influence of the streets.

Piet was also embarrassed that women were supporting him.

"Since I'm the only man in the house," he said one time, "I should be the provider."

He and various gang members occasionally robbed stores and stole food. Sometimes they caddied at different golf courses, but they now had to be careful. The police were enforcing laws which gave them power to arrest any black man found "loitering" in white areas. Frustrated by the meager tips he was receiving from stingy rich white people after spending the whole day lugging heavy bags and chasing after balls, Piet and his fellow gang members sometimes attempted to steal golf bags and rob whites, a crime for which they could have been sent to jail for a long time.

Piet was saved from the dead-end life of gangs and stealing when his older brother, Reuben, took him aside and told him all about the hardships of prison.

"It's like slavery, young brother," Reuben said. "Whatever little freedom you now enjoy as a fourth-class citizen is taken away. You spend days working on chain gangs. The Boers beat you up at random. They can even kill you and nothing will be done to them. You never want to end up in the slammer doing time, young brother, it's not worth it. So stop leading the sort of life that is sure to land you there."

Luckily, Reuben backed up his sound advice with finding Piet a job at a garment factory near the bakery where he worked. But before Piet could take the job, he needed to have the proper permit. So I spent several weeks shuttling between his former school, the clinic, and government offices begging for the proper stamps, certificates, and papers allowing him to legally hold a job. Fortunately I wasn't given too much of a hassle because with my last savings I bribed a Zulu man who worked as a clerk at the offices and lived in our yard.

Piet was paid very little at his job as a garment worker—about R12 ($4) a week—but it was better than the dangerous life of the streets and gangs. He augmented his salary by filching irregular trousers from the factory, which he sold or gave to needy relatives.

As soon as her baby was old enough to take the bottle, Bushy started hunting for jobs. She found one as a maid serving tea in the offices of a large company on the outskirts of Alexandra. Bushy having a job relieved Piet of the enormous responsibility of paying for most of our family expenses of food, rent, and fuel, and he was able to save enough money to afford *lobola*.

His wife was a sweet, short woman named Thandazo ("Prayer"), Joyce's sister. We all crammed into the two-room house because Piet could not afford a shack of his own. It was not long before I realized that Piet was an abuser. Thandazo was a bit lazy, and Piet began beating her for neglecting to cook, clean the house, or wash laundry.

"All you do all day is sleep and eat!" he would shout at her, whenever he came home from work and found laundry scattered all over the floor, dirty dishes piled up, and the bed unmade. He would then whip her with a belt or slap her. Sometimes he would beat her so badly that her eyes were swollen and she could hardly walk.

I always tried to intervene whenever the beating occurred in my presence. I didn't want to be like other mothers who actually goaded their sons to beat their lazy wives. But Piet would shove me away. "Butt out, Mama, or I'll beat you too!" he would threaten.

Piet's abuse stemmed partly from the stress and pressures of having to support a wife and contribute to the family on a pittance, and partly from bad habits. Shortly after he began working, he started drinking and betting on horses. When I asked him why he did those things, seeing they were likely to ruin his life, he said, "I'm not making enough at work so I need another way to earn money."

"But gambling isn't a way to earn money," I said. "It's a sure way to lose it."

"There's always a chance that I'll strike it big," he said. "How else can I make enough money?"

"By working."

"But I already work seven days a week, including overtime," he said. "Still I don't earn enough to support my wife and child [he and Thandazo now had a child], let alone help you and Bushy. I need to make more money somehow. You don't want me to start robbing people, do you?"

"No, I don't."

So I turned a blind eye to Piet's gambling. Of course he lost more often than he won, and I found myself having to support him, his wife, and son on my wages as a gardener. But I was in a way glad that at least he was not a *tsotsi*, as many young men his age were. That sort of life always led to an early grave. Young men were dying like flies in the ghetto, at the hands of each other.

But a greater killer of young black men was still to come, mowing down women and children as well, by the hundreds. The only crime of the thousands who died was that they were black and dared to fight for their freedom, to demand a better life, to want to be treated like human beings in the land of their ancestors.

The year 1976 changed more than the political landscape of South Africa—it left most black people with a different sense of who they were. It made them more determined, meaner, more reckless, and more desperate. It touched the lives of everyone, young and old, from every tribe, and permanently changed the way we lived. Many of us were destined never to come out of the nightmare alive, but those who did had harrowing stories to tell.

28

FLORAH

THE NIGHTMARE
YEARS

The year 1976 seared itself into the consciousness of most South Africans. It was a watershed year. It irrevocably altered the social and political landscape of South Africa. It forever changed my life. I finally came of age. Ritual school was supposed to make me into a woman, but it was the rebellion of 1976—when students in ghettos all over South Africa rose up and demanded that apartheid stop enslaving their minds—that matured me.

Like most people, I was swept into the rebellion by the rush of events. I didn't even understand what it was all about until later. All I knew was that the illegal white minority government we despised had just announced that black students had to be taught all subjects in Afrikaans, the hated language of our oppressors.

Students in Soweto led the battle against the Afrikaner decree. On Wednesday, June 16, a phalanx of policemen had opened fire, unprovoked, on a crowd of about ten thousand students marching peacefully through the streets, killing several of them. As soon as news of the massacre reached Alexandra, students in tribal schools all over the ghetto instinctively knew that the cause of Soweto students was their cause also.

The next day, June 17, I went to school as usual. But one could sense the tension and excitement in the air. Principals and teachers advised students to remain calm, to do nothing foolish, but our seething rage made us ignore them and stream out of classes into the streets.

Students from various tribal schools quickly joined each other in common cause. In the past we had been rivals, divided by tribe and by class, but now we were comrades, united in the same struggle against a common oppressor.

"Away with Bantu [Black] education! Stop feeding our minds poison! Away with apartheid! *Amandla Awethu!*" We chanted as we marched in protest along the dusty streets, our ranks swelling each minute by the unemployed, *tsotsis,* the homeless, the hungry, the poor, and anyone who saw the uprising as the perfect opportunity to loot, to terrorize, and to kill.

We soon became a mob run amok. We attacked everything identified with oppression or exploitation. We smashed, looted, and burned government buildings, stores, buses, and any delivery truck we encountered in our defiant march. We especially targeted businesses owned by Indian and Chinese merchants, many of whom we felt had grown rich and arrogant from exploiting us.

I was part of a mob of over two hundred. As we moved from street to street, from one target to another, we sang freedom songs and chanted the hallowed names of those who had devoted their lives to the liberation struggle: Steven Biko, Robert Sobukwe, Nelson Mandela, Walter Sisulu, Winnie Mandela, Govan Mbeki, Joe Slovo.

These names had been unknown to most of us, but we chanted them with passion and with pride, making up for all those years we were forbidden to even utter them. We had no chosen leaders. Older students and anyone who was brave enough to be the first to smash a window, or hijack a delivery truck, or throw a stone or petrol bomb, instantly gained followers and influenced the course of the rampage.

Within a week, what had begun as a student rebellion over inferior education was transformed by our anger and abject poverty into a battle against the apartheid system, an endless orgy of looting and pillaging and burning to satiate our rage and hate. By falling into this inescapable trap of rioting and chaos, we became sitting ducks for the hundreds of police and soldiers who were swiftly dispatched to overrun Alexandra and seal it, as a way of protecting panic-stricken whites in the neighboring suburbs who thought a black revolution was under way. Whites were reported to be arming themselves to the teeth or fleeing the country in droves.

We had no idea that the simple words *Amandla! Awethu! Power to the People!* could so frighten whites that the government would, before 1976 ended, unleash its awesome military power on children armed only with anger and stones, resulting in over five hundred dead. Hundreds more were detained without trial and tortured. Thousands fled into exile.

Of the hundreds who died, one was a close friend, Mashudu, the fifteen-year-old daughter of a tailor on 13th Avenue who had two wives. One wife was in the homelands, and the second, Mashudu's mother, lived with the man in Alexandra and had five children—two girls and three boys.

Mashudu's father—a short, gray-haired, soft-spoken man—was also the landlord's caretaker. He collected rent, settled disputes between neighbors, and made sure we kept our shacks clean. Mashudu's father often loaned the family money whenever my father had gambled away his last cent. He also arranged the rotating schedule for the cleaning of the two outside latrines serving nearly a hundred people in the different families who lived in the yard. He fined and evicted all those who shirked their communal duties. He was a terror to children who misbehaved, and his favorite form of punishment was whipping with a cane or pinching one's ears.

A few days after the student-led rebellion turned into an all-out riot, mobs of blacks, armed mainly with rocks, bottles, petrol bombs, and an occasional gun, began fighting running street battles with riot police riding in armored cars and armed with tear gas and automatic rifles. Mashudu, fearless and adventurous, wound up in the thick of things.

At first the government didn't take the uprising seriously. It kept insisting that the rebellion in the ghettos was the work of communist agitators, that black schools should stay open. This was a ploy to take students off the streets and confine them in the classroom, where they could be more easily controlled and, if need be, arrested in surprise police raids.

Mashudu, Joyce, and I would leave home early in the morning pretending we were headed for school. In reality we would skip school and join giddy mobs marching from street to street, breaking into stores and torching government buildings, while chanting black power slogans and singing revolutionary songs.

We were young and daring. We were not fully aware of the consequences or dangers of what we were doing. We had been sucked into the vortex by the energy, the joy, the exuberance, the madness of the chaos. Everything gave us an exhilarating sense of freedom. We had no fear of death. We thought ourselves invincible. As bullets zipped past our heads, and as tear gas canisters landed in our midst and we fled for cover, we thought it great fun and couldn't wait to get back home and relate the stories of our adventures to incredulous family members and those peers we called cowards for staying home.

When my father heard that I had been part of a mob during the day, he thrashed me. "If I ever hear that you've been out in the streets again," he said, "I'll make sure you remain bedridden until this whole silly thing is over. Who are you to think you can defeat the whites? You'll only be sitting ducks."

My father was partly concerned for my safety, no doubt. But he was also carrying out instructions the regime had been broadcasting to black parents to discipline their children and not allow them to be misled by "communists and terrorists." This was clearly an attempt by Pretoria to exploit tribal customs for political gain. The regime knew that parents traditionally had absolute control over their children, and thought it possible that the rebellion could be quelled by appealing to conservative traditional values.

But Mashudu and Joyce paid no heed to traditional values. They were born rebels. They continued sneaking out of their homes and joining mobs who roved about the township perpetuating the anarchy and rendering the ghetto ungovernable, as the ANC exhorted in its clandestine radio broadcast from Lusaka.

One day I asked Mashudu if she wasn't afraid of getting killed.

"We all have to die someday, Florah," she said. "And before the riots came people were dying everyday in the ghetto. Hunger killed them, *tsotsis* killed them, the police killed them, and diseases killed them. All because of apartheid. Now we are smashing the apartheid system to pieces."

"But aren't your parents mad at you?"

"My dad warned me to stop," Mashudu said. "But my mother told him to leave me alone. She's pleased that I'm bringing her lots of things. I've already brought home blankets, dishes, stereos, sofas, and other things we can't afford."

Joyce gave a similar rationale for daily taking to the streets. But my mother remained adamant that I not join mobs.

"But we need food and things too, don't we?" I said.

"Yes, we do," she said, "but I don't want you to get killed either. Your life is worth more than all the blankets, food, and furniture your friends are bringing home. Those things can be replaced, but you can't be replaced."

"But you let Johannes and George join in the protests," I said. While I and my sisters remained grounded, my brothers came and went as they pleased.

"I don't like them jiving for power either," my mother said ("jiving for power" was my mother's description of rioting). "But they're boys and can take care of themselves."

"That's not fair," I said.

"Tell that to your father."

So I stayed home, spending my time gazing longingly through the small kitchen window at the turmoil outside, or helping my mother and other women from the neighborhood attend to hollering children and infants being choked by the stinging tear gas. We would dab their eyes and noses with rags soaked in water to give them relief. The soldiers had taken to lobbing tear gas canisters into yards in an attempt to confine blacks indoors. But many homes and shacks were so flimsily built that the tear gas sipped in through cracks. One infant even suffocated to death from tear gas, and the gas also wreaked havoc on the elderly and those with asthma.

At the end of each day of rioting, if there wasn't too much tear gas outside, I would be among the group eagerly congregated around Mashudu and Joyce, as the two recounted their daring exploits and exciting adventures. My mother saw the hold that Mashudu and Joyce had on me, so she went to speak to both their mothers.

"My daughter is not your problem, Musadi," Joyce's mother said. "So leave her alone."

Mashudu's mother said essentially the same thing.

One afternoon Mashudu was shot while with a mob that was looting a Chinese store. My brother Johannes and Joyce were with her. Joyce came running home crying and screaming. She said Mashudu had been shot, that blood was all over her gym dress, and that after she had been shot the police had dragged her body and dumped her into a truck, along with other dead and wounded.

Joyce wasn't sure whether Mashudu was only wounded or dead.

"But she didn't move after the bullet hit her," Joyce said.

The truck, loaded with moaning bodies and mangled corpses, did not go directly to the clinic or mortuary. Instead it had roamed all over the township for several hours, picking up more wounded and bloodied bodies and corpses, and piling them upon each other. The soldiers who drove the truck paid little attention to the cries for help from the wounded. Those who were lucky to be alive at the end of the day had been taken to hospital and placed under arrest while being treated. The dead were dumped at a makeshift morgue at the police station.

Parents recounted horror stories of searching for their children among rows of corpses.

When Mashudu's mother heard of her daughter's fate, she wept uncontrollably, "Oh, my daughter, my poor daughter! What have they done to you?"

Mashudu's father, though grief-stricken too, simply said, "I warned you woman, that you should keep that child inside the house like the other mothers did theirs. But you were more interested in the goods she was stealing than in her safety. Look now what's happened. You have only your greed to blame."

But that wasn't the end of the pain for Mashudu's mother. She and her husband went to the police station searching for their daughter's body. After the agonizing process of inspecting various disfigured corpses, they at last found their daughter. She was dead. She was still wearing her school gym dress, which was caked with dried blood.

They had to pay for the corpse before they could take it home for burial. An autopsy revealed that she had not died instantly after being shot, but an hour or so later from untreated gunshot wounds.

The memory of my friend Mashudu stayed with me through the years. And whenever I was in pain, confused, or in need of strength or courage to do something, I would think of her. Mashudu was a born rebel, unafraid to die.

Mashudu was on my mind when I ran away from home in the summer of 1979 because I could no longer stand my father's abuse. Our latest confrontation involved a kitchen I had bought with money I earned from working as a cashier at Checkers, a grocery chain.

I was now the family breadwinner. My brother Johannes had left the year before for America on a tennis scholarship. Before his departure, while he still worked for Barclays Bank in Johannesburg, he had paid my way through secretarial school when black schooling became sporadic because of the violence and boycotts. At the time, Johannes told me that vocational training was one way for me to stay out of trouble and to prepare myself for the future, uncertain as it was.

"The riots will be over someday," he said. "And you'll need an education or some skill to make a life for yourself."

"But what about the call for 'Liberation before Education?'" I asked. "Student leaders say we should only go back to school after we've won our freedom. Otherwise all those who have died since 1976 would have died in vain."

"Freedom may be a long time coming," Johannes said. "But even when it does finally come, it can only mean something to those who are educated and can take advantage of it. Freedom will mean very little to people who can't read or write, or don't have the qualifications to hold the jobs now monopolized by whites."

I had always respected my brother. I heeded his advice. He had succeeded against great odds, by doing things that were unpopular or brought him ridicule and even endangered his life, things like reading books, shunning gangs, and playing tennis with whites. I went ahead and took the secretarial training course, for which he paid in full.

Now that I was working at Checkers and he was gone, I attempted to fill his shoes by helping the family. We were now a family of eight. The responsibility of supporting so many people on a meager salary of R80 a week was daunting, which is why I often stole groceries, or, as we blacks were fond of putting it, paid myself the wages I deserved.

This is how I did it. On a Friday or Saturday, the busiest days in the store, I would ask either my brother or sister to come and buy groceries. They would fill shopping carts with steaks, chicken, rice, peanut butter and jam, cereals, toilet paper, soap, and numerous items we couldn't afford, and then they would check out through my lane. I would pretend to ring up the items, whereas in reality I only rung up one or two, and my siblings would end up paying a few pennies for groceries worth over a hundred rands.

It was this sort of "help" with the groceries that freed up enough of my wages to enable me to make a down payment on a new kitchen unit as the first step toward refurbishing the shack. I meant it as a surprise to my parents. I thought they would be pleased that I was spending my earnings helping improve our lives instead of buying things like clothes and shoes for myself, as some young people who worked did.

My mother was thrilled with the purchase but my father saw things differently. He was furious.

"I don't want that damn thing in my house!" he inveighed.

"But the child meant well, Jackson," my mother said. "She wants us to be better. You should be proud of her instead of castigating her."

"Shut up, you," my father snapped. "I said I don't want that damn thing in my house and that's final. If I find it here I'll chop it to pieces with an axe."

The kitchen unit was to be delivered in a few days.

"But why are you against our improving our lives?" I asked my father.

"Because it's a damn waste of money, that's why," my father said. "If we need any furniture, I'll make it."

"You'll make it!" I cried, rolling my eyes. "What have you made to improve this dump?" My father was a jack-of-all-trades and master of none. He always bragged about his skills as a carpenter and builder, but he had done little to improve the appearance of the various shacks we'd lived in. Yet he opposed my mother's and my attempts at home improvement.

I was in a dilemma. I couldn't send the unit back because I had already made a down payment on it and the Indian store where I bought it had an "all sales final and no refunds or return" policy.

The kitchen unit was delivered Saturday afternoon while my father was away drinking. As soon as he came back and found it in the kitchen, he dragged it outside in a downpour and left it to soak.

"Tell the store where you bought it to come pick it up," he said.

"Damn you," I cried, as I stood helpless and drenched next to the kitchen unit. "I hate you! You're so stupid you don't even realize that this dump of a place needs improving! Only animals like you can stand to live in this shack the way it is."

"You can insult me all you want," my father hollered from the door. "But that damn thing won't come into *my* house."

Distraught, I ran to Granny's place, weeping. I found Uncle Piet home and told him what had happened. We waited for the rain to stop and then he accompanied me back home and confronted my father.

"Either you let this kitchen unit be moved back into the house or I'll beat you up," Uncle Piet said to my father, as he menacingly shook a fist in his face. The two were standing face to face by the door. Uncle Piet towered over my father. In a fight between the two, my father would be no match for Uncle Piet, who had been toughened by his years with street gangs.

"You have no right to tell me how to run my house," my father said in a fake loud voice, trying to hide his fear of Uncle Piet.

"And you have no right to abuse my sister and her children," Uncle Piet snapped back. "Now get out of my way before I throw you aside."

My father meekly stepped aside, muttering curses under his breath.

Uncle Piet, my mother, and I proceeded to haul the kitchen unit back into the house.

"Now get this straight," Uncle Piet said to my father after we had moved the kitchen unit. "This unit stays right where it is. If you try to take it out again, I'll come and kill you, understand? I mean it. I'll kill you, so help me God."

The kitchen unit stayed but I could not. Afraid of Uncle Piet, my father started making my life miserable. He constantly threatened, criticized, and yelled at me. The psychological abuse became unbearable. Running away, I felt, was the only solution.

I stayed away from home for more than a year, living with Florence and her husband in Soweto, working at various part-time jobs. No one knew where I had gone. I believe I would have stayed away indefinitely had my mother not gone mad.

29

GELI

I'M DRIVEN INSANE

My daughter's running away left me devastated. I felt so helpless and overwhelmed with responsibility, and I had nowhere to turn. She had been my chief aid. Her income had been indispensable. She had helped me with groceries and rent payments because Jackson no longer spent any of his money on the family. She had also paid the medical bills of family members who got sick because we had no health insurance. She had been my emotional support in trying times.

And I had relied on her to keep her younger sisters away from the temptations of the streets and early sex. But now she was gone. I had to deal with everything alone, including paying off the kitchen unit that had led to her running away.

I cried every night. I prayed. I wished my son Johannes had not gone to America. It had been nearly three years since he had left, in August of 1978. Since that time I had only received two letters from him. He sent them shortly after he arrived in America to tell the family that he was safe and missed us. Since then there had been only silence.

It later turned out that the police began intercepting the letters he wrote to us as soon as he became an activist and went about telling Americans about the true condition of black life in South Africa. He and other South Africans living and studying in America did this in the face of an intense propaganda campaign by Pretoria designed to deceive the American people into believing that nothing was wrong with apartheid, and that blacks were happy as fourth-class citizens.

I could not turn to relatives for help because they were consumed and overwhelmed with their own troubles. The riots had led to wholesale layoffs of black workers living in townships in and around Johannesburg. Blacks from the homelands who were apolitical and more obedient to white authority were hired as replacements. Reuben lost his job, and so did Piet, even though they were not politically active. To be from Alexandra was often enough to earn one a dismissal. Piet and Reuben were able to find new jobs, which paid less, only after they pledged to their white employers that they would not take part in any political activities, and would not honor any calls for strikes or boycotts, even at the risk of their lives.

With nowhere to turn, and with Jackson continuing to waste his life in drinking and gambling, I took my troubles to one of the priests at the church. I expected advice and hoped for consolation from him, as other priests had given me in times past when I had gone to the them about family or work-related problems. But this priest wasn't a true man of God. For some reason he didn't like me.

"I won't pray for you," he said bluntly, almost shouting at me. "You're a bad influence on the wives in the church. You're constantly complaining about your husband. A woman should never speak ill about her husband. She should honor and obey him, as the Bible says. So return to your husband, woman, and do his bidding, and you'll find peace."

The priest proceeded to quote Scripture to support his demand that I return to bondage and abuse.

I went back home crestfallen. Yet I was determined to do everything I could to keep my family together or die trying. Not only was help not forthcoming from Jackson, but he was constantly blaming me for having allowed Johannes to go to America.

"I told you that too much education and playing that silly white man's game called tennis would ruin that boy," he harangued me one time. "Now we're lost without him. We'll never see him again. He may as well be dead. And it's all your fault."

"But in America he'll attend university and be able to get a good job when he comes back," I said, despite doubts that my son would ever return to South Africa. "What would he have amounted to had he stayed here?"

"Wasn't he already working at the bank and earning good money?" Jackson retorted. "What did he need more schooling for? Hadn't he already learned enough? Had he continued working for that bank, which treated its black and white employees the same, he would be well on his way to the top by now. We would be living in a mansion and well taken care of. So don't bother me about support. I wouldn't even have to work if Johannes were still here."

A further proof that I would get no help from Jackson and should expect none came when he was struck by a delivery van. He wasn't badly hurt, but his arm was twisted and he couldn't work for weeks. A shrewd neighbor, who knew how to sue for damages in accidents, helped get Jackson a settlement of nearly R100 from the driver's insurance company. Jackson gave me none of the money. He didn't even give the man who had helped him a penny to show he was grateful. Instead, he gave the money to a *shebeen* queen in the next yard for safekeeping. The *shebeen* queen was crafty. She kept giving Jackson drinks for free until one day she told him that all his money was spent.

The heavy responsibility of supporting the family alone forced me to take the only job I could find—cleaning offices at night. I set off for work around five in the afternoon and returned home around four in the morning. I was part of a cleaning crew of five women, and we walked all the way to work, even in winter. It took us an hour and a half to cover the distance. We were particularly concerned about safety during the trip back, afraid we'd be raped or killed in the dark. Ever since the riots and wholesale layoffs which swelled unemployment, Alexandra was rife with thugs and rapists who infested a particular strip of Alexandra we had to cross on the way home.

During the day, instead of sleeping and resting, I had to work. I baby-sat a group of children whose parents were away working the day shift. As a result, I got only one or two hours of sleep a day. I would sometimes fall asleep while operating the heavy cleaning machines, but despite the strain, I kept plodding on. Weekends also offered no respite. On Saturday I did laundry and shopping, then spent all Sunday at church, praying for God's help, and for my daughter Florah to come back home.

My prayers were answered. One day word reached me that Florah had been spotted entering a shack in Soweto. I sent Piet to go fetch her. Piet traveled by bus and train all the way to Soweto, found the shack, and knocked at the door.

Florah, when she opened the door, was so shocked at seeing her uncle that she could only exclaim, "Oh! Uncle Piet!"

"I've come to take you home," Piet said. "Your mother needs you. She's very worried."

"Okay," Florah said, "I'll come with you. First let me go pack my stuff."

Florah went into the back room, slipped out through the back door, jumped a fence, and disappeared. She stayed at the home of a friend until a bewildered Piet left, realizing that she had once more gone into hiding. But a week later Florah realized that she was wrong in staying away and leaving me without help. She came back home crying, and promised never to run away again, even with Jackson's tyranny.

Shortly after Florah returned, Jackson did the unthinkable. Unemployed and needing money to support his heavy drinking, he rented out a corner of our already overcrowded two-room shack to one of his drinking buddies, Mathebula. Mathebula and his family of six had just been evicted from their own two-room shack, smaller than ours, which the landlord wanted to subdivide into four shacks so he could quadruple his rent income.

So many people were without permits to qualify for decent housing that they were willing to pay anything for a roof over their heads. Unscrupulous landlords took advantage of the situation by evicting tenants of larger shacks so they could split them up to accommodate the unending demand for housing.

Mathebula, his wife, and five children—four sons and a daughter—all squeezed into the already overcrowded ten-by-fourteen-foot kitchen that was sleeping quarters for my six children.

"How can you do this?" I asked Jackson. "We don't have enough room as it is for the family."

"It's my house," Jackson said. "I need money, and you refuse to give it to me. Mathebula will pay me rent."

"And where will your children sleep?"

"Florah has a boyfriend," Jackson said. "They can go live with him." Florah had just begun seeing Collin.

"But they aren't married yet," I said.

"Then let her boyfriend bring me *lobola*," Jackson said.

Though I was against letting my daughters live with their boyfriends before marriage, I allowed Florah to because twelve people now slept in the kitchen. There was no privacy. At night the table and chairs had to be moved into the bedroom or piled upon each other to make room for sleeping. My children packed themselves like sardines on one side of the kitchen near the old coal stove, while Mathebula and his family did the same on the other side.

Mathebula so liked the arrangement that he began talking about how nice it would be if one of his sons married Florah so our two families could be permanently united. I was appalled by this proposal, and saw it as part of Mathebula's plan to gain a permanent foothold in our shack. He knew he had Jackson, then thoroughly alcoholic, under his thumb as he was constantly buying him drinks. But he was wary of me.

Mathebula had a reputation as a wizard. I feared that he might resort to witchcraft to gain his end. Shacks were at such a premium that people did not hesitate to kill for them. But I placed my trust in the Lord, and daily I prayed fervently that He protect me from Mathebula's supernatural powers.

One day I started getting splitting headaches. They grew progressively worse. I couldn't think, I couldn't remember anything. Soon I was unable to work at my night job or care for the children during the day. My income vanished. Granny helped look after my children, and George skipped school to caddy at the white golf courses. The tips he earned, along with Florah's meager pay working at a flower shop, kept the family alive. By now I was totally incapacitated.

Then I started talking to myself. I refused to wash. I would get up in the morning and walk up to the entrance of the yard, where I sat all day picking up stray pieces of paper and "reading" them aloud to passersby, thinking they were letters from my son in America. Knowing I was illiterate, people would laugh at me, which angered me, and I would curse them. In better moods I would sing songs to myself about how pretty and kind I was. At other times I sang church hymns or, convinced I was a priest, I would deliver fire-and-brimstone sermons to the dogs scavenging among the garbage rotting along the streets.

Whenever strangers walked past, I would accost them and exhort them to repent because the kingdom of God was near. Sometimes I would greet complete strangers thinking I knew them. Other times I did not recognize people I knew and would suspiciously scan their faces when they addressed me.

Sometimes I spent entire afternoons staring into space, or imploring God to come down from heaven and destroy the world because it was so full of pain and evil-hearted people. I began suspecting family members of trying to poison me, and refused to eat anything they gave me.

Each time my children gave me food to eat I would "see" Mathebula come into the room, replace my food with a pile of shit, then slink away before anyone could see him.

"This is shit!" I shouted at my children. "Why are you giving me shit to eat! Do you hate me, my children?"

"No, Mama," they would say. "This is not shit. It's porridge with meat."

I would grab the food and throw it away.

Finally Florah and George, bewildered and terrified by my behavior, concluded I was a danger to the family and to myself. They approached Jackson for advice, but he wanted nothing to do with a demented wife. During the year and a half I was insane, he pretended I did not exist. He did nothing to help me or to provide for the children.

George and Florah took me to Tembisa Hospital, where I was confined in the mental ward for three months. Doctors and nurses didn't know what was wrong with me. They couldn't find the cause of my insanity. They transferred me to General Hospital, where it was the same story: they could find no organic cause, and I was released. There were hardly any psychiatrists or psychologists for blacks, so many of those with mental problems were often left to themselves. Because medical experts could not diagnose or cure my sickness, my children became convinced that I had been bewitched.

Florah consulted with my mother, who decided to take over the search for my treatment. She came to the shack and saw how Jackson had completely neglected me, and how Mathebula and his family had taken over the shack.

"I don't like the looks of that man," my mother muttered, as she helped me pack my belongings. She took me to her place. Thus began my eighteen-month ordeal from insanity to recovery, a harrowing experience which left me convinced, beyond a shadow of a doubt, that witchcraft does exist, and that it can be deadly, and that faith in God and in my ancestors helped me overcome the evil.

30

GRANNY

WITCHCRAFT IS
DEFEATED

Once I saw the terrible state my daughter was in I doubted if I could ever find a cure for her madness. She seemed far gone. Aside from her ravings, she had grown emaciated, veins protruded on the side of her skull, and her eyes bulged. She hardly ate anything, claiming that all food given her was either poisoned or shit. She refused to walk to the outhouse because she said her legs were on fire. She frequently wetted and soiled her underwear like a little child, before I could bring her a bucket. From time to time she would scream in terror, claiming Mathebula was after her.

"There he is, there he is!" she would scream, pointing into empty space and staring with horror-stricken eyes. "He wants to kill me. Look at his fangs. They're dripping blood."

At other times she would holler that Mathebula's putting shit into the meals I was giving her, or replacing her tea with urine. One day I prepared porridge and meat and brought Geli some. She glared at the food and began accusing me of conspiring with Mathebula to poison her.

"So you're his accomplice too!" Geli said. "You want me dead, don't you?"

"No, my poor child," I said reassuringly. "I'm your mother. How could I ever want to kill you?"

"Then why are you giving me this shit to eat?"

"This isn't shit, my child," I said. "It's meat and porridge. Look, I'm eating it too."

I took a bite.

Geli let out peals of maniacal laughter. She pointed at me and said, "Ha, ha, ha! She's eating her own shit! She's eating her own shit!"

I got up and pretended to leave, but as soon as I was outside, I went to the side window and peered in. I saw Geli sidle closer to the food, hesitate, sniff it like a dog, hesitate, cautiously taste it with a finger, then take a couple bites. I smiled with relief. She took a third bite, shook her head in disgust, then moved away from the dish. I came back in and ate the rest of her food, while she stared at me.

There were good days and bad days. Some bad days were filled with Geli's screams about Mathebula armed with an axe and coming to murder her. Whenever she "saw" him coming she would attempt to bolt out of the shack. I'd have to grab her, restrain her, and keep all doors and windows locked.

On other bad days she would scream that her feet were on fire. She couldn't walk. Each time she attempted to stand or walk she would collapse like a bundle. The bad days were worsened by Jackson's behavior toward his children. Whenever he was in a bad mood he would storm about the house breaking things. His children would flee to my home after he had chased them around the house with a *sjambok*, telling them to go join their crazy mother. As a result I now took care of two families, and we were all cramped in my shack's two tiny rooms.

Good days—which were few and far between—would be when the children were back at home. Geli spent these days lying quietly curled up on the bare floor, or sitting with knees drawn up, talking to herself or singing church songs. She had stopped going to church since she became deranged, and from time to time church members came to visit her. But strangely, Rachel never came.

Months went by. George and Florah wrote letters to Johannes in America informing him of their mother's condition. We couldn't call him as we had no phone; besides, a call to America would have cost us a month's food allowance. But as with earlier letters sent to Johannes, these brought no reply. We were at a loss as to what could have happened to him. Was he dead? Would he ever come back home again?

I dared not tell Geli that there were no letters from Johannes. Daily, in her ravings, she would talk about her dear son, saying he was the only one who loved her, and that when he got back from America a rich and powerful man, he would build her a new home and take care of her.

Years later we found out that Johannes had received and replied to all our letters, but the Pretoria regime had intercepted every one of his replies as a way of punishing him for his activism against apartheid.

Florah and Collin now supported the family, along with Maria, who had quit school before completing junior high because she became pregnant. She was now working as a maid, filling in for her mother until she got better.

One day Geli miraculously regained her senses. She awoke very early in the morning. As usual, she had slept curled up on the floor and I had gone to sleep beside her to keep an eye on her.

"I had a dream, Mama," she murmured.

"What was it about, my child?" I asked in a groggy voice.

"I dreamt I went to church by myself to pray. While I was on my knees praying, an angel of God came to me. The angel had huge, white wings. She approached me and said, 'Magdaline, Magdaline, today all your sickness is gone. You are well. You won't be sick anymore.' As the angel spoke I saw Mathebula and his daughter running away."

Geli paused. I was intrigued by her dream, its coherence, and the fact that as she spoke there was a calmness in her face, in place of the agitation, nervousness, and pure terror of past months.

"What then happened, my child," I asked, now fully awake and sitting up, "after Mathebula ran away?"

Geli went on. "I said to the angel, 'How can I be better? My feet are still burning, like fire.' The angel then replied, 'You have been made whole. God has vanquished your enemies and put out the fire in your legs. When you wake up, go to the bathroom, dress up, eat, and go to church.' After the angel spoke to me I awoke."

"Do you want something to eat, my child?" I asked, not knowing what to say.

"Not now," Geli said. "First I must go to the bathroom."

"Should I bring you the bucket?"

"No, I don't want the bucket. I want to walk to the outhouse."

I grew afraid. The latrines were at the other end of the yard. Was all this story about a dream a ploy to run away?

"Let me take you there," I said.

"No, I can walk there by myself."

She stood up without much difficulty, though she was so gaunt and wasted her bones protruded and I could see every rib and vertebra in her spine as she bent over to put on her dress. She took a roll of toilet paper, stepped outside into the dawn, and walked to the cluster of latrines at the back of the yard. I followed cautiously close behind. She went into one of the latrines and was inside for so long that I feared she might have escaped through the bucket hole.

"Are you almost done, dear?" I asked, leaning against the door.

"Yes, Mama."

Soon Geli emerged and when she saw me standing by the door she smiled and said, "Don't worry, Mama, I won't run away. There's no need to run away anymore. God has defeated Mathebula."

Back at the house she asked me to boil some water in a kettle and pour it into the washtub. She washed herself for the first time in months, scrubbing herself with soap and a *scrop* brush (scrubbing brush with thistles) from head to toe and washing her grimy hair with care. When she was done, the water was black with dirt. She then asked me for her favorite church outfit—a white shiny dress with frills, and a white hat with a broad brim. As she was dressing, she said, "Mama, I want to drink tea."

I speedily made tea and put it on the table.

"I want bread too."

I got her some brown bread left over from a week ago. It was crusty but not yet moldy. She drank all the tea and ate all the bread. I stared in amazement. There was no talk of shit or poison. When she was finished she said, "Mama, I'm still hungry. I want porridge. And I want more bread. Remember, I haven't eaten much in a long time."

As Geli kept asking for food, I wondered, Is this a prelude to her dying? I remembered hearing that before some people died they ate up a storm at the behest of their ancestors.

"Are you okay, my child?" I asked.

"I'm fine, Mama. I'm ready to go to church."

"But why go to church?" I said. "It's the church that tried to kill you." I was referring to the presence of Rachel at the church.

"It's not the church that tried to kill me, Mama," Geli said. "It's people with evil in their hearts."

"Can you get there by yourself?" I asked. The church was four blocks away from my shack, way over on 13th Avenue, in the next yard from where Geli lived.

"Yes I can," said Geli. "But first I have to go to my house and see my children. I haven't seen them in a long time. Are they all right?"

"Yes, they're fine," I said, and quickly added, "but you can't go to your house yet! That wizard Mathebula is still there and he'll kill you!"

"No he won't," Geli said calmly. "He's now powerless against me."

"Please don't return to that cursed house yet," I begged Geli. "It's better you go to Giyane first. There your sister Mphephu can wash away whatever evil remains in your body. She can help you gain weight and fortify you to face your enemies. She can give you *muti* to protect you against Mathebula should he come after you again."

"The God of Israel is enough protection, Mama," Geli said. "He's assured me I won't come to any harm. But I'll do as you say."

She then promised to bypass her house and go directly to church.

But she asked me to fetch her children in the meantime so she could see them when she returned from church. She also agreed to make the journey to Giyane to see Mphephu.

I knew that my daughter was on the way to recovery when I heard how fervently she sang hymns praising God. The following line was constantly on her lips: "There is forgiveness through Christ, and life everlasting."

PART VI

31

FLORAH

WHY I BELIEVE
IN WITCHCRAFT

Throughout the length of my mother's madness I never once doubted that she had been bewitched. The inability of doctors to find a cause for her insanity only confirmed what I had long ago concluded from the Mathebula's actions.

My belief in witchcraft dates back to my childhood. I grew up in a world where most people believed in the existence of the *baloyi*—witches and wizards—and their dreadful crimes were commonplace.

As a child I would listen spellbound and terrified as my parents related stories about witchcraft. They warned us to beware of the witches and wizards, who were the source of so much trouble, sorrow, pain, and death. We were especially warned to watch out for the Mai-Mais, tall men with filed teeth, who carried sacks as they prowled around kidnapping unwary children and taking them to remote places in the homelands, where they killed them and made *muti* out of various parts of their bodies.

These warnings were not groundless. A *shebeen* owner in our neighborhood was a known Mai-Mai customer. He kept a human skull with his illicit hootch as a means of improving its appeal. And the bodies of murdered people sometimes had parts missing. My mother constantly warned us as children never to eat food from the homes of strangers because the food might be voodooed. Whenever I complained of feeling ill, the first thing she would ask was, "Did you eat anything strangers gave you?"

Then there were the elaborate ceremonies that took place in our home whenever a *nganga* was summoned to cure an illness which baffled white doctors, to protect the house, to propitiate our ancestors without whose blessings all sorts of calamities would befall us.

Ngangas were imposing and awe-inspiring personalities. I was fascinated by their elaborate costumes and paraphernalia: animal skins, feathers, beads, bladders tied to their hair like balloons, pouches of *muti,* divination bones, strange incantations.

While my parents and life in the ghetto taught me to believe in the supernatural, at school, despite a curriculum designed by apartheid to reinforce tribalism, we were taught that witches and wizards didn't exist, that witchcraft was a bunch of poppycock, that we were now living in a world ruled by science, biology, physics, Christianity, and modern technology.

Our teachers daily insisted that witchcraft was superstitious nonsense that had to be rooted out by education and Christianity. They pointed out that we were living in the twentieth century and not the Middle Ages, that South Africa, despite apartheid, was a modern country, and that there were such things as laws of nature, which couldn't be suspended, violated, or interfered with by puny human beings for their petty ends.

Yet many of these teachers, while publicly dismissing and denouncing witchcraft as superstitious balderdash, privately believed in it. To them, as to most black South Africans, witchcraft was a reality beyond dispute, whether or not they had personally experienced its nefarious effects. Even die-hard skeptics of witchcraft frequently found themselves face to face with phenomena and events that defied reason and rationality. One such person was my aunt Nkensani, Aunt Bushy's childhood friend, who had gone on to become a teacher at the school I attended.

"I didn't use to believe in witchcraft," she once told me. "I considered it a bunch of rubbish, and those who believed in it were fools. I would laugh whenever I saw people consult *ngangas* and witch doctors. Then I saw witchcraft at work with my own two eyes and I had to believe."

Nkensani had a younger sister who was a fine student and had just passed her matriculation exams. She was headed for university the following year. She was outgoing, full of laughter, had everything that she wanted, and looked forward to becoming a teacher or doctor.

One afternoon, a few days after she received her exam results showing she had passed, she went to a nearby store, bought a gallon of paraffin, poured it all over herself, lit a match, and instantly became a human inferno. She was dead before anyone could douse the flames.

Nkensani was shocked and bewildered. Her sister had shown no sign of being depressed or of having any problems. On the contrary, she had been happy at the prospect of going to university, was full of energy, and passionately loved life. Nkensani and her mother, Elsie, were puzzled over the mystery. Elsie suspected witchcraft, but Nkensani dismissed the idea.

"How then do you explain your sister's death?" Elsie asked.

"There must be some rational explanation," Nkensani said. "Maybe she was upset or something. Maybe she had problems we didn't know about."

"I knew my daughter well, Nkensani. She kept no secrets from me. I would have known if anything were bothering her, however slight. And she was your sister. Did you detect anything wrong?"

"No, nothing at all. That's why it's incredible that she could have taken her life."

"I understand why you don't believe in witchcraft," Elsie said. "You are educated and a teacher. You live a modern life with television sets and airplanes. Witchcraft to the likes of you is something primitive, a form of superstition. I'm not asking you to believe without proof. But if it could be proven to you that witchcraft was involved in your sister's death, would you believe?"

"If it's solid proof, then yes, I'll believe."

There was a famous *nganga* in Komatipoort. While Nkensani's sister was in the mortuary awaiting burial, she and her mother paid the famous *nganga* a visit. The *nganga* requested R500 as payment for her services, but she told them that they should pay her only if they were convinced and satisfied. This was important. The lucrative practice of *ngangas* is rife with crooks and charlatans out to make a buck. These frauds can easily be detected by their insistence that they be paid up front. Genuine *ngangas*, who are few, first want you to test them, to be satisfied about the potency of their powers, before you pay them a cent.

A genuine *nganga* can, without having met you, tell you every detail of your life, from childhood to the present, describing where you've lived, your favorite clothes and food, your preferred manner of sleeping, and even the latest dreams you might have had. They can provide you with such intimate details about your life only you could possibly have known.

When the Komatipoort *nganga* told Nkensani about her whole life, she gradually became convinced that there was more to *ngangas* than meets Western scientific eyes.

But there was still more startling evidence to come. The *nganga* hung a white sheet against a bare wall. She then began muttering incantations, and images of various persons began appearing on the sheet, as if she were showing a home movie. It was not a trick and there was no hidden projector. These images were appearing on the strength of the *nganga*'s incantations. "Do you know this woman?" the *nganga* asked Nkensani and her mother, pointing to the image of their neighbor.

"Yes," they said.

"Don't tell me who she is," the *nganga* enjoined. "Just observe."

"Do you know who that is?" the *nganga* asked as a second figure appeared. This time it was a man.

"Yes," Nkensani and her mother said. It was Nkensani's brother.

"What are the two doing?"

"They are shouting at each other," Nkensani said.

The woman stopped shouting, went into the house, talked to Nkensani's mother, and on her way out she furtively dropped something like a tissue on the floor, which the *nganga* said contained the deadly *muti*. Soon thereafter, Nkensani's sister is seen burning and the neighbor is laughing fiendishly at the gruesome sight.

Overcome with emotions, Nkensani begged the *nganga* to stop.

"I've seen enough," she said, wiping tears from her eyes.

There was a long pause. No one spoke. Finally, Nkensani said, "Just one more question. What was the woman's motive for killing my sister?'"

"Jealousy," the *nganga* said, "simple jealousy. You know that the woman has a daughter, right?"

"Yes." The woman had a daughter who was Nkensani's sister's age. The two had been friends of sorts, and competitors.

"And did you know that her daughter became pregnant and dropped out of school?" asked the *nganga*.

"Yes," Elsie replied.

"Her mother was bitter that her daughter had no future while yours was headed for university," the *nganga* said.

"Just for that she killed her?" Nkensani asked, incredulous.

"Yes," the *nganga* said. "It may not seem an adequate motive to you, but to that woman, whose heart is corroded with envy and jealousy, it was motive enough."

Nkensani was now overwhelmed, and she trembled with rage. She wanted the neighbor's daughter dead. She wanted the witch woman to feel what her own mother was feeling at the loss of her daughter.

"I want revenge," Nkensani blurted out.

"Are you sure?" asked the *nganga*.

"I'm sure."

"No! No! Don't do that, my child," Nkensani's mother interjected. She had been sitting silent for some time, mesmerized by the *nganga's* performance.

"What!?" Nkensani shot back. "We didn't come all this way and pay all this money for nothing. Didn't you see with your own eyes what happened? That evil woman bewitched my sister. She must pay for the crime. God will forgive me for seeking revenge. He'll understand my pain."

Nkensani then turned to the *nganga* and asked, "Can you do it?"

"It will cost you a great deal," the *nganga* said.

"I have money," Nkensani said. "I can pay. I'll give anything to avenge my sister's death. Can you call up the images of that woman and her daughter?"

There are several methods of working voodoo on someone. One way is through direct poisoning, or *sejeso*, where you mix deadly *muti* with food or drink intended for the person you mean to kill. A second method is to obtain the intended victim's belongings—such as underwear, a hat (as in my mother's case), or a favorite piece of clothing—and voodoo the objects. Some powerful wizards can even voodoo someone using only the person's footprint or shadow. A third method is to conjure up a person's image so it appears on a white sheet or a bowl of water, and then stab it with a knife or needles. The instant you do that, the person, wherever he or she is, feels a sharp pain and dies.

People protect themselves against witchcraft in various ways. My daughter Angeline and I tie strings treated with *muti* around our waists, which we never remove. Other people wear similarly treated armbands. Some people, before moving into a new house that others might covet, hire *ngangas* to come treat it with *muti* so no evil can enter through the door or windows. Even football (soccer) teams, boxers, and other professional athletes consult *ngangas* for *muti* so as to be one up on the competition.

One *nganga* in Durban specializes in this sort of protection. He is consulted by whites as well as blacks. He has grown so rich he owns a mansion, his own helicopter, nearly a dozen wives, a Mercedes-Benz, cars and trucks, liquor stores and *shebeens*, and even has a school for his many children.

But Nkensani simply wanted revenge, and she was willing to pay for it.

"Do you have R2,000?" asked the *nganga*.

"I don't have it now," Nkensani said. "But I can get it for you."

"No, please don't do it," Nkensani's mother pleaded.

"I want revenge," said Nkensani, consumed with rage.

"No, don't," Nkensani's mother begged.

"I say I want revenge."

"Don't do it, please, my child. God is alive. He knows what that evil woman has done. He'll punish her. Don't damn your soul with her blood."

"God helps only those who help themselves," Nkensani said. "We must do something or this dastardly murder will go unpunished. Before we came here I would have agreed with you that we shouldn't seek revenge for my sister's death. I didn't believe in witchcraft then. Now I do. Now that I know the bitter truth, that there are evil people in this world, I'm prepared to fight them with their own weapons."

"God will avenge your sister's death," Elsie said. "Take my word for it. I swear it upon my soul. Please, please, don't seek revenge."

"Don't give me that, Mama," Nkensani said angrily. "Suppose you were poor and you sat in a windowless hovel all day. Would God bring you food, money, clothes, the good life? No, He wouldn't. You would have to get off your ass and go looking for them. Only then would He help you find them. As I say, 'God only helps those who help themselves.'"

In the end Elsie prevailed upon Nkensani to leave the revenge to God. Though Nkensani was enraged by the murder of her beloved sister, she wouldn't have killed for revenge. She wasn't the evil sort. She was cast in Granny's mold. Elsie and Nkensani paid the *nganga* the R500 and returned home, emotionally exhausted from the revelations.

The day of Nkensani's sister's funeral arrived. The evil neighbor came to attend the funeral, and when Nkensani saw her she confronted her and said, "Are you satisfied? My sister is dead, just as you wanted."

The neighbor didn't answer, but she had a guilty look on her face.

"Why are you here?" Nkensani demanded. "Do you plan to kill the rest of my brothers and sisters too? Maybe you plan to kill me next, is that it?"

Without replying, the evil neighbor abruptly left the funeral.

32

GELI

REVENGE IS MINE,
BUT I WON'T TAKE IT

Like my cousin Nkensani, I too had the opportunity to exact revenge against those who had bewitched me. But like Nkensani's mother, I wanted no revenge. Since becoming a Christian I no longer believed in demanding an eye for an eye, a tooth for a tooth. If those who had wronged me deserved punishment, I believed God would mete it out in His own sweet time. I didn't feel I had the right to sentence anyone to death.

The day following my miraculous recovery I awoke in my mother's shack. I again asked for some food. She gave me porridge and meat and I sat down and ate voraciously. I was still as thin as a reed. When I walked in the streets people thought a gust of wind would blow me away. My legs were particularly shrunken, as the skin clung to the bones. But though my body was weak, my spirit was strong, because my faith in Christ remained unshaken.

Friday arrived—it was rainy and cold—and my sister's daughter,

Mavila, came to take me to Giyane, as my mother had arranged. We were to travel there by bus, a distance that would take nearly twelve hours. Just as we were about to leave Mavila had second thoughts.

"What if Aunt Geli starts screaming about Mathebula and tries to jump out the bus window?" she asked my mother. "How would I cope with a maniac? I'm not strong enough to restrain her. And I'm traveling with two children."

"Don't worry about me," I reassured Mavila. "I'm cured. Nothing will happen."

But Mavila wasn't convinced. She pleaded with my mother to let Piet accompany us. She agreed. Piet, Mavila, her two children, and I boarded an evening bus for Giyane. Throughout the long journey Mavila remained apprehensive. Each time the bus stopped to let passengers go to the restroom, Mavila's apprehension reached a peak. She eyed me warily, and her body tensed, as if ready to grab me if I started hollering about Mathebula. Piet told her I would do no such thing.

"She's done it before," Mavila said. "She's mad. We'll be in serious trouble if she starts acting up and assaults white people. We could be thrown in jail."

But I didn't act up. At each stop I went to the bathroom by myself and returned to the bus without incident.

When we arrived at Mphephu's place in Giyane no one was home but her youngest son. Mphephu hadn't been told the time of our arrival. Messengers were sent to fetch her from the neighboring village. When Mphephu arrived and saw the condition I was in—withered body and protruding eyes—she was shocked and doubted if she could help me.

"Why did mother send her to me?" she asked Piet. "She looks ready for the grave. I have never dealt with a case like this before. To be frank, I doubt very much if I can heal her."

"Mother said you were her last hope."

Mphephu feared I might be possessed by *swikwembus*—ancestral spirits. Having *swikwembus*, ranting and raving because the spirits are possessing your body, is one sign that your ancestors want you to become a *nganga*. If you ignore their demand and don't undergo initiation rites and become a *nganga*, you remain permanently insane.

Mphephu sought to avoid the responsibility of finding this out, so she said, "I know of another *nganga* in the village who can treat Geli if she has *swikwembus*. I'll take you to her."

While I rested from the journey, Piet and Mphephu set off to the home of the other *nganga*. Villages in Giyane were far apart. There was no public transportation and few cars, so journeys had to be made on foot, over mountains and harsh terrain. To reach the nearest store, for instance, one usually left early in the morning and did not return until late afternoon.

Dissatisfied with the first *nganga*, Mphephu and Piet went on to a second, who, after consulting his divinatory bones, essentially repeated what the first had said: "You, Mphephu, are the one chosen by your ancestors to heal your sister. No other *nganga* can."

Again Mphephu doubted the advice and off they went to a third *nganga*. She simply did not want to bear the responsibility of having to attempt to treat a challenging and complicated case like mine. If she failed, her reputation as a *nganga* would suffer. Like Jonah fleeing from the task God set before him, my sister led Piet on an arduous wild-goose chase from village to village in search of a *nganga* who would let her off the hook.

"You're the one chosen to help your sister," the fifth *nganga* said. "It's your destiny."

"But my sister is VERY, VERY sick," Mphephu said. "My powers are inadequate. They might be ineffective because she's kin. She may even die at my hands."

"Don't worry about your powers," the *nganga* said. "Your ancestors chose you and will give you whatever powers you need for the task."

"But my sister may have *swikwembus*," said Mphephu. "And you know it's taboo for a relative to initiate another into becoming a *nganga*."

"No, your sister doesn't have *swikwembus*," the *nganga* reassured Mphephu. "She has the Christian God within her." One couldn't be a *nganga* and a Christian at the same time. "Unfortunately, evil people have poured harpies and demons into her flesh and she needs to have it purified. Her soul is fine. The Christian God has seen to that. Your task is to purge the evil that has attacked her body."

One sign of the evil attacking my body was my emaciated condition. My sister's task was to remove the poison that Mathebula and his accomplices had placed in my body, which had sucked out its vitality.

The fifth *nganga's* explanation finally convinced an exhausted and hungry Mphephu. She returned home and promised to start the treatment the next day. Guided by our ancestors, who at every step of the treatment told her exactly what to do through the divinatory bones, she went to the forest, dug up special roots to make *muti*, boiled some of it, and, when it had cooled, poured it into a special gourd and handed it to me to drink. Every night she would build a fire from special kindling gathered from the forest, burn the rest of the *muti* over hot coals, and, trapping the pungent smoke under a blanket, make me inhale it. I would sweat profusely while under the blanket.

Gradually, I began regaining some of the weight I had lost. Mphephu continued her treatment, digging up *muti*, burning it, and having me inhale the smoke. One day she informed me that the time had come for those who had bewitched me to be smelled and driven from my body. She again boiled *muti* and gave it to me to drink. She then started sniffing the air close to me, starting near my head, then proceeding down the rest of my body, attempting to catch the scent of the evil spirit. As she did so, she waved a *chovo*—the mane of a lion twisted around a small stick like a feather duster.

Each time Mphephu encountered evil in a part of my body, her personality changed and she would assume the personality of the perpetrator of the evil.

Finally Mathebula was expelled from my body. From Mphephu's entranced body came the unmistakable hoarse, deep, bitter, almost guttural voice of Mathebula, muttering in despair as he fled. "I've been defeated. I'm going now. I'm washing my hands of you. I'm never coming back. You've escaped my grasp. . . ."

"Go, and never return," Mphephu said, once more assuming her own personality.

"This which is unconquerable," Mathebula murmered as his image faded into the darkness. "She can't be defeated. I made the attempt and failed. She's bested me."

"Go, you cursed, misbegotten thing," Mphephu said to Mathebula's evil spirit, "you don't belong in Geli's body."

It amazed me to see the battle between Mphephu and the evil Mathebula for the possession of my body. One time she was Mathebula, then she was herself, then she became Mathebula's again, then herself again, and so on. Had the witchcraft in my body been put there by a witch in the form of a cat, Mphephu would have purred like one; a wolf, she would have howled like one. She would have easily assumed the mien of any other animal or person used in perpetrating the witchcraft.

The *muti* treatment continued every day for nearly two months. One day I started vomiting. I continued vomiting for several days until my body was cleansed. I was now completely cured, except for one thing: revenge.

A few days before I was to head back to Alexandra, Mphephu said to me, "Now that you know the truth about your enemies, what do you want me to do?"

"Protect me and my family from further mischief," I said.

"Is that all?"

"That's all."

"Don't you want revenge? Are you simply going to let them go scot free, after what they've done to you?"

"I'm not a witch," I said. "I'm a child of God. I harbor no malice toward Mathebula. I want no revenge."

"But your ancestors must be satisfied," Mphephu said. "They will want revenge. And what about the pain that wizard caused you? They intended to kill you, you know."

She proceeded to explain that Mathebula wanted our shack for himself and his family, and thought that with me out of the way, it would be easy for him to handle Jackson, who was always drunk.

Mathebula was also angry with me for having rejected his older son's request to marry Florah, a request Jackson had already agreed to.

"I know they wanted to kill me," I said. "But Christ prevented that. He led me to you and gave you the power to cure me."

"You know, Mudjadji," Mphephu said, using my maiden name, "you're so kindhearted that it's impossible to understand why anyone would want to harm you. The only thing left for me to do to complete the cure and prevent a relapse is to send the mischief back to its perpetrators."

"Please don't do anything to harm Mathebula or his family," I pleaded with Mphephu.

"The Gods will decide," Mphephu said.

Mathebula's punishment was so severe it made me weep, despite what he had done to me. A week after my return from Giyane, two of his sons were killed and the third badly wounded. His eldest son was stabbed to death by unknown assailants on his way home one night, leaving behind a wife and three children. A few days later his second son was stabbed by a jealous man in a *shebeen* not too far from where we lived, following an argument over a woman.

The third son was ambushed by *tsotsis*, who ripped open his stomach with knives and left him to stagger home clutching his bloody intestines in his hands. It was a miracle he survived. As soon as he was sewn up and released from the hospital, his father sent him to the homelands, where he hoped the boy would be safe from the uncompromising forces of revenge that were eager to punish the son for the sins of the father.

Following the loss of his two sons and the wounding of a third, a chastened and contrite Mathebula left our shack with his family and built one of his own in a nearby alley.

33

GRANNY

A POLITICAL
LESSON

Geli's troubles didn't end when her madness was cured. She had still others to face, equally pressing, stemming mainly from the pressures of supporting her family and keeping it together. Jackson had now totally relinquished the responsibility. His main occupation had become drinking. He had been permanently laid off from his job, when his employer shut down the company and left for overseas, as many whites were doing.

After returning from Giyane, Geli resumed her grueling work schedule of cleaning offices by night and running a day-care center at her home. At the same time, she had to watch over her daughters, who were growing up during a time of great turmoil in the township.

It was the mid-1980s. Black rage and protest were a daily fixture, and violence was rife all over the townships. Almost every day, the police were firing on protesters and arresting people. Martial law was declared, Alexandra was cordoned off, and the media kept out. Soldiero were brought in and went from street to street, house to house, searching for guns, interrogating people, and arresting hundreds of youngsters. At the same time, ANC and Inkatha supporters battled each other for turf and control of the township, leaving scores dead and wounded and whole sections of Alexandra in ruins in what became known as the Six-Days War.

Black schooling once more came to a standstill. Children as young as eleven had little to do but stay at home, join protest marches, attend mandatory funerals, party, and indulge in sex, while their parents were away at work or searching for food. As a result, many young girls became pregnant, among them two of Geli's daughters—Maria and Mirriam. Maria had a son at fifteen. And before he could marry her, Calvin, the father, was shot dead by an assassin's bullet at the same time that Florah's Collin was shot.

Mirriam's pregnancy was an even greater shock. At seventeen, she was a devout churchgoer and still a virgin. She was very active in the choir and youth programs. She hated jiving for power and kept away from those who did. The very thought of sex disgusted her and she would cry and plug her ears with her fingers whenever her sister Florah told her about boyfriends.

Then one day, as she put it, it happened. It was her first sexual encounter. The man who got her pregnant was a Zulu auto mechanic in his twenties who continued sleeping around even after having a son by Mirriam. He stopped when Geli warned him that he stood to lose his son if he continued his philandering. He even quit his low-paying job, traded his greasy overalls for a white shirt and tie, got a respectable job as a clerk, and began supporting his son.

I admired the way Geli handled her daughters' unexpected pregnancies. It showed that she had come a long way from the days when she, like myself, would refuse to discuss sexual matters with our daughters because of taboos. Geli didn't force them to have back-alley abortions, which would have endangered their lives, nor did she kick them out of the house, as some mothers did, calling them a disgrace or blaming them for something that wasn't entirely their fault.

Instead she urged Maria and Mirriam to visit family planning centers and get birth control. Both went, and nurses at the family planning center recommended they get periodic injections of Depo-Provera.

Geli also talked to them about their future, especially now that they had children to support.

"Don't rely only on the fathers of your children to take care of you," she said to Mirriam and Maria. "Go back to school so you can get jobs and be able to stand on your own two feet, just like your older sister Florah is doing."

Mirriam heeded the advice and attempted to finish high school. Maria, on the other hand, was too embarrassed to return because she was now a mother, so she started working at various piece jobs.

Jackson took the news of his daughters' pregnancies differently. He was furious with them, called them irresponsible whores, and threatened to toss them out of the house if their boyfriends didn't promptly pay *lobola*. He was particularly severe with Mirriam. Her pregnancy had apparently botched his plans to marry her off to one of his drinking buddies, Joseph, a stodgy, leathery-faced old man who wanted to buy a virgin as a third wife, in the vain hope that his youth would be restored.

No longer working, Jackson was in the habit of sponging off Joseph. Each time Joseph bought Jackson drinks, he would say, "You don't owe me anything. Count the money as *lobola* for your daughter Mirriam."

Jackson apparently agreed to this arrangement. One day Joseph told Florah that he was now almost done paying *lobola* for Mirriam and would soon claim her. Florah was shocked and told Geli. Geli confronted Jackson.

"Is this some sort of joke?" she asked. "Have you really sold Mirriam for liquor?"

"You've no business telling me what form of *lobola* payment I can accept for my daughters."

Geli was stupefied. She said, "Aren't you ashamed to sell your daughter to someone old enough to be her grandfather?"

"I was older than you when we got married."

"And I've regretted it the rest of my life."

"But you're my wife now."

"What sort of a father are you?"

"They're my daughters. I know what's best for them."

"Hasn't it occurred to you that they're my daughters too?" Geli retorted. "And over my dead body will you sell any of them to fat, toothless old men for drinks."

Mirriam somehow heard of this. A month later she was pregnant by the auto mechanic. I think that Mirriam may have turned to him as a way of escaping from being sold by her father to a fat old man she didn't love. Her fears of marrying an old man with many wives may have been heightened by the fate suffered by one of her close friends, Mavis.

Fourteen-year-old Mavis was the youngest of five and the only girl in her family. She was a dedicated student and attended the same school as Mirriam and as Bushy's daughter Fikile. The three always walked home together after school. One day they arrived at Mavis's place to find all her belongings packed and a strange old man wearing a loose, faded gray suit and a Stetson hat with a feather, sitting with her mother in the shack's kitchen.

"This is your husband," Mavis's mother told her, as soon as she entered the shack, before she even had time to change. "He's come to claim you."

"My what?!"

"Your husband, I said," Mavis's mother said sharply. "Now wipe that stupid expression off your face and get ready to leave with your husband. Your belongings are already packed."

Mavis's mother was an authoritarian and ill-tempered woman. She had no husband, and used to whip Mavis at every turn. Mavis feared her and always did as she commanded. Mavis hardly knew the old man. She had only caught glimpses of him among her mother's customers. He had the habit of purchasing liquor from Mavis's mother on Sundays, his day off from his job as a kitchen boy in the suburbs, and would not request change whenever he had any due.

"Put it toward my *lobola* payment for your daughter," he would say.

The old man already had four wives in the homeland and wanted Mavis as his "city wife." And incredible as it may sound, Mavis's mother had determined for whatever reasons that her only daughter should be married to this old man. So poor Mavis sadly changed out of her gym dress, then asked her friends Mirriam and Fikile to help her carry her suitcase and thick duffel bag, packed with her belongings, to the bus station.

The old man with the feathered hat proudly led the way to the bus station, with Mavis, Fikile, and Mirriam following a few paces behind. As they neared the bus station, Mavis whispered to Mirriam and Fikile that she was planning to run away, that under no circumstances would she become the concubine of a toothless old man. Mirriam and Fikile encouraged her to do so. They discussed a strategy. A short while later Mavis went up to the old man, still walking a little ahead.

"Excuse me, my dear husband-to-be," Mavis said in a false, honeyed voice. "My friends and I are thirsty. Do you mind if I run to the cafe over there and get something to drink?"

"Not at all, my love," the old man said. "Do you want some money?"

"If you don't mind."

The old man gave Mavis a R5 note.

"Get me some too," the old man said.

"Okay," Mavis said as she left for the store. She never came back. Fikile and Mirriam, in on Mavis's plan, disappeared with her suitcase and duffel bag, leaving the old man standing alone and bewildered. Mavis went to her boyfriend's place. Her mother, when she heard what had happened, vowed to kill Mavis if she ever returned home.

While young girls like Mavis and Mirriam were running away from home or bearing children out of wedlock, Alexandra remained under military occupation. During the day, battalions of armed soldiers in the yellow armored trucks called *caspers* and *hippos* patrolled the streets, and at night, glaring searchlights flared up in the ghetto sky. Tear gas sprayed all over the ghetto confined people indoors and deprived them of sleep. The tear gas was particularly hard on little children and the elderly, and a couple of people even died from its effects on weak lungs. The government was going all out in its ruthless efforts to crush black resistance against apartheid.

At first I didn't understand what the young people hoped to gain with their daily protests, in which so many of them were being killed. I faulted them for making a bad situation—black poverty and suffering—worse, by burning stores and staying away from school, by calling for stay-aways and strikes when people needed every penny they could slave to survive, and by getting themselves shot, killed, crippled, arrested, and tortured. I had seen it all before, and it seemed so futile.

"Apartheid has always existed, in one form or another. It's a way of life. Nothing you can do can ever change that. My generation tried and failed," I said one evening to Florah and her friend Joyce, who had fled to my place because soldiers were swarming in her neighborhood, indiscriminately arresting young people in an effort to stamp out the daily protests.

"But Granny," said Joyce. "We have no choice but to fight the Boers [rednecks]. They have taken our land and we have no rights."

"I know that," I said. "But getting yourselves killed won't solve the problem."

I proceeded to recount the various failed attempts by blacks to defeat white power. I recounted how, in the days of my grandparents and their parents, black warriors fought against white people and sought to drive them off our lands and back into the sea from whence they came. These warriors were brave and had previously won impressive battles against enemy tribes. But they were no match for white people armed with guns.

"But we now have guns too, Granny," Florah said.

"Yes, you do," I said. "But how many white people have you killed with them? Haven't you instead been shooting each other?"

"We're becoming more disciplined, Granny," said Florah. "As soon as we are united we will form a mighty army that will defeat the whites."

"That's what our people always said back in the old days," I said. "They claimed our great numbers would defeat the whites, but that hasn't happened."

"It will happen," said Joyce. "The only way whites can defeat us is by dividing us. Divide and conquer is their strategy. That's why blacks in Alexandra are fighting each other. We've been divided by the Boers."

"But we are often the ones who divide ourselves up," I said. "We hate and denigrate each other because of our tribal differences. That makes it easy for the government to pit us against each other. That's what happened in the fifties and sixties."

I paused to reflect on how, during those momentous decades, members of other tribes were suspicious of the ANC because it was dominated by Xhosas; how, after the ANC was banned and went underground, various tribal leaders cut deals with Pretoria to create their own homelands and preserve their own power; and how urban blacks often looked down on their tribal brethren, who were more loyal to tradition, easily cowed by white power, and less politically active.

"What happened in the fifties and sixties, Granny?" Joyce asked. "We weren't yet born."

"Those decades were a turning point," I said. "They marked the beginning of serious black resistance to apartheid. I was a single mother then and working piece jobs in the suburbs. Alexandra was rife with political activity. The first challenge to white power the people made was with the bus boycott of 1957. The bus company had raised fares from 3 to 4 cents, which was a lot for most people. Remember that rent for a shack in those days was about 50 cents and wages were around R1 a week for most people. Our leaders told us not to ride the buses until the fare was brought down. Almost the entire township obeyed. People walked as much as twenty miles to work, even in bad weather. Even when employers threatened to fire them they continued walking. Eventually the bus fare raise was scrapped."

"That's what unity can do," Joyce said, applauding enthusiastically. "It can topple the system."

"Not so fast, Joyce," I said. "It's one thing not to ride buses. Most people considered that a minor sacrifice. After all, we were accustomed to walking. But when our leaders demanded that women stop carrying their passbooks, that was another matter altogether."

"But passes are degrading," Florah said.

"We knew that. Our leaders demanded that the pass system be abolished. White women don't have to carry passes, why should our women? they said. In 1959 our leaders called on the people to defy the pass laws by not carrying passes. They made a show of burning them in public bonfires. Many people were scared of burning their passes. Without them they could lose their jobs and their homes. I didn't burn mine. In fact, I started carrying mine on my head whenever I left the ghetto to show the policemen that I still had one. That way they would leave me in peace and allow me to go to work. Other women did the same."

"But Granny," Joyce said, "sacrifices have to be made if the struggle is to succeed."

"That may be true," I said, "but not too many people were willing to sacrifice their livelihood. People were afraid and confused. They felt whites were all-powerful. I remember some people hiding their passes under mattresses each time ANC and PAC [Pan African Congress] activists came and demanded them. Whenever people got arrested under the pass laws they blamed themselves instead of the system."

"Why, Granny?" Florah asked. "Didn't they see it was the system that was to blame?"

"They saw and didn't see," I said, shrugging. "I guess we were so used to oppression that carrying passes seemed normal. Many of us thought that if only we kept our passes in order we could avoid trouble. Of course, there was no way a black man or woman could keep his or her pass in order for long. The government was constantly coming up with new laws to make the stamps and permits in our passes invalid. Families couldn't stay together, work became difficult to find in white areas, children could no longer be sent to neighborhood schools, and people were daily being deported back to the tribal reserves—all because our passes were not in order. Then there was the daily terror of the midnight pass raids from the Peri-Urban police."

I paused to take snuff. I felt a bit tired. I sent Florah to fetch me some water in a mug. It was nearing midnight, and the girls planned to spend the night at my place, as it would have been dangerous for them to attempt going home given the turmoil in the streets. I was only too glad for their company, as Piet and his wife were away.

I had never before talked politics for so long. In fact, I disliked politics, in part because I didn't fully understand what was involved and had seen little change in our lives brought on by politics. But I had lived through the experiences I was now recounting to Florah and Joyce, and they had left an imprint on me and changed my life in many ways.

And Florah and Joyce were very eager for this history lesson because they had never learned it in the schools. After taking sips of my water and making myself more comfortable on the floor where I sat, flanked by Joyce and Florah, while the sound of gunfire and the rumble of *caspers* echoed in the distance, I resumed my story of the black struggle for liberation.

"Our leaders did try to show us the connection between our miseries and apartheid. But many of us were uneducated and didn't fully understand things. Some of us were downright afraid of the consequences of knowing the truth. It was a slow learning process. And many mistakes were made on both sides. Many of us at first were suspicious of our leaders. We were told that they were only troublemakers, that they were rich and therefore could afford strikes and boycotts. And terrible things happened to people who joined the ANC or PAC. They would disappear in the middle of the night. They were arrested and beaten up in jail. Some even died there."

"Were most people afraid to join as a result?" Florah asked.

"Yes, very afraid," I said. "You often didn't know if the person asking you to join was sent by the leaders or was an *impipi*, an informer, working for the police. There were many *impipis* in those days. One of them even got Nelson Mandela arrested."

"We know of Nelson Mandela, Granny," Florah chimed. "We sing songs about him and his courage whenever we march at funerals."

"When Mandela and his people started talking about guns and bombs, people grew afraid. We knew many would die as a result."

"That's the price of freedom, Granny," Joyce said.

"But how can you be free when so many of you are dying?" I asked. "When so many of you no longer go to school? When so many of you are giving birth to children without being married? Is this the way to build a nation?"

Florah and Joyce had no convincing answers. They and their generation were confused too, despite their energy, rage, and determination. Yes, I was old-fashioned and didn't have their political sophistication or courage, but I believed the future lay in education and having values. The younger generation had to have a sense of respect and morality, it had to be disciplined and patient, it had to know right from wrong, to work hard at acquiring the skills and the knowledge to take over the running of the country when the whites were defeated.

Members of the younger generation had to work hard if they didn't want to end up as maids, kitchen boys, tea girls, alcoholics, teenage mothers, tsotsis, garden boys, garbage collectors, and garden weeders (as I did). That's why I was so proud of my grandson Johannes. Despite growing up in a horrible environment, where the only role models for him were his irresponsible father and street gangs, he fought to make a better life for himself, using education as a weapon.

He was incredibly single-minded in his determination to achieve his goal. At first I was among those skeptical that this education he was devoted to would lead him anywhere. But then, like his mother, his greatest ally, I went on faith. That's why, at the end of each work day, when I was tired and faced with having to walk home for over an hour, I never forgot to ask the white people whose gardens I weeded if they had old newspapers, comics, and books I could give to my grandson who loved to read. When I was given any, I placed them in a box—they were often heavy—and proudly lugged them home. When Johannes was done reading the newspapers, I exchanged them at the corner butcher shop for meat. The butcherman used the newspapers to wrap meat for customers.

One time, when I stopped by a shady tree to rest during the long walk home, curiosity made me leaf through some of the books in an attempt to find out what so engrossed my grandchild, but all I saw were black-and-white marks which made no sense to me. Yet to my grandchild, books more than made sense. They so enraptured him he sometimes forgot to eat. They had the same power over his mind as the bedtime stories his mother and I had entertained him and his siblings with when they were growing up.

My employers often asked me what I did with the old newspapers and books. "My grandson goes to school and loves to read," I would say with pride. They would be surprised—most whites thought black children didn't love learning—but would condescendingly congratulate me for having "a fine grandson."

Such praise from white people filled me with pride and made Johannes very special to me. He was also special for another reason. When he was just sixteen months old he saved my life. I had taken him from his mother for the day, and we were riding in a packed train to visit relatives in Soweto. He was strapped to my back as we stood near the door of the jam-packed evening train. A *tsotsi* behind me somehow got hold of the ends of my *doek* (head scarf), and was stealthily trying to strangle me with it. But he didn't have enough slack because Johannes had the rest of the *doek* in his hands and refused to let go. It was the noises Johannes was making as the *tsotsi* tried to wrench the *doek* from his tiny hands that alerted me to his deadly intent. I started screaming for help, and the *tsotsi* panicked and fled through the packed coaches.

As the years went by without Johannes returning from America, I wondered if I would ever get to see him before I died.

34

FLORAH

GOING TO AMERICA

As the second child born in my family, I became very close to my brother Johannes. I always looked up to him. At school, whenever teachers wanted to challenge me to do my best, they always reminded me that my brother had been an exceptional student. In all his years in lower and higher primary school, he was either first or second in class. This put a lot of pressure on me, but still I was very proud of him.

When Johannes left for America in 1978, on a tennis scholarship arranged by Stan Smith, the American tennis professional, I spent a lot of time reflecting on what had made him turn out so different.

I remember the hard time my father constantly gave him when he was a teenager for striving to be different. He would shout at him, chase him out of the house, burn his books, and accuse him of trying to be white, often for very trivial things. For instance, the family was in the habit of sharing a face cloth and eating the same meager meals because we were poor. When Johannes found an after-school job at a Chinese butcher shop, he bought his own face cloth. He forbade anyone to use it, because he said sharing things like face cloths spread disease. He was very much into hygiene when he reached high school and started reading all those books with big words. He even advised my mother not to borrow the neighbor's diapers to use on her children. He also started buying nutritious food such as cereals, eggs, and vegetables, and would cook his own meals, which he invited us to share.

My father wanted none of this independence in his house. He was the lawgiver and things had to be done his way. Another thing which particularly rankled my father was my brother's habit, once he reached high school, of reading or doing homework when others were asleep because that was the only quiet time in the crowded shack. My father would castigate him for this, insisting that he was wasting candles. So what did my brother do? He went out and bought his own candles to read and study by.

Often I did not understand why he so loved knowledge. No one else in the family did. While many of his friends spent their money on clothes, movies, and girls, he bought mostly books.

He almost got killed for books. During the rebellion of 1976 he ran back to a library—the only one we had in the ghetto—that an angry mob had set afire, in order to save a few books. While preoccupied with rummaging among the charred remains, he failed to notice an armored vehicle packed with soldiers rumble into the complex. He narrowly escaped being caught and shot by leaping into a nearby ditch, still clutching books in his hands. Everyone at home was shocked by his behavior and thought him foolish and reckless.

But though I didn't understand his love for books, I saw how learning changed him. He always dressed neatly, even in secondhand and patched clothes; he always spoke about trying to become a gentleman, which was one reason he took up tennis. While his friends were chasing after girls and experimenting with liquor and sex, he was either with books or on the tennis court.

In fact, I remember the many times he would come back home

almost in tears because his peers had called him a sissy for not doing what they did. Sometimes I was embarrassed when he walked away from bullies instead of fighting them. He was known as the neighborhood coward. Even my father constantly called him effeminate because of his nonviolent nature and his strange habits of neatness, reading, playing tennis, and speaking English.

I was proud of him. Deep down in my heart I knew that he was none of those things people were calling him: a sissy, a nerd, an imitation white man, a coward. He was simply groping for a better life. And he proved many people wrong when the very things they had denigrated him for—tennis, books, and English—earned him the friendship of caring whites who helped him get a tennis scholarship to America.

Suddenly parents all over Alexandra bought their children rackets and wanted them to learn tennis. For a while the tennis courts became a favorite hangout as youngsters flocked there for free tennis lessons conducted by whites who had coached Johannes. My brother George even trained to become a coach. People began looking at the family with different eyes and treated us differently, including relatives who had wanted to have nothing to do with us because of our poverty.

They wondered how a member of such a destitute family could have gone to America, a place many people in the ghetto considered a magical world where the average black was as rich as the athletes and entertainers who regularly visited South Africa to perform in places such as Sun City, and lived in mansions, dressed expensively, and drove fancy cars. This was the America people saw in the movies and read about in magazines like *Ebony*. This was the America everyone in the family, including Granny, longed to see. This was why we had believed that Johannes would become a rich man simply by going to America.

So when—after he had been gone nine years, after my mother had given him up for dead because letters from him never reached us but were intercepted by the police, after the nightmare years of the mid-1980s when so many blacks lost their lives in the daily violence of the ghettos—word reached us that Johannes was alive and a writer of books, and wanted us to come visit him, the entire family fell down on its knees and thanked God and our ancestors for the miracle. Finally, we would see the Promised Land, the land whose streets were paved with gold.

As arrangements were made to get us to America, Granny assumed all along we were going there by train. She had no conception of flying. For most of her life she had traveled on foot, and occasionally by bus, car, and train. Modern technology still bewildered and terrified her. She became quite apprehensive as the day of our departure for America approached, especially when she learned that we would be traveling in a "huge manmade bird" that would fly at terrific speed through heaven.

"I'm not ready to go to heaven," she said with a concerned look. "I'm not dead yet."

Yet despite her fears, Granny was determined to go to America to see her favorite grandchild.

We spent the eve of our departure—June 25, 1987—at the suburban home of Gary Beukes, an Afrikaner businessman who had befriended the family and had helped us get tickets, passports, and visas. Money for our tickets had been wired from America to Gary by some generous black woman I had never heard of before—Oprah Winfrey. We were told that Oprah had read my brother's book, *Kaffir Boy*, and been so moved by its story that she offered to bring us over to America for a family reunion after a nine-year separation.

The whole extended family turned up for the farewell party at Gary's house. Even Grandpa John, Granny's former husband who was now nearly blind, was there. Granny's anger toward him had softened somewhat, especially as his third wife, Melinda, had recently left him after seducing a younger married man from down the street.

People swam in a pool for the first time and we stuffed ourselves at a huge dinner prepared by Gary's wife, Carol, and their maid, Gladys. Carol had been to America before, so she gave us a crash course on American culture. She startled us by informing us that we would find no apartheid in America. Granny and my mother were especially bewildered. They wondered how in the world they would be able to function in a world without apartheid, having lived under the system all their lives.

Next we learned basic greeting phrases and etiquette. The thought of having to speak English all the time, because no one in America spoke Shangaan or Venda, made Granny and my mother frantic to brush up on the pidgin English they had learned from years of working for white people.

Then we had tips on the proper use of showers, telephones, and electricity, none of which we had at home. When it came to learning how to properly use knives and forks, Granny became so exasperated at not being able to get any food into her mouth using a fork that she dropped the damn thing and resumed eating with her fingers, as she had done all her life.

Next came television. Gary and his wife told us that in America we were likely to appear on television. My siblings and I were thrilled at the prospect. Most black South Africans considered American television the ultimate in glamour and sophistication. Television had only been introduced in South Africa in 1976, and provided just three boring basic channels. Most blacks didn't start owning sets until several years later because they were so expensive. A typical family would have had to toil years to afford a small black-and-white TV set. But prices gradually came down and the quality of the shows improved when American programs were imported. Before, the menu had been mostly sports—rugby, cricket, soccer, bowling—a sprinkling of home-grown shows and endless government propaganda. With lower TV prices and foreign programming, there was an explosion in the purchase of television sets by blacks in the ghettos. We bought one huge color set on layaway and powered it with a car battery. Even the poorest blacks somehow managed to get a set. It became a sort of status symbol.

But now television for most has become a necessity. One finds, even in the crudest of shacks, without electricity or running water, battery-powered TV sets in front of which ragged men, women, and children sit mesmerized, as they imbibe movies, programs like "Dallas" and "The Cosby Show," and soap operas, most of them dubbed in Zulu, Sotho, or Afrikaans.

Children in our family became so enamored of the television that each time Granny or my mother attempted to entertain them with folktales, as they had done when I was growing up, no one had the patience to listen.

"Granny, you're making too much noise," my daughter Angeline would say. "I can't hear the TV."

"Your stories are old-fashioned," Maria's six-year-old son would add. "We see better stories on television. Why should we listen to your boring ones?"

Granny, my mother, and most older folks lamented the advent of television. They blamed it for the deterioration of family life, for the loss of values, and for the increase in violence, especially among the youth, because the programs which always have the largest and most captive audiences were the ones with the most violence and mayhem.

On June 26, 1987, Gary picked us up in Alexandra and drove us to Jan Smuts Airport for an evening flight to Frankfurt, Germany, where we would wait eight hours for a connecting flight to New York. None of us had ever flown or even set foot inside an airplane. Granny's dread increased. At the sight of the jumbo jet she almost bolted. My mother and I had to grab her, each taking one arm, and continue through the airport toward the gate.

With each step, a panic-stricken Granny kept muttering prayers and saying, "There's no way that huge bird is going to fly into the air with *me* inside. What if it falls down? Protect me, oh my ancestors."

We did our best to reassure her that planes routinely flew with hundreds of people inside and didn't just fall out of the sky. We reached the gate and began boarding. Granny gingerly stepped in the jet, walked like a zombie to her seat, sat rigidly on it, and clutched its armrests for dear life, even before the plane took off. As the plane accelerated, raised its nose, and glided into the air, Granny shut her eyes and grabbed my arm. Meanwhile, my siblings and I were bug-eyed with wonder at the magic of flight, and ooohed and aaahed as the plane gained altitude.

Several minutes later, as the plane gradually leveled, Granny slowly opened one eye. And finding that the plane was still in one piece, she opened both eyes wide and marveled, along with the rest of us, at the enchanting world above the clouds.

"Is this heaven?" Granny asked.

"Yes, Granny," I said.

"Am I dead?"

"No, Granny," I said, "you're very much alive."

She and my mother were so awed by the magnificent view of the thick, fluffy, white cloud against a dazzlingly blue sky that they expected any moment to see God and the heavenly host robed in dazzling array and singing hosannas. No one slept during the entire flight to Germany.

America proved to be everything we had dreamed it would be. It was vast, rich, bewildering, luxurious, and full of surprises. At the airport, when we saw my brother Johannes for the first time in nine years, we embraced and wept.

I was particularly thrilled to meet my new *Skwiza*, Gail, whose lovely pictures Johannes had sent us. Oprah Winfrey, who had made our reunion possible, was to us just another well wisher in the giddy crowd. We had never seen her before and hardly knew about her fame and fortune. To us she was simply a loving, caring human being full of *rirhandu* (the milk of human kindness). She had a tall and handsome boyfriend named Stedman.

When Johannes later explained to us that Oprah had risen through hard work from a childhood of abuse and poverty to become one of the richest and most powerful women in America, earning millions of dollars a year—an amount of money so vast we couldn't conceive it—we believed America to be truly the Promised Land. Only the Promised Land would allow blacks like Oprah to succeed in ways we never dreamed of in South Africa. In South Africa, people worked their fingers to the bone and still didn't earn enough for survival. I wondered how long it would take me, with my wage of R400 ($150) a month, to earn the millions Oprah had.

But Oprah was very generous. She put us up in a fancy hotel, all expenses paid, sent us shopping for anything we wanted at Alexander's, flew us down to North Carolina, and then on to Chicago where we had a triumphant family reunion on her show, before millions of viewers across America.

During the two months we were in America we attended my brother's wedding on Long Island, in which I was a bridesmaid and got to have my hair done for the first time at a real beauty parlor, and on Sundays we went to various churches, which had either all-black or all-white congregations, just as in South Africa. Yet all the blacks and whites we met, in both the North and the South, showered us with love and were eager to hear our story of life in South Africa.

The family was quite shocked when Johannes showed us American ghettos. We never dreamed that such places existed in America. The poverty and hopelessness of many of these places reminded me of the ghettos back home.

"How could such places exist in America?" I asked my brother as we were driving down to Hilton Head, South Carolina, to visit Stan Smith and his family.

On the way, we drove through black areas with ramshackle homes, boarded buildings, pot-holed streets, garbage piled up on the sidewalks, and men, women, and children in the grip of the same dismal conditions I thought unique to South Africa. Yet right next to these ghettos were white suburbs full of the comforts and luxuries of white suburbs in South Africa: parks, nice homes, well-kept streets, supermarkets, gardens, hospitals, and happy children playing about the streets. This was all very confusing, especially as so many blacks in South Africa believed that American apartheid had been abolished a long time ago.

Johannes began explaining to us the complicated history of black life in America. During our stay he read us books and showed us videos about slavery, the Civil War, lynchings, the Ku Klux Klan, Jim

Crow, the civil rights movement, race riots, the Great Society pro-grams, and the problems of America's inner cities—drugs, violence, teenage pregnancy, the disintegration of families, police brutality, and endemic poverty. For several days the family was shocked and bewildered by contradictions in America, and the many similarities between black life in South Africa and in America.

At the end of our eye-opening and sobering course on the history of racism in America, Johannes asked us, "Well, what do you think about America now?"

He was surprised by my answer. "Despite all these horrible and shocking things that have happened and still happen to blacks in America," I said, "I would still prefer to live here than in South Africa."

Everyone in the family agreed with me.

"Why?" Johannes asked.

I replied that there were jobs in America, that blacks had the right to vote, that blacks were not being shot daily by the police, that there were no segregated schools, hospitals, buses, trains, toilets, parks, libraries, or graveyards, and that many blacks were succeeding, despite the obstacles they faced.

"You should see Alexandra now," I said to Johannes. "Conditions are worse than when you were there. Unemployment is over 50 per-cent. There's no schooling. There are over two hundred thousand people in the one-square-mile ghetto. Crime is rampant. There's no police force so people kill each other with impunity. The situation is thoroughly hopeless. I agree that compared to white Americans many black Americans have it bad. But compared to most blacks in South Africa, they are in living paradise."

When I was in America I had long discussions with my sister-in-law Gail about women's issues. I told her things I had never revealed to anyone before. I told her about the abusive relationships I had been in, about the beatings, and about the struggles women went through in South Africa. She was shocked by most of what I had to say.

"It sounds like most women are treated like slaves in South Africa," Gail said.

"At times I feel the same way too."

Gail then went on to tell me about the women's movement in America, how over the years it had fought for women's rights.

"For instance, abortion is legal in America," Gail said. "It's regarded as a woman's right."

I was amazed. I told her about back-alley abortions, about my friend who became so distraught over an unwanted pregnancy that she tried inducing an abortion by swallowing a packet of laxatives. She got so sick she had to be rushed to the hospital. She ended up having the baby, a girl, whom she named Laxa to remind herself of the terrible ordeal.

The knowledge I gained from learning about the struggles of women in America made me realize that I and women like me in South Africa were not strange in fighting for our rights. It helped strengthen my resolve to keep fighting to be independent, never to tolerate abuse from men, and always to speak my mind to let them know how I felt and what I wanted, despite what tradition and custom dictated.

That's exactly what I did after I broke up with Walter and met Sipho in 1991. Like myself, Sipho came from a poor, large, and close-knit family. He and his five brothers and parents were forced to flee their home when waves of Inkatha *impis* from a nearby hostel, armed with machetes, spears, *knob-kierries*, and guns, went on a rampage burning and vandalizing homes, in a desperate grab for territory in their bitter struggle with the ANC for control of the ghetto. The security forces did little to stop the mayhem or disarm Inkatha. When the orgy of violence and terror ended a few weeks later, eleven people were dead, hundreds injured, and over three thousand left homeless. The section of Alexandra where this devastation took place came to be known as Beirut, and became a sort of no-man's land.

Sipho was about my age and worked as a floor manager at a trouser factory. As a secretary, I earned more than he did and that bothered him, but I told him he would have to get used to it, as there was no way I would quit my job to cater to his manly pride.

I remember the conversation we had on our first date.

"I have this problem with men," I began. "My past boyfriends were unfaithful to me. I hate infidelity. I won't tolerate it in our relationship. It hurts too much. And it's degrading. So before we start anything or go any further, we have to be honest with each other."

"I too hate infidelity," Sipho said. "My former girlfriend slept around, so I left her. I promise I'll be honest in our relationship."

"I take you at your word," I said. "And please don't make me regret trusting you. The reason I say all this to you is because I want to have a future—together if possible, alone if necessary. I don't want to play house anymore. I've been playing house too long, for eight or nine years now. I'm sick and tired of it. I'm nearly thirty. Either I marry a man I can trust or I lead my life alone with my child and try to find a house or apartment on my own. Being a single mother won't be easy, but I'll make it. I now know that I don't have to have a man in my life to be happy, though having one who loves and respects me would be nice."

I could tell from Sipho's silence that he was a bit surprised at my assertiveness. I went on.

"I saw what happened to my grandmother. She was abandoned by a man for another woman. She found herself with a brood of children, without support, and spent her whole life slaving to raise them alone. For over fifty years she's had to scrape and beg to stay alive. She doesn't know what being fulfilled as a woman means. She's never known a moment's happiness in her life. Then I saw what happened to my mother. She was forced to marry an older man she didn't love, who abused her and showed her no respect. Had she had a choice she would have gone to school, worked, been independent, married the man she loved, and her life would have been quite different from the hell she's been through. She might not even have gone mad. So I don't want to turn out like either my mother or grandmother, or to repeat my own mistakes. So which will it be? Will I be the only woman in your life or should we go our separate ways?"

"You'll be the only one," Sipho said, "and I mean it."

"Thank you," I said. "And you'll be the only man."

Though I took Sipho at his word, I took precautions to ensure he kept it. First I changed his friends, for I didn't like the behavior of most of his old buddies one bit. Many were married and yet they had girlfriends. I knew their wives, so each time these men brought their girlfriends to the shack I now shared with Sipho (which I had inherited from Granny when she took over my parents' old shack after they moved to a Habitat for Humanity house), I would take the women aside and try to talk to them.

"Are you aware that these men you're with have wives and children?" I would ask.

Many simply shrugged and replied, "Yes."

"You dare say yes!" I would scream at them. "How dare you come to my home with another woman's husband! Get out of my house, you trash, you home wrecker!"

Needless to say, these girlfriends hated me, but the wives of Sipho's so-called friends liked me, and a greater bond of solidarity formed between us.

"We have to stand up for each other," I would often say to them, "or else we'll forever be hurt by men and pitted against each other. We let men get away with cheating by not saying what we think when we see a married man with a girlfriend."

One day Sipho told me that some woman in the neighborhood who was engaged to be married was trying to seduce him.

"I can't believe it," I said to Sipho. "She's one of my closest friends. She's even asked me to be a bridesmaid at her wedding."

Sipho was surprised at the news. "I keep telling her that I'm not interested," he said, "but she won't leave me alone. She does the same with my friends."

Incensed, I marched straight to where the young woman lived and, finding only her mother at home, I said to her, "You need to talk to your daughter. She's about to get married yet she's chasing after other women's boyfriends. She's after mine. What am I supposed to do? Chase after her husband-to-be?"

The mother was shocked and said she would talk to her daughter.

As I was leaving, I met the young woman coming through the

gate. "What do you mean trying to seduce Sipho?" I said.

"I don't know what you're talking about," she said evasively.

"Yes you do. If you don't stop, I'll telephone your fiancé and tell him all about you. I doubt if he'll want to marry you after he finds out what a slut you are."

"Florah, please don't do that," she pleaded. "I didn't mean any harm, honest. I was just flirting with Sipho."

"You have no right to flirt with other women's men," I said, "especially when you're about to get married."

"I won't do it anymore," she said. "Will you promise not to tell my fiancé?"

"Well, . . . " I said.

"Please!"

"Okay."

She was relieved. "Will you still be my bridesmaid?" she asked.

"I don't know about that," I said, "after what you've done. But I'll think about it. It depends on you, you know."

The woman stopped trying to seduce Sipho, my anger against her cooled, and I attended her wedding as one of her bridesmaids. She's now happily married, and as far as I know, she isn't fooling around. She's probably too busy slaving for her husband's family as a new *makoti*.

35

GELI

MA-MAHAFA'S SON
IS BURNT ALIVE

The time I spent in America was the happiest of my life. For the first time since I was born I breathed freedom. I understood what it meant to be treated as a human being. I learned much about my rights as a human being and as a woman—rights I never knew I had. To apartheid I had always been a laborer to be exploited, and to my husband I had been property to be lorded over. But now I knew that I was a person, an individual.

I lost a lot of my illusions about the good life for blacks in America, but in the end I agreed with my children that America, with all her faults and shortcomings, was a lot better than South Africa. I hope to settle there someday, so I can be near my grandchildren.

What most impressed me about the Americans I met, black and white, was their faith in God and their love of learning. They went to church on Sundays. They knew how to read and write. So when I appeared with my family on a Christian show called "The 700 Club," and my son told the producers about my fervent desire to learn to read and write, they generously gave me a learning kit consisting of booklets and tapes. I started the lessons immediately. They were difficult, but I was determined. I was undeterred by some of the hilarious mistakes I made.

"Give me your address," the voice on the tape would say.

"Give me your dress," I would repeat.

The help I got from my children made such mistakes fewer with time, and I was soon able to read and write the alphabet and my name. I was thrilled. My life's ambition is to be able to read the Bible, the living word of God, all by myself.

The more similarities I saw between the struggle for freedom by blacks in America and in South Africa, the more I became convinced that education was the key to the future. I saw that in America, as in South Africa, most of the blacks who were successful were educated, and that those who remained trapped in poverty were often uneducated.

I was proud of myself for having persevered in educating my children, despite not having attended school myself. Many Americans asked how I did it, given the hard life I led. The only answer I could give was that as a mother I simply wanted a better life for my children. I couldn't stand by and see them destroyed by apartheid. I did the best I could to sustain their hope for a better life. But I always added that I couldn't have done it without faith in God.

I didn't succeed with all of my children, but at least Johannes's accomplishments proved that my efforts have not been in vain. And through him there is hope for the rest.

That's why, when my son Johannes told me he wanted Linah, Diana, and George to remain behind in America to continue their education, I heartily agreed. Linah and Diana were bewildered and confused by a great deal in America. At the thought of not returning home to a familiar world and their friends, they burst out crying. I insisted they stay.

"What is there for you to go back to in South Africa?" I said to them. "Having children out of wedlock? Jiving for power? Being killed by the police? There's no future for you in South Africa, so you stay right here with your brother and get that education."

It was very painful for me to leave them behind. They were my darlings, my consolation. Also I wondered how their father would react when I told him I had left them in America without consulting him.

The day we left, many tears were shed. I prayed all day for God to take care of my children, as He was the one who could protect, guide, and comfort them, with me so far away.

When Florah, Granny, and I arrived back home, we all wished we had somehow been able to stay in America, for once again we had to deal with the painful realities of black life in the ghetto—violence, soldiers, poverty, desperation, tear gas, witchcraft, hopelessness, death, hunger—and with Jackson.

Jackson was furious when I told him I had left Linah and Diana in America.

"Why the hell did you do that?" he fumed.

"I left them so they could go to school there," I said. "They have no future here. I don't want them to end up having children out of wedlock."

"Damn the school!" he shouted. "Weren't they attending school right here at home?"

"Do you call it going to school when they were roaming the streets and jiving for power?" I asked.

"You forget that those girls are *my* children," Jackson said. "You had no right to leave them without my permission."

"They are my children too. And I did what was best for them. If you want them, go to America and get them."

Strangely enough, Jackson never asked why I had left George behind. This led me to conclude that his main interest in Linah and Diana was the fact that they constituted *lobola*. He knew that in America men didn't pay *lobola*, because Johannes had told him so when he called to say he was getting married.

It turned out that when I was in America, Jackson had terrorized family members who had remained behind. Mirriam and Maria had been left behind because their passports came late, and both were nursing newborns. Angeline, Florah's daughter, and Given, Maria's firstborn, stayed behind with them.

The day after we left, Linda Twala, Gary's contact in the township and a close friend of the family's, had given Mirriam R250 for groceries and R50 each to Jackson and Maria. Linda was one of the kindest and beloved men in Alexandra.

Jackson immediately went to the *shebeen* and bought himself and his buddies drinks. After his money was spent, he came back home and demanded more from Mirriam.

"Don't give him any, Mirriam," Maria said. "That money is for groceries while Ma is away." Maria spoke while she sat on the bed in the kitchen, breast-feeding her premature, three-day-old baby, Tsepo ("Faith"). Tsepo was so tiny and fragile he needed constant attention.

"Shut up you!" Jackson shouted at Maria. Turning to Mirriam, he said, "Now, give me the money, damn you."

"Maria has the money," Mirriam stammered.

"Let me have that money, Maria," he said in a threatening voice. "Let me have it or I'll *donder* [thrash] you."

Maria said no. Jackson, furious, stormed into the bedroom, grabbed his *sjambok*, and came after Maria, who was still breast-feeding. When she saw Jackson she hurriedly placed the squealing Tsepo on the bed and leaped up to defend herself.

"Now give me the money before I thrash you," Jackson demanded.

"I told you that that money is for groceries!" Maria said defiantly.

Jackson raised the *sjambok* to strike Maria on the head, but she ducked in time and the blow landed with a thud on the bed, inches away from the infant. An enraged Maria threw herself at Jackson and grappled with him, punching and scratching his face, and butting him with her head. While the two wrestled, Mirriam, whose own baby was tied to her back with a shawl, grabbed Maria's baby and ran outside. Angeline and Given fled from the shack, screaming.

Maria fought Jackson with the fury of a tiger. As the two went at it fiercely, Mirriam ran next door and summoned a neighbor, a middle-aged woman who in the past had intervened in fights between Jackson and me. The neighbor pulled Jackson away from Maria.

"Shame on you, Jackson," she said. "What's possessing you? Are you mad? Don't you see your daughter is nursing? Why don't you pick on somebody your own size?"

"She needs to be taught a lesson," Jackson said. "She gives me no respect."

"To get respect from your children you must show them respect."

An embarrassed Jackson slunk out of the house, muttering curses under his breath. Maria and Mirriam kept their distance until I returned from America. When I heard what Jackson had done in my absence, I was furious and confronted him.

"When will you stop abusing the children?" I said.

"These children disrespect me," Jackson said. "Especially Florah and Maria. They must leave this house and go live with their boyfriends. I won't be ruled by women."

"Those children are going nowhere," I said. "And if you don't leave them alone, I'll hire *tsotsis* to kill you, so help me God. I'm tired of your abuse, Jackson."

Jackson was stunned.

"So you want me dead, heh?" he said.

"No, I don't want you dead," I said. "You're already dead. You died a long time ago. You killed yourself with alcohol, gambling, and neglecting and abusing your family."

I kept praying to God for Jackson to change his bad habits. I refused to give up hope on him. I don't know why. Maybe because I believed that hope was synonymous with life. Jackson gradually began to see the light. He must have realized that he was getting old, that he no longer had the energy to run around acting like a young man, that if he didn't change his ways, his children would forever be ashamed of him and shun him.

Also, years of hard drinking were beginning to take their toll on him. He was constantly getting sick. And Johannes, despite what Jackson had done to him when he was growing up, still loved him as a father and sought ways to help him. Johannes showed love for his father by arranging for us to move from the shack on 16th Avenue to a larger house built with the help of Habitat for Humanity. Johannes sent us monthly checks to pay the mortgage and Jackson and me to live on.

All this must have contributed to Jackson's decision to turn a new leaf. He stopped drinking and gambling, and began accompanying me to church from time to time. I could not thank the Lord enough for this minor miracle, for which I had waited all my married life.

But life for the family continued to be hard, especially for my three daughters. Mirriam resumed school and I cared for her baby boy, Sibusiso ("A Blessing"). Maria, now a mother of three, grew tired of working at piece jobs and wanted to start her own business. So she thought of attending sewing school. I spoke to Johannes and he sent her some money and bought her a sewing machine.

Florah's relationship with Sipho continued to grow, and there was talk of marriage, despite their struggles to make ends meet. I became very close to my granddaughter Angeline, even though by custom she was the grandchild of her father's parents. But something happened to make Florah decide to permanently keep Angeline and to shun Collin's stepmother.

Apparently before Collin was murdered, he had taken out a life insurance policy, making Angeline his beneficiary in the event that he died. Because he and Florah were estranged at the time, Collin didn't inform her of the life insurance policy. But his stepmother and father knew of it.

Shortly after Collin was buried, when Florah was living with me and struggling to care for Angeline as a single mother, Collin's stepmother came and asked for Angeline's birth certificate, saying she needed it to resolve some family matter and would bring it back.

Not suspecting anything, Florah gave it to her. She and her husband then took the birth certificate, went to a neighbor who had a daughter about Angeline's age, and asked to "borrow" her for a day. According to Collin's sister, Tembi (meaning "Promise"), who was close to Florah and told her the story, Collin's stepmother paid the parents money so their daughter could masquerade as Angeline. Florah later heard confirmation of this from the little girl's mother who stopped her one day to "unburden her conscience," as she put it.

They then took the little girl along to the life insurance company, where they presented her as Angeline. They produced Angeline's birth certificate as "proof of identity." The insurance company went ahead and gave them the money. They never gave a penny to Angeline.

When Florah heard of this, she was enraged.

"How could they do this to their own granddaughter?" she said to me.

"I don't know, my child," I said. "I can think of no other reason but greed."

"What should I do?"

Florah was afraid to confront Collin's stepmother and father directly, fearful that they might bewitch her or hire *tsotsis* to murder her. She didn't know how to get hold of a lawyer and even if she did there was no money to pay for the service. She telephoned Johannes in America and asked for advice. Johannes told her of Susan Bazilli, his friend from Canada who was a feminist, lawyer, and journalist. Susan had recently come to South Africa to defend a group of black men from Alexandra in a treason trial. During the long trial, which ended with the complete acquittal of the ten defendants, she became very active in championing the rights of African women, organizing various conferences on women's issues, and editing a collection of essays titled *Putting Women on the Agenda*.

Susan was kind enough to find time from an important case to attempt to help Florah regain Angeline's inheritance. Susan wrote several letters to the insurance company exposing the fraud, but the company said it could do nothing because the money had already been paid. It was a matter between Florah and Collin's stepmother, the company said.

Aware that people in the ghetto were murdering and bewitching each other over money, I told Florah to drop the matter.

"It's not worth losing your life over money," I said. "God knows what they have done. He will punish them."

Faith in God continues to be the rock of my life. I take all my troubles to Him and find the greatest comfort in Him in times of affliction. He has answered many of my prayers. He's kept me and my children alive. He's given me a new home, with two bedrooms, electricity, and plumbing. He has sent four of my children to America to be educated and to improve their lives. And He's changed Jackson's life.

I believe that none of this would have been possible if I had not joined the Twelve Apostles Church of God. And for this miracle I have Ma-Mahafa to thank, the same Ma-Mahafa who had been my drinking buddy and had wanted me to have lovers so I could support myself and my children.

Ma-Mahafa had her share of faults, but the Lord, who works in mysterious ways, chose her to lead me to greener pastures. That's why when her son was burnt alive, I grieved for him, despite the sordid circumstances of his life, which led many to say he deserved to die such a hideous death.

Ma-Mahafa's youngest son, Herman, was the terror of the township. He thought himself invincible because he wore voodooed armbands. He robbed, stabbed, and killed people, and abused women. One night he met a couple walking down the street. He approached them, told the man that he wanted his girlfriend, and when the man refused to let her go, he ripped his stomach open with a knife, forcibly took his girl, and left him clutching his guts.

One day, as we were leaving church, I said to Herman's mother, "How can you, Ma-Mahafa, a woman of God, allow your son, your own flesh and blood, to commit such horrendous crimes?"

"Ma-Johannes," Ma-Mahafa said, "people tell all sorts of lies about my son."

"Do you mean the whole township is lying about your son?"

"I know people hate my son," Ma-Mahafa said, "but they can never harm him."

Ma-Mahafa refused to believe reports of her son's crimes partly because he was her favorite child. She apparently wasn't worried about rumors that people wanted to kill him because she thought him protected from harm by the voodooed armbands he wore. Many notorious *tsotsis* and killers wore such *muti*-treated armbands, which they obtained from witch doctors.

I knew it was only a matter of time before justice caught up with Herman, voodooed armbands or no voodooed armbands. His victims and their loved ones so loathed him they wanted to see him dead. The Comrades who sat in the People's Courts heard a constant stream of complaints about his crimes and barbarities. But apparently none among them had the courage to bring Herman to justice.

Then one day someone finally summoned up the courage. Herman had tried to rob and stab a Rastafarian man, who escaped alive and went and got his friend. Together, armed with a container of gasoline and a box of matches, they went in search of Herman. As they approached his shack he saw them through the window and sneaked out the back door. They chased him as he fled into a cluster of shacks. Herman drove the occupants out of one of the shacks and locked himself in.

That was a deadly mistake. The Rastafarian and his friend soaked the flimsy shack with gasoline and lit it. It exploded in bright orange flames that leaped into the sky. By this time a crowd of onlookers had heard that the notorious Herman had been cornered. They congregated to witness the spectacle and applaud the fact that finally Herman was getting his due.

The shack burned for some time, with Herman still holed inside. The crowd grew excited. A chorus of shouts—"Burn him! Burn the bloody dog! Burn the devil!"—reverberated through the air. Suddenly Herman emerged, having stabbed himself in the neck with a dagger. As blood spluttered from his wound, he was heard swearing, "I'd rather kill myself than die at the hands of you dogs!"

He staggered about the yard with blood oozing out of his thick neck, then collapsed. Instantly the vengeful, bloodthirsty mob pounced on him. It was a grisly sight. People hacked at him with shovels and pick axes. They bludgeoned him with slabs of concrete, kicked him, and spat on him as he writhed on the ground. Finally they poured the remaining gasoline on him and set him on fire. He never screamed, he never uttered a cry for help. Had he cried for help no one would have come to his rescue. He had no friends. Not even the police intervened to save him, for they knew of his notoriety. They simply drove past the macabre scene several times.

Herman had been cornered, bludgeoned, and burned around noon. His mother returned from work four hours later and was informed of the ghastly attack on her son. She went to the site and found his charred, smoldering, and bloated corpse. Incredibly, the corpse still had spasms of life. Ma-Mahafa could not bear the suffering of her son, so she cut the voodooed armbands, weeping as she did so. He died the instant the voodooed armbands were removed.

While Ma-Mahafa mourned her son's death, the community rejoiced. People celebrated in the streets. *Shebeens* gave out free beer. Men and women drank to each other's health and peace while comparing scars from wounds inflicted by "that Herman dog."

When Herman died, I thought of my son Johannes in America. I wondered if, had he remained in South Africa amid the diabolical forces created by apartheid, which turned young men like Herman into bloodthirsty fiends, he too would have become a *tsotsi*, a robber, a killer. Or would he have been among those who celebrated and rejoiced as another human being burned to death?

36

GRANNY

PHUTHADICHABA
("GATHERING OF NATIONS")

Herman's fate makes me wonder about the future of South Africa and that of the younger generation. I'm old now, nearing ninety, and may not live to see the "new South Africa," the Promised Land that we've all dreamed about and fought so hard and long for.

Everywhere around me, despite the promise of a new dawn, I see ominous signs that things are falling apart. Families are disintegrating, the community spirit is dying, little girls are having children, alcohol abuse is rife, neglected and abused children without homes glut the streets, and people no longer care about each other in ways which even when apartheid was at its worst allowed us to survive and hope and fight to improve our lot.

One sign of things falling apart is what is happening to old people. In the past we used to age gracefully, revered by the community, taken care of by our children and in return making our contributions to the extended family by passing values to the young and doting on our grandchildren. Through the telling of stories as the family gathered around the fireside, or as we basked in the sun surrounded by our grandchildren, we passed on the noble and beautiful culture and heritage of the African people.

But little of that goes on now, as families fall apart. Now most of us old people feel unwanted and abandoned. We are having to make it on our own. The lucky ones have meager pensions of as little as R150 (about $55) a month to cover everything: food, rent, clothing, medicine, transportation. I am fortunate to have other sources of income. My grandson Johannes sends me a monthly allowance of $50, and I also receive another $50 from an American woman named Susan Heumphreus and her friends, members of a community book club in Fairfield, California. They began sending me the money after they had read Johannes's book *Kaffir Boy* and had been touched by the hardships suffered by people like me.

I and most of my peers often find ourselves having to use our pensions to help our unemployed sons and daughters pay rent, buy food, care for their children, and attempt to pay off their ever-mounting debts. Some of us are even robbed of these monthly checks by our own children, who are addicted to drinking and gambling.

This is not what old age is supposed to mean in the African tradition. But the world of filial piety is gone. Apartheid has changed and wrecked it. We now find ourselves, in our declining years, when old age is supposed to have brought us dignified rest, having to either continue working, beg, or rely on charity. Most of us cannot work. Some of us are over a hundred years old. Many of us are in our eighties and nineties. The bones are tired, the energy is sapped, the eyes no longer see well, the ears are nearly deaf, and the mind is waning, though the spirit is still willing.

That is why most of us flock to the Phuthadichaba ("Gathering of Nations") care of the aged center. The center has become our last refuge. But its name is a bit misleading. It's nothing like a retirement or nursing home. Such places are still a rare luxury for most elderly black South Africans. Phuthadichaba is more of a makeshift feeding center, an alley-way soup kitchen, operated by Linda Twala, a dedicated community activist who has been helping the poor in Alexandra since the 1960s.

Linda is a friend of my grandson Johannes. He owns a garbage collection company while at the same time operates four feeding centers across Alexandra. They give a little nourishment to the thousands who otherwise would go hungry each day. Hunger and hopelessness are the biggest problems in the overcrowded ghetto, which is now swarming with refugees fleeing violence and poverty in the homelands and civil war in Mozambique.

Each morning the elderly congregate at Phuthadichaba, which has become the heart of social activity for the aged in Alexandra. Here we gather to reminisce about the old days, when Alexandra hadn't yet degenerated into a slum and blacks still owned land and did not live like animals. We swap family stories, sing hymns, and attend informal prayer services. When there is something for our community to celebrate, such as a birthday, a wedding, or a birth, there is much singing and dancing, and great joy in our hearts, as we share in the few pleasures still left to us.

Back when Phuthadichaba was still well funded, Linda and his assistants, aware that most of us were on fixed incomes or had no income at all, periodically doled out food packages, clothing, and blankets to those of us who could make it to the center.

There are often nearly a thousand of us, from every corner of Alexandra. Phuthadichaba doesn't discriminate, all tribes are welcome. We have among us Xhosas, Zulus, Shangaans, Vendas, Tswanas, Ndebeles, Sothos, Coloreds, Nyasas, Pedis, and even the Portuguese from Mozambique. Even the elderly from Inkatha and ANC break bread together at the center, while their grandsons and granddaughters wage war against each other.

Linda knows most of us by name. Each day he drives around the township in his van before the midday meal, inquiring among the shacks for any "oldies," as he lovingly calls us. He stops to pick up dozens of us along the way as we struggle to make it to Phuthadichaba on crutches, canes, or by leaning on our great-grandchildren.

Once a month, whenever funding allowed, Linda and his assistant volunteers handed each oldie a bag of groceries that included sacks of sugar, tea, mealie meal, oil, and other staples.

One year, the center organized a fun walk. The grand prizes for the winners were two color TV sets, a dinner set, and a wristwatch. I remember the race well. There was great excitement as men and women as old as one hundred creaked their rusty joints in preparation for the race. I was right there at the starting line, on my toes when the countdown began.

"On your mark, get set, ready, go!"

It was supposed to be a simple brisk walk around the block to let us get some exercise. Instead, it turned into a fierce battle for those television sets, which cost more money than any of us had in savings for old age.

Old women and men with canes and on crutches, whom I had seen struggle to take as much as a step because of arthritis and weak joints, whizzed past me on either side, like sprinters in their prime. I increased my stride, struggling to keep up while my lungs felt like bursting and my joints threatened to fall apart.

I was beginning to gain on the leaders when a pack of old men came out of nowhere and stormed past me with elbows and knees flailing. I had known most of them for decades, and lately many had been bedridden, unable to walk, but now they were as swift as greased lightning. The crowd of oldies, amid shouts and screams of encouragement from the younger spectators, limped, caned, and crutched their way around the block so fast that dust billowed in our wake. The winners of the television sets were in their nineties. They proudly received their prizes during an elaborate awards ceremony. I didn't win anything, but I had a good time.

Another time, we held a beauty contest, and men came spiffed up in suits, ties, ironed white shirts, and shined shoes. The women were also elaborately dressed and some even had makeup on.

Those were the good old days, when Linda had enough funding for prizes, blankets, and food packages. Now the laughter and joy has been replaced by the sort of hunger and desperation I never thought

I'd live to see, as the number of destitute in Alexandra and throughout black South Africa has swelled into the millions.

One measure of how much worse things have gotten is that before
1992, the year Linda's funds began drying up, we were accustomed to
receiving whole loaves of bread at noon each day, and full meals on
Fridays. There were always enough loaves to feed the hundreds who
flocked to the center. If bread ran out, more loaves were immediately
purchased and brought to the feeding station so no one went away
hungry.

Even the hundreds of orphans who flocked daily to the center—
children as young as three who had lost their parents to the horrendous violence in the ghetto—were fed and thus kept from digging
through garbage dumps, begging, or prostituting themselves for food.

But all that has changed. Now funds are so limited the elderly no
longer get whole loaves. We receive only half a loaf. Sometimes just
one-quarter of a loaf. Now orphans wait in long lines that flow
through the long, narrow yard and pour out onto 17th Avenue, then
along several blocks—all for a single slice of bread that is supposed to
fill their empty bellies for the day.

To avoid being at the back of the line when the bread runs out, the
elderly often arrive at seven or eight in the morning to sit on
makeshift benches, some in an open garage to keep out of the sun,
and others under lean-tos made of wood and zinc, until the center
opens around noon. Linda still insists that the custom of respecting
the elders be observed, despite the hard times. So the oldies are given
their slices before the young, with the assumption that they will
share it with their grandchildren should bread run out before they
receive any.

Because the loaves inevitably run out while hundreds remain
unfed, melees erupt every day bread is distributed. When the supply
of slices of bread starts running low, word spreads like wildfire
through the huge crowd of people still waiting for their share. Panic
and pandemonium often break out. Sometimes I've been caught in
the middle of all the pushing and shoving, as people frantically tried

to grab bread out of the hands of volunteers, or wrench it from each other.

When the shoving and pushing begins, however, the volunteers handing out the bread usually stop until order is restored. With so many people desperate for a piece of bread, and facing excruciating hunger if they go without, the panic is often hard to control and fights sometimes break out. To know that just a little money would make such a difference in the lives of so many breaks my heart.

But Linda is undaunted by the enormous task of sustaining hope among the poor of Alexandra, especially the aged and children, who are his primary concern. He has added to the activities of the center. There is now a Sunday school for children, so the orphans can have a place of worship. There are over thirty gospel choirs, with as many as sixty members each, that meet every Tuesday.

Linda even has dreams of building a retirement village for those senior citizens who are homeless or in need of twenty-four-hour care. Most of us cannot even imagine living in a place designed exclusively for the elderly, heated in the winter, cooled in the hot summer, with regular meals, with an indoor bathroom and perhaps showers and rocking chairs. What a paradise that would be, especially since most of us live in tiny, overcrowded shacks with a multitude of relatives.

Every oldie was excited to hear that land had been purchased and the building plans had been drawn up. But disappointment followed. The dream had to be deferred. Linda didn't have enough money. For many oldies who have since departed this life for the realm of our ancestors it remained only that—a dream. Linda is trying very hard to raise enough money to continue the project. He recently received a donation of about $15,000 from the British Consulate, but that was only enough to break ground and pour the cement foundations for the buildings.

The government of Pres. F.W. de Klerk has refused to help. It even abruptly ended its support for the feeding center, declaring that feeding old people and orphans in the townships was no longer a "priority." The government now defines a priority as a project that creates jobs and promotes economic growth. Keeping people from starving accomplishes neither, the government says.

It is my fervent prayer that a black government, which we oldies hope to elect when we cast our first ballot in 1994, as free men and women, proud citizens of the new South Africa, will remember the wisdom of our ancestors, which says:

A nation that ignores its elderly and neglects its young cannot long remain a nation. For the strength of a people lies in cherishing the past and safeguarding the future.

EPILOGUE

While the chief motivation for writing this book has been personal—namely, to record the experiences of three women who are intimately connected with my life—it is clear that the struggles of Granny, my mother, and sister Florah, though uniquely their own and African, have much in common with the struggles of women everywhere.

The oppression of women is not limited to South Africa or Africa. It is global. It is economic, social, domestic, political, traditional, cultural, and sexual in nature. In many societies, women are second-class citizens; they are regarded as property and treated as minors; they are exploited as workers; they are denied equal rights with men in marriage, in education, in the home, and in the workplace; they have been stripped of control over their own bodies; they are emotionally and psychologically abused; and they are battered, raped, and killed, often with impunity.

Those women with the courage to seek redress in the courts, when they are fortunate enough to enjoy such a privilege and have the education to know what their rights are, seldom receive justice because of their gender.

Though impressive gains have been made in many countries in the struggle for women's rights, battles continue to rage everywhere, and the war is still far from being won. And in some places one step forward has been followed by two steps backwards. These battles are fought in different ways, as women are not monolithic but are separated by race, culture, color, ethnicity, class, language, and so on.

This book has particular significance for the new South Africa. As I was writing it I was struck by the pioneering role women have played in African society, despite being oppressed and caught between two different ways of life: the traditional and the modern.

Because of having to shoulder the enormous responsibilities of working and raising families while living in a society dominated by men and by apartheid, women are constantly called upon to reconcile the often conflicting claims of two worlds. In that unique role they have attempted to weld the two into a harmonious, progressive whole, so that the anachronistic in tribal life is discarded, while the useful is preserved, to anchor and sustain the community in the turbulent, materialistic, and ever-changing present.

Women have been more the pioneers of a new order than men because they have a more intimate knowledge of the demands of daily life and of survival, and are readily adaptable. Men, on the other hand, particularly those emasculated by apartheid, have tended to cling to customs and practices that have long outlived their usefulness and serve only to oppress, retard progress, and destroy. A case in point is my father. He kept insisting that tribal law be supreme in the house, even when the world in which we lived was no longer tribal.

He did this in part because under tribalism, his power and authority—in other words, his manhood—were unchallenged. His word was law and his wife had to know and keep to her place. But the arrival of the white man forever changed this sort of arrangement, which, despite its shortcomings and flaws, served society at the time.

Men like my father have to adapt to the future—a future that is murky and uncertain. While apartheid has finally been abolished, at least on paper, and the African National Congress, armed with a radical and progressive agenda for change, is poised to assume power and plans to transform South Africa into a nonracial and nonsexist democracy, most blacks continue to lead lives of desperation and hopelessness. They see no future, so they either live for the moment or cling to the past.

One measure of how conditions have deteriorated is that in Alexandra—where Granny, my mother, and sister Florah have spent most of their lives—the population of the one-square-mile ghetto in the early 1980s was roughly 120,000. By 1993 it had mushroomed to over 300,000. Aside from the few middle-class blacks who live in modest comfort in the improved parts of Alexandra, where houses have up to three bedrooms and there's enough to eat, most Alexandrans live in overcrowded shacks, amid poverty that defies description.

Unemployment in Alexandra stands at over 50 percent. There is no welfare safety net or universal health care. Schooling since the mid-1980s has been sporadic at best, with the disastrous result that few young blacks are being equipped for productive lives and positions of leadership in a postapartheid South Africa.

The sad story of Alexandra is repeated across the four provinces of South Africa and in the tribal reservations called homelands, where the legacy of apartheid has doomed communities and generations of blacks to a life of grinding poverty, degradation, illiteracy, squalor, and violence. Conditions don't show any sign of improving soon, despite the prospects of a black-led government.

It is in this larger and grim context that the oppression of women should be seen. Women constitute 53 percent of the South African population of 35.2 million. Nearly two-thirds of black households are headed by women. An estimated one thousand rapes are committed each day, three hundred thousand illegal abortions are performed each year, and one psychologist estimated that 60 percent of husbands routinely beat their wives.

As the stories of Granny, my mother, and Florah clearly illustrate, the violence against women and their degradation, subjugation, and exploitation are deeply rooted in the nature of South African society, shaped as it has been by the powerful forces of apartheid and patriarchy. Over the years these two forces have served to entrench sexism and the inferior status of women in virtually every sphere of life. Forced removals, lobola, Influx Control, the migratory labor system, the homeland system, polygamy—all have hit women the hardest.

But things have begun to change. The revolution that overthrew apartheid also served notice that the days of patriarchy are numbered. Women, who fought and sacrificed and died with men in the national freedom struggle, are demanding that their agenda no longer be ignored, postponed, or compromised. They are insisting that their emancipation not be regarded as incidental to the overall liberation from apartheid. The two struggles are indivisibly linked.

Politically active and vocal women are producing impressive results. The ANC now regards the championing of women's rights as an integral part of its agenda as it works to transform apartheid South Africa. To this effect, the ANC, as a government in waiting, has solidly committed itself to using the power of the state to eradicate patriarchy and sexism.

Already the ANC has enshrined women's rights in constitutional guidelines for a postapartheid South Africa. Women, albeit not enough of them, now occupy powerful positions within the movement, and are vigorously advancing their agenda to ensure that they are liberated and empowered not on paper only but in fact.

They want to ensure that South Africa doesn't go the way of many independent states in Africa where women contributed as much as men to the overthrow of colonialism and yet find themselves still oppressed, discriminated against, and treated as second-class citizens.

Achieving the complete liberation of women is a daunting task for any society, especially one in which the roots of sexism and patriarchy run deep, and where tradition, custom, the legal system, and political power have for many years been used as tools to enslave, denigrate, and brutalize women. The defenders of the status quo between men and women won't give up quietly, just as those of apartheid didn't.

But it is the firm hope of the majority of South Africans of all races that the battle for women's rights will be fought with the same determination, courage, and resolve as the battle against racism. Racism and sexism are, after all, twin heads of the same monster. They inhibit progress, enervate a nation, stunt human growth—both must be slain and buried if true equality, democracy, and justice are to be attained.

Of all the countries in Africa, South Africa, as it strives to usher in a new era, has the best chance to accomplish this imperative and long-overdue task. I look forward to the day when the struggles and sacrifices of Granny, my mother, Florah, and countless other women—the unsung heroines of the black liberation struggle—will be vindicated by the equality of women in every facet of South African life, public and private.

INDEX